Crafts, Capitalism, and Women

❁

Potter and her granddaughter with a piggy bank. This potter shows a piggy bank that she has recently completed. The bank has not yet been painted with slip, nor burnished. She made the body as a pot and then enclosed it. Her daughter modeled on the ears, snout, and legs. It is 26 cm long and 18 cm in diameter.

Crafts, Capitalism, and Women

The Potters of La Chamba, Colombia

Ronald J. Duncan

University Press of Florida
Gainesville · Tallahassee · Tampa · Boca Raton
Pensacola · Orlando · Miami · Jacksonville · Ft. Myers

Library of Congress Cataloging-in-Publication Data
Duncan, Ronald J.
Crafts, capitalism, and women : the potters of La Chamba, Colombia /
Ronald J. Duncan.
p. cm.
Includes bibliographical references and index.
ISBN 0-8130-1774-2 (alk. paper)
1. Indian women potters—Colombia—La Chamba—Economic conditions. 2. Women,
Black—Colombia—La Chamba—Economic conditions. 3. Mestizos—Colombia—La
Chamba—Economic conditions. 4. Pottery industry—Economic aspects—Colombia—
La Chamba. 5. Sex role—Colombia—La Chamba. 6. La Chamba (Colombia)—
Economic conditions. 7. La Chamba (Colombia)—Social conditions. I. Title.
F2269.1.L18D86   2000
331.4'8663986136—dc21   00-008954

The University Press of Florida is the scholarly publishing agency for the State
University System of Florida, comprising Florida A&M University, Florida Atlantic
University, Florida International University, Florida State University, University of Central
Florida, University of Florida, University of North Florida, University of South Florida,
University of West Florida, and Florida Gulf Coast University.

University Press of Florida
15 Northwest 15th Street
Gainesville, FL 32611
http://www.upf.com

To the memory of Nina S. de Friedemann,
the distinguished Colombian anthropologist
and sister of my wife, Gloria, who introduced us to
fieldwork in Colombia, who accompanied us on our first
trip to La Chamba, and who collaborated with us
throughout years of research on the traditional arts and
crafts of that country. Her decades of research, writings, and
advocacy for Afro-Colombians helped shape scholarship
and social policy in that country
in the last quarter century.

CONTENTS

ILLUSTRATIONS

Figures

TABLES

FOREWORD

Ronald Duncan's engaging study of potters in La Chamba, Colombia, adds luster to his earlier research on ceramics in a different Colombian village. He offers a well-rounded view of the town, including its cultural and social history; the markets that surround it; household, family, and gender relations; pottery making, artisans, and apprenticeship; and the difficult conditions in which the people live. For Duncan, the study of pottery provides a window to see the whole community and the connectedness of village life. But he does not claim, nor does the ethnography suggest, that the village of La Chamba is a bounded unit or atom of society; the reader will find that it is linked historically, spatially, and conceptually to larger realms. One value of the book is its functionalist style, showing how this form of study can be carried out in today's global world. Duncan has a fine eye for capturing cultural similarities between La Chamba and other areas in Latin America, from Mexico through Central America, and the Isthmus. Much of his ethnography resonates with my knowledge of Panama and comparable places: the centrality of the nuclear family, the prevalence of common-law marriage, the importance of the *compadrazgo* (godparenthood system), gender divided tasks. In recognizing these themes Duncan returns us to the established anthropological aims of discovering and describing the extent of cultural traditions, of comparing and contrasting within culture areas, of relating the general to the particular, and of illuminating local findings against a broader backdrop. These authorial touches add to the book's appeal. But I was most fascinated by his description of pottery making and styles, and the cultural patrimony within which they occur. Duncan starts with the local classification of ceramics—traditional, tableware, "fine"—and shows how these distinct pieces are made by different generations (from older to younger), are sold in different markets, and provide different monetary returns. The markets seemingly work in concentric circles: the traditional forms appeal to nearby country folk or agriculturalists (*campesinos*) who buy them locally; the tableware is desired by urban workers in city markets; and the fine pieces are used and displayed by wealthy consumers in Bogota, the United States, and parts of Europe. Innovations are most rapid for the fine pieces, slower for tableware, and least frequent for the traditional pieces. These spatial, style, class, market, innovation, and financial distinctions are nourished by the historical patrimony that provides the matrix of production for all the ceramics. In prehispanic times, the indigenous populace made functional and funerary ceramics; after the Conquest, this style was continued in the functional pots that are still produced today by elderly women; in the 1940s, as transport improved, potters began to supply urban markets with low-cost tableware, because metal cooking pots had begun to supplant the traditional ceramic ones. Recently, the youngest generation has been making one-off fine ceramics, using magazines and other glossies as well as traditional images for inspiration. The cultural symbolism of the ware, which draws on nostalgia and memory, unites style with potter and markets and provides an identity for consumers. The top-line ceramics—adorned with animals or figures of agricultural fertility—are bought by urbanities who desire a remembrance of rural Colombia, visualized as the pacific countryside, a simple life, closeness to nature, and authentic culture. They are buying a share in the patrimony of an imagined community. These innovative and expensive pieces, made by younger women as a challenge, are used for serving festal meals and are kept for domestic display as tokens of the national legacy, so linking their owners to other patrimony holders in Colombia. (Ironically, the "traditional" cultural foods these ceramics are used to serve do not come from the La Chamba region; and the people of La Chamba eat their festal foods from modern creamware!) In contrast, the traditional pieces, which are made by older women and bought locally, suggest the warmth and closeness of the hearth, home, and family that eats together daily. Readers will also be intrigued by Duncan's account of the connection between form and function in pottery. I had never considered how pots must be shaped in relation to their role in cooking and storage, and to the human body when they are used as carrying vessels. I also understand better how round and flat bottom pots are not only differently made and emerged in differing cultural traditions but also are related to type of house floor where they are used! At a larger level, the study displays the intricate and complex relation of the communal and market realms of economy. Pottery making, a female occupation, is learned through apprenticeship. Mothers teach their daughters to work consistently and carefully, and through the years women learn how to mine clay, prepare it, make pots, and fire and finish them, while carrying out their domestic tasks. The women potters are individual artisans, not members of a production line, and even those working in the most traditional styles innovate by trial-and-error practices. New forms or styles are the private property of their makers, however, others can use them if they are taught the design by the innovator. But pottery making is a "low" occupation whose cash returns (except for the finest artistic products) are below normal wages. Women make pots at home to supplement the returns of other household members engaged in agriculture and wage work: they help maintain the household and meet its necessities. With its low capital input, "freely" learned technology, and relatively inexpensive raw materials brought together in the household—where work efforts are distributed and shared among unpaid females—pottery making provides domestic cash and a subsidy to the larger market. Pottery making, in my terms, is part of the "base" that supports an economy. This pottery base is uncosted in monetary terms but contributes much to local well-being—from useful goods to self-worth to forging a special identity through innovation—and to the larger market through the low-cost goods provided. I invite the reader to enjoy this study of potters, which provides a window on local life in La Chamba, on Colombia and its history, and on the construction of all economies.

Stephen Gudeman

PREFACE

This book examines one of the most important ceramics communities in Colombia. The women potters of La Chamba make prehispanic, indigenous-style coiled ceramics that have been adapted to their mestizo world and to capitalist commercial practices in recent decades. The primary purpose of this book is to describe the forms and working techniques of La Chamba ceramics in terms of its history and the contemporary social environment of the work. As my wife and I became involved in the community, it became obvious that the study could not be limited to techniques and design. The potters told us their social and economic stories, which became an integral part of the research. This is an attempt to describe ceramics making in the real-life social and economic context in which it occurs.

The potters are women, and the fact of their gender affects their work and their relationship to the larger economic world. The people of La Chamba have always been open with us in telling the story of their ceramics making, and I thank the members of the Silva-Prada family, the Sandoval family, and the Avilés family, and the many others who collaborated with us in this research. People demonstrated techniques, talked about clays and kilns, discussed their family histories, and encouraged the study of their community. The *chambunos* (people of La Chamba) are proud of the reputation of their ceramics for high quality, but at the same time most are frustrated with the low economic returns from their work. This study addresses issues that will be of interest to professionals and students interested in anthropology and archaeology, Latin American studies, women's studies, development studies, and crafts.

My wife, Gloria Abella De Duncan, an artist, was the principal collaborator for the research in La Chamba. She is from Colombia originally, and we lived in that country for ten years, during which time I worked with international organizations and did research. We made all but one of the field trips to La Chamba together, and she also assisted me in some of the archival research. She reviewed my process of analysis and writing to guarantee the accuracy of information and interpretation, and she prepared the illustrations.

At various stages this research was funded by the USIA-Fulbright Program (1983), the Universidad de los Andes (1985–86), the International Development Research Centre, Universidad Javeriana (1986–87), and the Hunt Fund of Oklahoma Baptist University (1994 and 1995). Professor María Teresa Guerrero, as director of the Program of Art at the Universidad de los Andes, and Profesor Miryam Ochoa, as director of the Graduate Program in Education at the Universidad Javeriana, provided support for the early stages of this research.

I would also like to thank Greta Friedemann for her assistence in collecting data on La Chamba and for reading an early version of this text. I want to thank the staff of Artesanías de Colombia (Crafts of Colombia), especially the director, Cecilia Duque, and the subdirector, Lucie Cajiao de Ruan, as well as Alexandra Díaz Rodríguez of the Centro de Investigación y Documentación (Center for Research and Documentation) for support to do research in the archives of the organization. I would also like to thank María del Carmen Benavides, director of the Museo de Artes y Tradiciones Populares (Museum of Popular Arts and Traditions) in Bogotá, for her assistance in making data available to me from the archives of the museum. I also thank Hector Mejía of the Departamento Administrativo Nacional de Estadística (National Administrative Department for Statistics) and Alida Narváez Daza of the Banco de la República (Bank of the Republic), both in Bogotá, for their able assistance in obtaining vital economic and statistical information. Barry Isaac, Kathryn Ledbetter, Bill Mullins, and Tómas de los Santos read chapters and made valuable recommendations about revisions. From the University Press of Florida I would like to thank the anonymous readers who made helpful recommendations to improve the manuscript, and I thank Gillian Hillis for her skillful oversight and direction as project editor.

I appreciate the permission of the following organizations to use materials: the JAI Press for some of the materials discussed in Chapters 1, 11, and 12, which were published in "The Economics of Crafts among Home-Based Workers: The Women Potters of La Chamba, Colombia," in *Research in Economic Anthropology,* volume 20 (1999), pages 197 to 219; the Banco de la República of Colombia for permission to use adaptations of two watercolors by Edward W. Mark; and Villegas Editores, Colombia, for permission to reproduce the photograph of Eduardo Sandoval's centerpiece from the book *Artefactos.*

Introduction and Fieldwork

The restructuring of the global economy in recent decades has impacted traditional craftswomen in non-industrialized nations as local economies have become increasingly money based. During my research among the potters of La Chamba, the women repeatedly mentioned their frustration at not being able to improve their economic situation. Their frustration as mothers trying to provide for their families is an expression of the problems that large numbers of home-based women workers are experiencing in the new global system. The women of La Chamba have few possibilities for income-producing work in a capitalistic society, so the opportunity to work is accepted even though the profits from making pottery are meager. This study is not only about women workers in La Chamba, Colombia, but much of it applies to home-based women workers throughout the world, whether it be the Americas, Asia, Africa, or Europe.

The dynamic between indigenous culture and the mestizo world is an important aspect of La Chamba ceramics making. Most artisans in Colombia today are identified as mestizos, but their craft traditions are primarily indigenous and not Iberian. Although the indigenous cultures of Colombia were never totally dominated politically or militarily during the Spanish colonial period, a further step in that direction may be happening today as mestizo people are encouraged by market forces to adopt mass-production techniques and forms of work organization. As a result, indigenous design styles and patterns of work are increasingly compromised. A contradiction exists in that entrepreneurs frequently use the "exotic" appeal of indigenous craft to create a market, even though the subcontracting system and the distribution networks used to market the crafts are typical of global capitalism today.

This study of La Chamba ceramics is part of my larger research plan to study traditional ceramics in Colombia, including the differences in men's and women's pottery systems in Ráquira (Duncan 1998), children workers in pottery (Duncan 1985a), descriptions of prehispanic ceramics (Duncan 1996, 1993, 1992b, 1989; Duncan et al. 1993), and historical ceramics (Duncan 1986, 1985b, 1984). The purpose of these various studies is to understand material culture as a measure of social organization and thought within a society.

La Chamba Ceramics

I first encountered La Chamba ceramics in 1972 in Bogotá, and I was struck by the clean, efficient lines of the design, the satin-smooth textures, and the saturated red and black monochrome surfaces. A few days after moving to the city that year, my wife and I visited the Museo de Artes y Tradiciones Populares (Museum of Popular Arts and Traditions), which exhibits the major crafts produced throughout Colombia. Work from La Chamba was displayed in the section on ceramics, and I stood before the pots intrigued by the graceful profile lines and the light reflecting off the polished surfaces. Some of the pieces were quite large, amphoras over one meter tall and storage pots that bulged out into diameters sixty centimeters wide. More than just functional pots, these were abstract sculptures, based on the geometric form of the sphere and curved profiles. Soon I saw smaller La Chamba bowls and pots in the *artesanías* (crafts) shops in El Chico, the boutique district of the city, and these were intended for use. Then we were invited for dinner at my brother-in-law's house, and we were served *ajiaco,* a traditional Colombian stew, in jet-black bowls from La Chamba. The satin black color was like that of classic Grecian pottery.

More than a year later, we had the opportunity to travel to La Chamba with Nina and Robert Friedemann and observe the making of this pottery and to see the kilns in which it was fired. The slick elegance of the pottery had led me to expect a village that would be visually more sophisticated than other small Colombian towns, but that was not the case. As we turned off the main highway and began the seventeen-kilometer ride down a rough dirt road, dust and heat dominated my senses. We passed kilometers of fields planted in sorghum, rice, and cotton, and a large, modern hacienda that reflected the wealth of the landowners. We passed pastures with cattle clustered together under the few shade trees to escape the hot midday sun. Along the road a few adobe houses with thatched roofs were built in shady groves of trees.

Just before reaching the town itself, we began to see the first dome-shaped kilns beside the houses. At the entrance to the town, the Artesanías de Colombia (Crafts of Colombia) building sat on the left side of the road. The combination of bamboo, thatch, and stone used in the building copied the traditional architecture of the region.

In the showroom of the center we saw pieces rarely seen in Bogotá, such as a sow feeding her piglets or a donkey loaded with water pots. One of these unusual pieces was a large, brilliantly burnished, iron red *tinaja* (water pot), which stood out from the hundreds of repetitively made soup bowls and cooking pots that filled the room. That *tinaja* showed that traditional craft techniques could be used to create beautiful individual pieces of ceramics. What was the origin of the design? How were the deep iron red color and the soft reflection of the light from the surface produced? When I was able to return to La Chamba years later to do research, no one was making those *tinajas,* but I did learn the techniques of design and craftsmanship that had been used to make them. I also came to know the complexity of the social arrangements and cultural heritage that permit the women to make this pottery.

Fieldwork in La Chamba

Although my wife, Gloria, and I observed ceramics production in La Chamba in the 1970s, ten years passed before we were able to do systematic research there. In 1983 I received an appointment in Colombia as a Fulbright Senior Lecturer, which permitted me to renew research on traditional ceramics in the country.

In 1985 we were able to initiate the systematic study of the ceramics of La Chamba, which we continued in stages until 1999. Since very little research has been published on the ceramics of this village or the larger craft tradition of the Tolima-Huila region of Colombia, doing research there offered the possibility of contributing to the knowledge of a little-studied area. During the 1985–86 research period, we identified types of pottery, representative potters working with the various styles of ceramics, and marketing outlets. We became acquainted with the five households of an extended family (the Pradas) in the central part of the village, which included three generations of women potters. Within that one extended family, the three major styles of ceramics were made, including traditional cooking pots, urban-oriented tableware, and the "fine ceramics" of the younger generation. We did the basic documentation of the stages of forming, burnishing, drying, and firing ceramics.

During this period, we also worked with two nuclear families who made traditional cooking pots and tableware, and who lived just outside of the village on the banks of the Magdalena River. The Sandoval family, including mother and daughter, make tableware and beautifully finished "fine ceramics" pieces. Next to them lived an older couple, Doña Julia and Don Roberto Avilés, who made traditional cooking pots. With Doña Julia we were able to document the traditional processes of clay preparation, pot formation, burnishing, and firing. In addition to the tableware made by the Sandovals, we were able to observe and document the evolution of the figurative work done by the son of that family, Eduardo, who lived in Bogotá but still brought his pieces home to fire.

Over the next few years, we repeatedly visited these families, especially the Pradas, and occasionally visited virtually all of the potters in La Chamba. During this period, Mercedes Mendez became an important guide for us, introducing us to the members of her extended family, most of whom lived on the edge of the village near Artesanías de Colombia. Mercedes was unmarried and only occasionally made ceramics, but her married sister made water filters and her aunts made tableware. They included us in their firings and taught us the art of properly balancing a round-bottomed cooking pot on the ground. Her stepfather bought ceramics from the local potters and marketed them in surrounding towns, and he showed me how he worked as a local middleman.

We did most of our research during the women's normal morning and afternoon working hours, but occasionally we would make night visits and sometimes be present for the nighttime firings that are done during rush periods. Gloria's presence was always necessary because as a man I could not make prolonged unaccompanied visits with women, so we normally went together to the potters' houses. Both of us interviewed them about their work, and I made the observation notes and wrote up the completed interviews. I also interviewed the men on firing procedures and other activities in which they are involved, such as obtaining wood and mining the clay for slip.

In 1986–87, the International Development Research Centre of Canada funded a project for us to study education and children's work patterns in La Chamba. This facilitated the collection of additional social and cultural information on the community. During this period, we visited the schools and interviewed parents and children about education.

In 1987 we did a household survey to collect data on family organization and work patterns in the 184 households that made up the village nucleus.

Gloria and I interviewed the potters in half of the households, and Greta Friedemann, an anthropology student, and Mercedes Mendez, the young adult daughter of one of the informant families, interviewed the other half. The survey was constructed to obtain information on gender and work within the household, division of labor between generations, patterns of collaboration between multiple women potters within households, and kiln sharing. This information complemented the participant observation and interviews that characterized the research with the various individual family groups.

The primary field data were collected during a series of research trips to La Chamba between 1985 and 1990, while we lived in Colombia. My field journals, covering the first three years, were stolen in 1988 in Bogotá, but I had written up the most important information in secondary documents. I collected additional information during shorter trips in 1992, 1995, and 1998. In 1999 we collected current market information on La Chamba ceramics and interviewed Eduardo Sandoval on his most recent work. The constantly changing value of the peso in Colombia over the last fifteen years has made it difficult to establish comparable prices from year to year. To provide a more stable point of reference, most prices are given both in pesos and U.S. dollars.

The research covered all areas of the community, and we personally interviewed most of the ceramics-producing families. Our fieldwork was also supplemented by other sources of information. The earliest study of the community was a thesis written by Carmen Lara (1972) for an anthropological degree from the University of the Andes in Bogotá; this focused primarily on the history and community organization of La Chamba, but it also included information on ceramics production. I consulted Lara's work extensively during the early stage of our research. Since then, Artesanías de Colombia has commissioned a number of specialized studies on La Chamba, and we have consulted the unpublished reports from those studies in the archives of the organization.

Our research as well as the other studies done in the community indicate that the last few decades have been a time of change and innovation in design styles and working patterns. These are adjustments that women have been making to the economic opportunities brought by the capitalist expansion of the last half of the twentieth century. Although the market pressures for increased production have led potters in other pottery centers, such as Ráquira, to abandon the traditional working styles associated with their communities, the women of La Chamba have made adaptations to recent market pressures that are consistent with their prehispanic, indigenous, and mestizo pottery tradition.

While we were doing this research, the potters of La Chamba repeatedly protested to us the inequities of the marketing system that gave them minimal returns on their labor. We observed their work and the dozens of pots and bowls they produced weekly, which were sold to middlemen as quickly as they could be completed. We also saw the minimal economic circumstances in which they live. However, in the analysis of the data, these issues became more salient. A woman's production unit, including herself and children or older relatives, in combination can work twenty hours per day to earn an income equal to the official daily minimum wage for men in commercial agriculture working an eight-hour day.

Why are these women paid so little for well-finished crafts when there is a strong market demand? Oversupply is one factor. Since many women have no other alternative for income-producing work, they dedicate themselves to ceramics. However, in Colombia other social factors are at work, including discrimination against rural, non-European people as well as gender discrimination against women, who are seen as housewives and not as professional potters.

The issue of ethics in the marketplace arises. Why is it acceptable that middlemen charge as much for one or two days of work as a woman and her entire family work unit can charge for three weeks of work? Human rights issues are not only political ones, they are also economic. The results of this research suggest that people who manage the economic system use it to their advantage, increasing their own income even though it means denying the women potters even a subsistence-level minimum wage. The potters recognize this situation and protest that they are not receiving a just return for their work. This study reflects these issues as part of the documentation and interpretation of continuity and change among the women potters of La Chamba. My interest on initiating the research in La Chamba was in the design and making of ceramics, but as I discovered the preoccupation of the women potters with their economic situation, I realized that the research also had to include that dimension to accurately reflect the social circumstances of the community.

Chapter Overview

Chapter 1 discusses the effect of capitalism on indigenous-mestizo traditions and home-based women workers, with attention to the particular case of La

Chamba. Chapter 2 describes the history of Tolima province, including the social history of the region and how it has contributed to present-day social and economic stratification. The community of La Chamba and its history are described in Chapters 3 and 4. Chapters 5 and 6 address the family organization and women's work patterns. Chapters 7, 8, and 9 examine the three styles of ceramics made in the community. The specific forms or shapes made within each style are described, setting each in its historical and economic context.

Chapter 10 considers the technology of clays, tools, and kilns. The final two chapters (11 and 12) describe and analyze the economic aspects of the production, including pricing, middlemen, and markets. The economic priorities of women in work are discussed along with their role as home-based workers within the subcontracting chains that have come to characterize the global economy.

This study of ceramics making as a contemporary rural craft permits an analysis of the dynamic of change in the craft as well as an analysis of the economic role of women in rural Colombia today. Although this research started as a study of the forms and techniques of making ceramics, the economic struggle of the women potters and their children became more and more apparent with each research trip that we made to the community. So the project became a broader study of mothers and children working together, using traditional indigenous pottery techniques to deal with the demands of the expanding market-based economy that surrounds them.

I

Women, Mestizo Craft Traditions, and Capitalism

Capitalism has a history of underpaid labor ranging from sweatshops and mill towns to home-based piece work, and the labor of women and children is a prominent part of that history. Today, women and children working at home in non-industrialized regions, such as La Chamba, are an underpaid labor reservoir that is helping fuel the expansion of craft capitalism in the emerging global economy. Along with the publicized cases of underpaid workers in the *maquiladoras* along the U.S.-Mexican border and in Asian sweatshops, there is a less visible world of home-based women and children workers in the crafts. Their economic exploitation is as serious as that of factory workers.

The exploitation of labor in Colombia has been documented since the Spanish colonial period, when indigenous people were required to perform unpaid labor for the Spanish. Today the same socioeconomic structure continues in place, featuring the mestizo descendents of those indigenous people working for subsistence-level wages in the market economy. This study looks at the mestizo women potters of La Chamba, Colombia, and their children, whose work is paid at rates well below the legal minimum wage of the country. They form a link in the global economy of crafts that has emerged in recent decades, with their production being exported to urban centers in Colombia, the United States, and other industrialized countries.

Home-based women workers (and the children who work with them) are the perfect laborers for craft capitalism because they can be contracted at low wages, and they will work "flexible" schedules according to market demand. Since women in many societies cannot leave home or their domestic obligations to work in wage-based jobs in factories or other workplaces, they instead do home-based work on contract to supplement the household income. Merchants and middlemen form subcontracting chains to hire these women, who are frequently paid less than the legal minimum salaries that they would be paid in regular jobs (Prugl 1996a, 43). Home-based work is characteristic of women who live in societies in which they are largely limited to house-based activities because of domestic obligations or patriarchal constraints.

La Chamba and Capitalism

The women potters of La Chamba are the underpaid producers of craft goods at the bottom of the socioeconomic structure in Colombia. As the mestizo heirs of the indigenous potters of the Department (state) of Tolima, they continue to use indigenous techniques to make largely indigenous vessel forms. However, they are also heirs to the history of Spanish conquest and colonialism, which defines their indigenous ancestors as the lowest caste of rural workers in the quasi-feudal economic system of their region. Although they are linked into the global economy today, their position at the bottom of their local society and economy remains the same as it has been for the last four hundred years. This caste is largely disenfranchised and disempowered, so they have little possibility of challenging their underremuneration. In recent years the source of their exploitation has shifted from the landlords who underpaid them for their agricultural labor to middlemen who contract them at less than official wages. Instead of being independent craft producers, the women potters of La Chamba are now proletarian contract workers.

Although they are mestizo (mixed culture) potters, they are also primary heirs to the Tolima-based precolumbian, indigenous cultural tradition, which is reflected in their ceramics making. Following the prehispanic indigenous pattern, only women make pottery while men are engaged in agriculture. The story of their evolution from prehispanic potters to ceramists in the global economy shows how indigenous traditions have been preserved by the women within this mestizo culture, as they have made adaptations to contemporary economic realities.

La Chamba is a village whose people are largely of indigenous descent; they represent the rural working caste of mestizos in the Departments of Tolima and Huila, Colombia. The semi-nucleated community, as it is presently formed, has existed for a century, but it has a much longer history and appears in Spanish colonial records as early as 1746 (Lara 1972, 36). The people of La Chamba have been affected by the major economic and political events of the last century, including La Guerra de los Mil Días (the Thousand

Days' War), La Violencia, the expansion of agrarian capitalism, the land invasions of the 1970s, and the formation of leftist resistance movements. During this time they have built their community, developed a lifestyle based on their socioeconomic context, and maintained their indigenous-style ceramics tradition. Patterns of housing, household organization, and institutional development reflect their heritage as the indigenous-mestizo descendants of the rural working caste in Tolima.

From the Spanish Conquest to the present the people of Tolima and Huila have been subject to the political, military, and economic dominance of outside powers. Similar to what is happening in other Andean countries (Miles and Buechler 1997, 3), the most recent influence has been the expansion of capitalism, first the agrarian capitalism that replaced their sharecropper economy and then craft capitalism. The latter has developed as La Chamba potters have become contracted workers for merchants and middlemen from larger towns and cities. Potters no longer determine what they will produce, nor where they will sell it. The market economy has increased the potters' incomes, but it has also led to long hours of underpaid work.

In recent decades, global capitalism has used the home-based women and children of subordinate social and ethnic groups in Africa, Asia, and Latin America as labor that can be contracted at less than subsistence wages. The contracting of people who are economically vulnerable because of ethnicity (for example, Indians), gender (women), residence (isolated rural workers), and age (children) all too frequently leads to exploitation in the form of wages below the officially established minimum. These workers accept the subminimal pay because they have no other alternatives for income in economies that are increasingly money based.

The women potters of La Chamba exemplify the process of change from indigenous traditions to contemporary capitalist patterns of work, economy, and community organization. This research shows how they have retained key aspects of indigenous material culture and work organization as they have adapted to national and international economics as home-based workers contracted to distant business interests. The evolution of the women of La Chamba from indigenous-mestizo village potters to potters working on contract in a global economy shows the changing position of indigenous peoples in the world as they make the transition from subsistence agriculture to capital-based economies.

Before the Spanish Conquest of the La Chamba area in the early 1600s, indigenous pottery was a domestic craft primarily supplying the needs of

household members and local markets. The craft retained this same character for two centuries following the Conquest. In the late 1800s La Chamba
potters began trading with broader regional markets, and by the 1950s they
had begun to enter national markets. By the 1970s they were completely
linked into the national economy as workers on contract who depended on
the market demands of larger cities. Although the techniques of making
ceramics in La Chamba are the same as the prehispanic-indigenous ones,
new styles have emerged in recent decades in response to the urban markets.
While La Chamba potters are heirs to the indigenous tradition of precolumbian ceramics, they are now mestizo, proletarian workers on contract to
merchants in Bogotá and other cities. This synthesis of two contradictory
systems, one tribal and ancient and the other capitalist and contemporary,
defines the ceramics culture of La Chamba today.

Ceramic Design as Cultural History

The visual design of ceramics in La Chamba has reflected its use in the
community at each stage of history, and there are four major stages in the
cultural evolution of La Chamba ceramics. These stages are tribal ceramics,
provincial ceramics, contemporary market ceramics, and "fine" figurative
ceramics. As the cultural and economic conditions of the people have changed,
they have altered the forms and designs of their pottery and the way it is
distributed. This has resulted from a synthesis of precolumbian and European traditions that can be seen in the cultural *mestizaje* or mixing of people
and traditions. La Chamba shares the evolution from precolumbian ceramics to contemporary market ceramics with other indigenous groups in the
Americas, including pottery centers in Colombia (Duncan 1998), Mexico
(Lackey 1982), Guatemala (Reina and Hill 1978), and the United States
(Wyckoff 1985).

   The first stage of tribal ceramics in the Americas existed in the prehispanic
period and included both undecorated functional ceramics and painted or
sculpted ceramics, which were a part of rituals and burials. For example, the
ideological underpinning of indigenous Pijao culture and ceramics in Tolima
(the region of La Chamba) focused on shamanism and the spiritual power
that the shaman represented. In the prehispanic crafts, this power was communicated through figures made in ceramics, wood, and gold (Simón 1981,
6:445; Reichel-Dolmatoff 1988, 102–7) and probably in the painted designs
on pots. Both the indigenous and mestizo people of today began with that
indigenous basis of culture, but this ideological foundation eroded under the

attacks of the Spanish and the establishment of Christianity. This led to the next stage of provincial ceramics during the Spanish colonial period.

Provincial country ceramics consisted of the daily functional ware of undecorated cooking pots (*ollas*) and water bottles (*múcuras*), which were tribal ceramics that local potters continued to make (see photographs 1.1 and 1.2). The loss of tribal identity during the colonial period by the Pijaos and their descendants was reflected in the loss of the traditional iconography of painted designs and figures in ceramics. The undecorated functional ware of the Pijao descendants changed very little under the Spanish because it continued to serve the same domestic needs of agricultural people for holding water and food. In La Chamba, these indigenous-style country cooking pots and bowls have continued to be an important part of ceramics production up to the present.

The third stage began in the 1940s and 1950s, when the potters of La Chamba began making urban market ceramics as Tolima evolved from a sharecropping economy to a capitalist agricultural economy. Just when the

Photo 1.1. *Ollas* (cooking pots). These are indigenous-style cooking pots made in La Chamba, primarily by the older generation of potters. The La Chamba *olla* is always made with a neck and a slightly flaring mouth rim. This form is the basic reference for vessel shapes in the village. These pots are ready to be loaded into the kiln. The larger ones are 40 cm in diameter and the smaller ones 30 cm.

Photo 1.2. *Múcura* (water jug). This is a prehispanic form, and it is used to carry water to the fields. A wooden plug is carved to fit tightly in the spout so that the water does not spill. This one will hold approximately two liters. The size is 30 cm tall and 16 to 17 cm in diameter.

men were becoming hired day laborers in industrial agriculture, new factory-made metal cooking pots became available to them. These new pots reduced their need for traditional ceramic pots. Although they continued making cooking and water pots for local markets, they created new tableware forms for urban markets, including casseroles, platters, and the traditional eating bowl. With that, the Colombian version of international craft capitalism became the dominant force in La Chamba ceramics, affecting work relationships, workshop organization, styles, and prices. Potters redefined their craft to meet the demands of emerging urban markets. It could not continue as an indigenous-mestizo craft making containers for local markets because it could not compete with industry. Gradually, La Chamba potters transformed their craft into a proletarian production system of low-cost handmade goods for urban markets. Since La Chamba potters were interested in ceramics as a source of income, they essentially became home-based production workers on contract to middlemen and market demand.

Out of this market approach to the crafts, the fourth stage of La Chamba ceramics has emerged, called "fine" ceramics locally. These one-off pieces (similar shapes made one-by-one by hand) include some one-of-a-kind (unique) pieces, and they are hand modeled with figures and special high-luster finishes. Some "fine" ceramics are for display rather than function, and they bring higher prices in national and international markets. Since these one-off pieces are made for urban bourgeois buyers, they are not used locally and only loosely refer to La Chamba traditions. This is an art form created from precolumbian, Spanish, and perhaps Chinese models to fit the imagination of buyers with urban cultural references, which specifically means well-to-do customers in Colombian cities and abroad. This is similar to the Pueblo potters of the U.S. Southwest converting their traditional weaving and pottery into market-oriented crafts in the early twentieth century (Wyckoff 1985:80). In this evolution from indigenous-prehispanic ceramics to the urban art markets of today, La Chamba potters have retained their indigenous roots, but they have also forged an adaptation to the contemporary economic world. All the while their identity with their indigenous heritage has eroded under the national acclaim for Spanish culture and simultaneous disdain for indigenous culture.

Indigenous Culture and the Myth of Hispanization

One way to invalidate a culture is to claim that it no longer exists. Urban Colombians generally consider the indigenous cultural tradition to be extinct or to survive only in small marginal groups in the mountains or jungles. To be Indian in Colombia means speaking the tribal language, practicing indigenous customs, wearing tribal dress, and living in a community identified as Indian. When they have an overlay of Spanish culture (especially language and religion), people are considered mestizo. Since Colombian national culture is heavily "mestizoized," indigenous culture becomes invisible and is forgotten in favor of the higher status faux Spanish identity.

The people of La Chamba think of themselves as mestizos, Colombians, Tolimenses, and Chambunos, rather than Indian, even though their indigenous heritage is apparent in the name of their town, their genetic makeup, their family organization, their techniques of ceramics making, their work organization, their residence patterns, and many other aspects of their language and material culture. Much, if not most, of mestizo behavior is indigenous in origin, especially in rural Colombia and in small towns and villages like La Chamba.

In Colombia, as in other parts of Latin America, the myth of hispanization has created the illusion that the prehispanic indigenous culture has not made a significant contribution to contemporary national culture. This myth suggests that mestizos are not Indian when in fact their genes and culture may be primarily Indian. It falsely suggests that Colombia is a European, Spanish society, rather than a mestizo, American society with primarily indigenous roots. This myth is perpetuated by the elites of European descent to camouflage the colonial nature of their domination of the disenfranchised majority of indigenous, mestizo, and mulatto peoples.

Carmen Lara's study (1972, 29) of the ceramics of La Chamba reflects this attitude by referring to the "extinction" of the Pijaos, suggesting no extant cultural or biological descent from them. However, in the same study she refers to several Pijao cultural characteristics that appear in La Chamba ceramics (p. 32), and she also refers to the "indigenous facial features" of La Chamba residents (p. 65). Although she repeats the commonly accepted idea of Pijao extinction, she has data showing the presence of indigenous culture and genetic heritage in the contemporary population. The confusion, I believe, results from the fact that the political and military apparatus of the tribe did become extinct, but the people did not. Such misplaced assumptions lead to erroneous interpretations of research results, and Lara, for example, fails to note that the mestizo ceramics of La Chamba are essentially indigenous. This invisibility of Native American culture and its influence in mestizo Colombia today began with the negative, ethnocentric rhetoric against the Indian people during the Spanish colonial period.

Negative Rhetoric toward Indigenous People

Initial references by the Spanish to the indigenous people of Tolima, the Pijaos, in the 1500s (Aguado 1956) gave them only passing coverage without the vilification that characterized later portrayals. When the Spanish declared war against the Pijaos in 1606, General Juan de Borja wrote to King Philip III justifying his use of genocidal military tactics (1922b, 134). He accused the Pijaos of being inhuman and villainous, and most notably of being cannibals. He seems to have believed that the accusation of cannibalism exonerated him and his men from their own atrocities. Later, as Fray Pedro Simón (1981) wrote his landmark historical account of the conflict in the 1600s, he used the same terms and arguments as Borja. He portrayed Indians in negative images that range from their being uncivilized to being inhuman. In so doing, he became an authoritative source of negative rhetoric toward indigenous peoples (Bolaños 1994, 30) and helped validate the rejection of indigenous culture that still characterizes Colombian society.

Eventually, this negative depiction of the Pijaos was generalized to all indigenous groups and became established as the Colombian national image of them (Bolaños 1994, 31f). Indigenous people and their cultures were defined as an alien "other" not acceptable to the Spanish. This rejection of indigenous culture led as well to the nullification and denial of indigenous cultural contributions, such as pottery. Since then indigenous cultural influences on the mestizo society of Colombia have been largely ignored, and mestizo village ceramics have been viewed more as a marginal activity by poor, uneducated *campesinos* (peasants) rather than as a reminder of the rich precolumbian heritage from which they are derived. Most indigenous agricultural people who adopted the Spanish language were redefined as mestizos, and gradually their indigenous heritage became invisible.

Colombia and Mestizo Culture

Colombia is an inherently mestizo nation, and indigenous influences can be seen particularly in the crafts, such as ceramics. Like the other Andean countries, Colombia has a substantial indigenous-mestizo cultural heritage and extensive crafts production. The relative importance of indigenous, Spanish, or African culture varies from region to region, and usually ceramics are a good measure of that variation.

Colombia does not have the predominantly European population and cultural patterns of the southern cone countries of Argentina, Chile, and Uruguay. However, claiming descent from European ancestors and affirming European cultural values is important among the educated elite in Colombia and the working classes that emulate them. Rarely do Colombian mestizos or mulattos claim, much less celebrate, their indigenous or African roots. This negative attitude toward non-European influences on national culture can be seen in the ambivalent attitudes toward indigenous-based crafts.

At the time of independence in 1819, Colombia had a population of just over 1.3 million people (Céspedes del Castillo 1992, 393) and 45 percent of that population was mestizo (ibid., 399). Another 35 percent was indigenous, making the overwhelming majority (80 percent) of the country Indian or mestizo. Fourteen percent were of Spanish descent, and 6 percent of the people were of African descent. Since independence the process of *mestizaje* (cultural and genetic mixing of Spanish and Indian people) has continued, while some limited immigration has added to the European population.

Although the Colombian census does not collect North American–style racial data, the census bureau, the Instituto Geográfico "Agustín Codazzi" (Augustine Codazzi Geographic Institute) has calculated (1969, xi) the composition of the population to be mestizo (47.8 percent), mulatto (24 percent), of European descent (20 percent), African descent (6 percent), and indigenous descent (2.2 percent). According to these calculations, 50 percent of the population is indigenous or mestizo while another 30 percent is African or mulatto (African and Spanish), making 80 percent of the population non-European. Since mixed-race people historically have been raised by their lower-caste mothers rather than their Spanish fathers, the non- European cultural influences are stronger than the Spanish ones. The Spanish-European cultural influences are strongest in the cities, and the indigenous-African cultural influences are strongest in the rural areas and small towns. Indigenous influences are predominant in the mountainous interior of the country, and African influences predominate in the coastal lowlands.

Although rigid racial categories are not used in Colombia, there is a system of defining skin color differences along a continuum of light-skinned to dark-skinned people. This follows the caste hierarchy of Colombian society, with the light-skinned Europeans at the top and the darker-skinned Indians, Africans, mestizos, and mulattos at the bottom. The four principal terms used are *rubio* (blond or fair-skinned), *trigueño* (olive-skinned), *moreno* (brown), and *negro* (black). The term *moreno* may be used to refer to people who have Indian background or people who have some African parentage because it describes a skin color without assigning a racial category. These are descriptive terms like the colors for eyes and hair rather than racial categories.

Other related terms are *mestizo* (mixed Indian and Spanish), *mulato* (African and Spanish parentage), *zambo* (African and Indian parentage), and *indio* (Indian). Marriage is preferred with a person of lighter skin color, which is called *mejorando la raza* (improving the race). Although *raza* means race in a generic sense, it is also used to refer specifically to indigenous people. So *mejorando la raza* means that dark-skinned indigenous people are improved genetically when they marry lighter-skinned people and give their offspring European characteristics. Similar attitudes are common in other Andean countries (Weismantel 1997, 32).

From the Spanish colonial period to the present, there have been continuing attempts to deculturate the indigenous groups. The campaigns to "pacify the Indians" during the Conquest and those to "integrate the Indians" today have essentially the same effect of eroding indigenous traditions in favor of becoming "modernized," "civilized," or "westernized." These efforts are in effect ethnocide (Friedemann, Friede, and Fajardo 1981, 50–51). However, rather than losing their indigenous traditions, the mestizo population of

Colombia has synthesized them with the public, Iberian cultural elements imposed on them by the Spanish and preserved them.

The public elements imposed by the Conquest culture include language, religion, political organization, social caste, and the system of property ownership. Within the first century of the Conquest, a modus operandi had been negotiated between the local indigenous populations and the Spanish about how to use those elements. The Spanish language was adopted as a lingua franca among the many tribes, but it incorporated important vocabulary from tribal languages, such as the place names Bogotá, Chamba, Guamo, Natagaima, and Coyaima. Although Christianity was adopted, tribal holy places were transformed into Christian holy places, and the Virgin Mary also acquired the semantic overtones of the mother earth figure.

Another important contribution of the Spanish was the formation of a unified government over the entire northern Andes region, including Colombia, Venezuela, Ecuador, and Panama. Simultaneously, the Spanish borrowed many elements of indigenous material culture (including crafts and building practices) and agriculture (corn, potatoes, squash, cotton, and rubber, among others). Although the Spanish dominated urban, official culture, the local regional and domestic aspects of culture continued to be primarily indigenous. That led to the regional cultures in Colombia being differentiated along the lines of the indigenous groups that made up the populations in the colonial period.

Ceramics and Region

The regions of ceramics making in Colombia today are identified according to the predominant cultural heritage of the potter, either Spanish or indigenous. Communities where men are the potters use Spanish techniques, and communities where women are the potters use indigenous techniques. There are four ceramics-making regions in Colombia, distinguished according to cultural origin: (1) the prehispanic-indigenous-mestizo tradition (Tolima and Huila with pockets of women potters in other regions); (2) the mestizo-Spanish-Moorish tradition from Andalusia introduced in the early colonial period (in the Departments of Cundinamarca and Boyacá, the southern highlands and Cauca Valley, and the lower Magdalena Valley); (3) the areas of poorly developed crafts (the Departments of Antioquia and Santander), which were settled late in the colonial era by northern Spanish groups (from Galicia, León, and Catalonia), and (4) indigenous ceramics.

The two cultural traditions (Spanish and Indian) that dominate the interior of the country can be seen in the styles of the pottery water pots, the

Spanish amphora and the indigenous *tinaja*. The Spanish-style amphoras exist throughout the lower Magdalena River Valley from Honda to Santa Marta, an area of significant Spanish cultural influence. This region was the main artery for commerce between Bogotá and the Atlantic coast until the mid-twentieth century, and these amphoras were shipped as trade goods up and down the river. Potters in Mompós (a lower Magdalena River port) still made these amphoras until recently (Perdomo 1965, 5).

In contrast, the prehispanic, indigenous *tinaja* was used primarily in the communities of the upper Magdalena River Valley, such as La Chamba, reflecting the predominant indigenous heritage in this region. Whereas the amphora is a tall form, the *tinaja* has a broader profile similar to the prehispanic cooking pot. It is a conical pot with a marked V-shaped profile, and it opens to a broad shoulder, then closes in sharply to the mouth (see Photograph 1.3). It makes a broad surface of water available at the top of the pot,

Photo 1.3. *Tinaja* (water storage pot). This *tinaja* is a "fine ceramics" version that has been made as a decorative pot with a high surface sheen. The size is 70 cm tall by 60 cm in diameter.

near the mouth, so that it is easy to dip water out of it. Differences such as
this one between the Spanish amphora and the indigenous *tinaja* are cultural
markers delineating the influence of Spanish and indigenous traditions. Although the mestizo villages of today share a common indigenous cultural
core, they are different from one region to another. Local agricultural needs,
the varying kinds of Spanish influence, and the preexisting tribal differences
contribute to these regional differences.

Mestizaje and Cultural Origin

Colombia has a tripartite cultural heritage that is Spanish-Moorish, Native
Colombian, and African. Given the cultural tensions in Colombia between
these three traditions, the struggle for the minds and actions of the people
produces regional divisions in Colombian society that are ethnically based.
These cultural divisions separate the upper and lower castes, urban and rural
communities, and even the gender roles of men and women. When the
Spanish Conquest cut off the trunk line of prehispanic ceramics, new growth
began in many directions, much like the new shoots on a pruned tree. As new
regional ceramic traditions developed, they took on their cultural identities
according to the degree of indigenous and Spanish influences.

On one hand, indigenous people who successfully resisted Spanish intervention, such as the people of the Amazon and the Sierra Nevada of Santa
Marta, have continued many of their traditions virtually intact. On the other
hand, the populations of the Andean mountain and river valley areas that
were subject to conquest and acculturation are now primarily mestizos.
Most followed a pattern of mixed resistance and adaptation to the Spanish
cultural presence in which they retained some aspects of indigenous culture
and borrowed others from the Spanish. The pottery of those mestizo groups
emerged as the village ceramics of today. One of the best indicators of indigenous influence on mestizo culture is the quality of the crafts, and the best
crafts in Colombia are from indigenous or mestizo communities.

The Indian-Spanish cultural mixture in mestizo communities varies from
one region to another, and it ranges from predominantly indigenous technology and pottery shapes to predominantly Spanish ones, depending on the
region and the gender of the potter. Although there is no tradition of purely
European ceramics in Colombia, men potters of certain regions have adopted
the Spanish style of ceramics making, especially in Boyacá and Nariño, while
women potters almost invariably use indigenous ceramics styles.

Indigenous men and women have historically had different patterns of acculturation and resistance to Spanish cultural influences. Women have retained their cultural identity more fully than men because they live and work in the house, where they are removed from foreign influences. Since indigenous men work primarily in public spaces controlled by Europeans, they have acculturated more to that world (Miles and Buechler 1997a, 8). The clothing choices of men and women from indigenous communities in Colombia, Ecuador, and Peru show this difference. Men more readily adopt Western-style clothing while women continue to wear indigenous dress. This gender contrast is also apparent in weaving technology because only women use the precolumbian-style loom, in contrast to men weavers who use the Spanish-style loom. Following this pattern, La Chamba women potters use indigenous working techniques, and most of their pottery forms are also indigenous. Since women retain much of indigenous culture and they are the primary socializers of each new generation, they perpetuate the indigenous traditions in mestizo societies.

Campesinos, Mestizos, and Caste

Campesino and *mestizo* are the two most common terms used to refer to the Colombian population. Virtually half of all Colombians are small farmers or *campesinos,* which means someone who lives in a rural area. In terms of cultural origin, half of all Colombians are mestizo. So the largest single group of Colombians is *campesino* and mestizo, like the people of La Chamba. The structural constraints on behavior imposed by the social system in Colombia affects access to education by these people, as well as limits their possibilities for work and mobility.

Colombia's rigid social-class system functions as a semi-caste system that locks certain people into their birth status. A person's caste status is determined first by their family name, with a few Spanish and other European names constituting the small elite group. The elite function as a closed caste, rarely admitting new members, and when they do, they are wealthy people of western European Christian origin. This group controls the capital markets and the political system in the country. Below them is a professional commercial class that is open and porous, and it includes people who are predominantly European in origin as well as lighter-skinned mestizos who are Eurocentric in their values. This group includes doctors, lawyers, and business people, as well as artists and intellectuals. The small Jewish and Arab populations in the country belong primarily to this class. People can gain access to this class through education and wealth.

The working classes are divided into clerical, technical, and service occupations in addition to the manual-work occupations. While the clerical, technical, and service workers constitute a class of trained workers that people can enter through education, manual workers are essentially a caste apart. They are typically more indigenous or African in origin, with their status determined by birth. Their geographic or social isolation within the nation frequently denies them access to the education necessary to enter higher occupations. The majority of craftspeople in Colombia fall into this group. Being a potter, weaver, or basketmaker is the result of being born into a group where this is the traditional occupation, and there is little or no opportunity for learning other occupations. In Colombia membership in the elite and in the group of the working poor functions like a caste into which people are born. The intermediate social groupings (professional, merchant, clerical) function as social classes in which some social mobility can occur.

Among the *campesino* class there is an important distinction between people according to their degree of Indian or African background. The more Indian *campesinos* from the Departments of Boyacá, Cauca, Huila, Nariño, and Tolima and the *campesinos* of African descent from coastal regions have historically experienced caste-like limits on their opportunities for education and mobility. They may be able to become professionals or merchants within their locality, but they can only rarely move out of their local regions to the national level. In contrast, the *campesinos* of European descent from the Departments of Antioquia, Caldas, Quindio, Risaralda, Santander, and Norte de Santander can move into the national professional and merchant class because of their European origin. So the *campesinos* of Indian-mestizo and African origin have caste limits that exclude them from access to the larger Colombian society and economy. Their caste status confines them to a future as working-class people with little hope of social or economic mobility. In terms of the craft occupations, people are born, not trained, to be potters or weavers.

From Indigenous to Proletarian Workers

Colombia's semi-caste system has been transformed in recent decades by the capitalist expansion, and it now serves to identify the proletarian workers who are needed for the new market economy. Néstor García Canclini (1990, 203) suggests that the indigenous ethnic groups in Latin America are being absorbed into a larger "popular" level of society that includes both urban and rural working classes. According to this view, the autochthonous indigenous cultures are blending into national proletarian cultures. The expansion of capitalism in recent decades has been the strongest influence in acculturating indigenous groups to the national societies since the Spanish Conquest. In Colombia even indigenous basketmakers in remote tropical rain-forest villages have now become proletarian producers of baskets designed by professionals in Bogotá for international markets. This process has been encouraged and supported by official development agencies.

García (1990, 13) juxtaposes the issues of tradition and development in Latin America, and he raises the question whether modernization should be the primary objective for countries in the region. As Latin America moves into the future, he predicts that traditional crafts will coexist with cellular telephones, computers, and other manifestations of the digital age (ibid., 200). Traditional cultures are developing and transforming themselves in the process, and he suggests that there are four reasons why traditional cultures are retaining their identities instead of being completely absorbed into national societies.

1. It is impossible to incorporate all of the population into a homogenized urban, industrial society, so some sectors of the society retain their local distinctiveness.
2. It is necessary to include traditional symbolic goods in the mass media to reach the people who are least integrated in the modernization process, and that process reinforces their identity.
3. Politicians use elements of traditional culture for political expediency to fortify their hegemony and legitimacy.
4. The popular sectors of Latin American society are indigenous and African, and they continue acting out their traditional cutlures.

Evidence of the persistence of traditional culture is in the prevalence of crafts in indigenous-mestizo communities, and the economic planners of countries with large populations of this type have begun to count their productive potential in national planning. Since indigenous-mestizo populations are primarily rural, their production is now recognized as a component in the rural sector of national economies. Traditional crafts have an important role in the developing economy of Colombia and many other countries.

Crafts and National Development

Economists frequently mention crafts for their potential role in Latin American development plans (Lauer 1984, 58ff; Urrutia and Villalba 1971, 1–3), but little mention is made of the role of women (León 1987, 84). Since the emergence of nationalistic ideologies in the 1920s and 1930s, traditional craft production has been recognized as a sector of the national economies and discussed in public policy debates. In Mexico indigenous culture has played a role in national identity since the revolution of 1910, and that country has been the leader in Latin America for official state support of traditional crafts (Lauer 1984, 69). Other countries have followed that lead and created official agencies to promote crafts for their economic potential. Ecuador and Peru created special offices within the Ministry of Industry; Guatemala and Bolivia each created a Comisión Nacional de Artes, Artesanías e Industrias Populares (National Commission for Arts, Crafts, and Popular Industries); and Colombia formed Artesanías de Colombia (Crafts of Colombia). These entities engage in activities that range from developing new technologies for increasing productivity to creating designs that are more marketable. They also create strategies for national and international marketing.

Craft work is an important source of employment in the mestizo-indigenous areas of Latin America, such as Colombia. Estimates from Artesanías de Colombia have suggested that there may be as many as 1.5 million craftspeople working in 458 of the 1,000 townships in the country (Montoya de la Cruz 1990, 15). In a survey of Latin American craft production in the early 1980s, Mirko Lauer (1984, 40) also estimated 1.5 million craftspeople in Colombia out of a population of 11 million workers. That figure represents almost 14 percent of all workers, the highest percentage in South America along with Ecuador and Peru, which have similar percentages of their labor force in the crafts.

During the period 1992–94 Artesanías de Colombia carried out a census of artisans in known craft centers within the country, but it included only people who devoted 70 percent or more of their time to crafts. This census identified 58,821 artisans (Artesanías de Colombia 1998, 22), suggesting either that the earlier estimates of 1.5 million craftspeople in the country were wrong, that almost all artisans work part-time, or that the number of artisans is dropping rapidly. In fact, all three explanations are probably true. Most artisans are rural and most are women, and both groups are usually bivocational (being artisans as well as housewives or farmers), meaning that they spend less than 70 percent of their time working in crafts. So the census criteria may have eliminated large numbers of craftswomen. However, the number of artisans may also be dropping rapidly as the national economy expands and people increasingly leave farms and small towns for urban employment. The census by Artesanías de Colombia demonstrates that the making of crafts is predominantly a small-town (16,689 or 28 percent) or rural (28,439 or 48 percent) phenomenon, accounting for a combined total of 76 percent of artisans. Only 13,693 (23 percent) lived and worked in cities.

In a study of crafts and development in Colombia, Miguel Urrutia and Clara Elsa Villalba (1971, 2) suggest that the primary purpose of economic development is to increase income levels. Simultaneously, they suggest that public policy should focus on transferring the traditional sectors of the economy to modern industries. Their position implies moving people into "modern" occupations or augmenting the productivity of the traditional ones. This means that craft workers must either abandon their occupation or mechanize it to increase their productivity and income levels. In this view of development, cultural patrimony is not critical because it does not lead to an improvement in the standard of living.

Urrutia and Villalba (1971, 2) argue that the craft sector has excellent potential for generating jobs with little capital investment. Comparing job-creation data from various industries, they noted that one new job in the chemical industry required an investment of 675,000 pesos, in contrast to only 9,508 pesos for one new job in crafts (ibid., 16), which means that jobs in the chemical industry required seventy times as much capital to create. From this point of view, crafts are a capital-efficient means of creating employment within a national development plan.

Although 57 percent of the workers in the nationwide study done by Urrutia and Villalba were in craft occupations, their work accounted for only 21 percent of the economic value of the production measured (1971, 50). Although crafts are a useful mechanism to eliminate unemployment, they do not generate higher incomes. Promoting crafts as a development strategy creates jobs and may serve to stem rural-to-urban migration by keeping craftspeople in rural areas, but it nevertheless traps people in poverty-level incomes. In non-industrialized countries like Colombia, craft is a system of handwork production and low-wage labor, and the labor-intensive quality of crafts makes them attractive to official planners as a complement to the industrial and service sectors of the economy (Urrutia 1985).

Education, Technical Assistance, and Development

Various official programs have existed in La Chamba from time to time to promote the production of market-oriented ceramics, including a technical school in ceramics in the 1940s, the SENA (Servicio Nacional de Aprendizaje, or National Learning Service) program in the 1960s, and the Arte-sanías de Colombia Center in the 1970s. Although none of the officially sponsored development efforts reached their announced goals, they did introduce new ideas that undoubtedly played a role in the subsequent changes in ceramic style. These development efforts along with the opening of roads into the town, the experiments of local people with new ideas of pottery, and the arrival of outside influences (such as the middlemen representing urban markets) combined to produce a climate of social change.

Non-governmental organizations (NGOs) have had very little presence in La Chamba. The nuns of the Order of María Inmaculada have taught literacy classes in the community, but they did little specifically to improve the situation for potters. Part of my own research was funded by the International Development Research Centre of Canada to evaluate work and education among children, but no project for intervention resulted from it. In general, NGOs have not been active with ceramics communities in Colombia, but technical-assistance missions from foreign countries have provided aid to artisans in Ráquira in the Department of Boyacá (assistance came from the United States and Japan; Duncan 1998, 29) and in Pitalito (this aid came from China), among others.

In general, artisans in Colombia have minimal educations, which affects their preparation for social change. Half of the artisans either have no formal education (17 percent) or have failed to complete the minimum of five years of elementary education (33 percent) provided by Colombian law (Arte-sanías de Colombia 1998, 23). This means that 50 percent of the artisans have little or no education, many being completely illiterate. A small minority (8 percent) have completed high school, and only 1 percent have done some study at the university level. This lack of education is consistent with the caste-like discrimination of the national society against the indigenous and mestizo populations who predomimate in rural areas in Colombia. Their lack of education locks them into lives of manual labor and low income, which benefits the large landowners and businessmen who are guaranteed a pool of cheap labor.

Most artisans have learned their craft from their parents (48 percent) or as apprentices in a workshop (14 percent), and one quarter (26 percent) of all artisans are self-taught, having received no training at all (ibid.). Thus, 88 percent of the artisans have had no training in their craft beyond the traditional knowledge of their group. Very few (7 percent) have received formal training in the techniques or designs of their craft. The rudimentary knowledge that many artisans have of their craft hinders them from developing the technical or commercial aspects of their work.

The economic development of recent decades has transformed most La Chamba potters into proletarian workers on contract, but some have been able to create a role as producers of village art (discussed below). There is a caste-like separation between village potters and university-educated ceramists, who are considered artists or designers rather than craftspeople. This separation reflects the social-class divisions of the larger society. In Japan, Canada, the United Kingdom, or the United States, it is common to find professional art ceramists referring to traditional forms and techniques in their work. That rarely occurs in Colombia because of the social barriers separating the professional art world in the cities from the village craft world.

Ceramics as Art, Craft, or Manufacturing

The intention with which ceramics are made and the concepts and techniques of making them determine whether they are fine art, village art, industrial design, or village craft. If ceramics are made as art with professional, university-trained esthetics, they may be shown in art galleries in the cities, but if they are made with the esthetics of village artists, they will be shown in craft stores as tourist goods. If ceramics are made as production goods with industrial design, they are considered as manufacturing, but if they are made with the inexpensive manual work of village potters, they are considered as crafts. Most La Chamba potters are village craftspeople making large numbers of repetitive forms, but a few of the younger generation are making special pieces called "fine ceramics," which are distinguished by their esthetic qualities in color, light, and form. So in La Chamba there is both village art and village craft.

The definition of art in Latin America, according to Néstor García Canclini (1990, 224–25), reflects the interests and tastes of wealthy urban people. This elite bourgeoisie sees the predominantly rural craftspeople as turning out repetitive work that has no special visual quality, in contrast to urban-based artists who create esthetic statements in line, form, texture, and color. To the bourgeoisie the social class of the ceramist is an important indicator distinguishing art from craft in ceramics.

In contrast to Garcia's interpretation of the difference between art and craft, Jean Clare Hendry (1992, 2) suggests that the line between the two cannot be drawn sharply because all esthetic activity is based on the special eye-hand coordination and skill with materials associated with craft. According to Hendry, craft can be art. The potters of La Chamba agree with Hendry because they understand that there is an esthetic difference between their "fine ceramics" and their regular production of tableware and cooking pots.

Historically, the terms "craftsman" and "craftswoman" have referred to an artisan in a subsistence economy who produces the domestic material goods required to sustain life, such as pottery for the cooking and storage of food. Craft is rooted in place, time, and tradition and is characterized by integrated work processes based on individually done handwork. Artisans have also been seen as independent workers who own their means of production, have a style of work, and control the disposition of their work. However, traditional rural, subsistence-oriented women artisans, working to produce baskets, pottery, and weavings only for their families, are rarities today, if they exist at all. Although La Chamba potters work with the techniques and work organization of traditional handicrafts, they now work on contract and sell their production to national markets. Is this craft or manufacturing?

Mary Helms (1993, 16) distinguishes between craftwork and manufacturing by saying that the former emphasizes the qualitative process of transforming materials while the latter emphasizes the quantitative process of production. She suggests that craft becomes industry when the production goals become more important than the act of transforming raw material into an artifact. She also points out the necessity of distinguishing between skillfully crafted material objects with esthetic qualities and ordinary crafted objects in which the utilitarian qualities dominate (ibid., 48).

In the global economic village, crafts are becoming a means of inexpensive hand production of goods that require little or no investment in machinery or other capital goods. This has changed the artisans' work from crafts infused with inalienable values to proletarian work having no value beyond the economic one. The traditional crafts are being transformed into systems of low-overhead manufacturing that use home-based women workers.

Home-Based Women as Proletarian Workers

As the rural economies of Andean countries have become increasingly capitalist in recent decades, the gender definition of labor between the Spanish and indigenous traditions has been sharp. The former has relegated women to the marginal role of supplementing the primary production of the household by men (Miles and Buechler 1997, 3–4). This is also true in Colombia. In a study of small farmers in the Department of Valle, in south central Colombia to the west of La Chamba, Cynthia Truelove (1990, 49) found that the role of women in subsistence production is declining on small farms. As a result, they are entering the "semi-proletariat" by doing piecemeal work on contract to Colombian corporations. So the subsistence family farm is being displaced, and women are responding by contracting out their labor as home-based workers. In La Chamba women contract their work to individual middlemen instead of corporations, but otherwise it seems to be the same subcontracting system that Truelove describes.

The practice of contracting home-based women in the crafts (especially ceramics and textiles) has led to their proletarianization as workers. They are compensated at less than minimum wages, which does not permit savings nor improve their standard of living. Even though home-based craftswomen live in a perpetual cycle of hard work and minimal compensation, many of them choose to make crafts because it is their only consistent source of income in economies that are increasingly money based.

The subcontracting system has converted La Chamba and other craft communities in Colombia into virtual factory towns, with the same abuse of the labor of women and children that occurred in milltowns in the United States in the nineteenth and early twentieth centuries (Morland 1958, 32). The primary difference between the factory towns described by Morland and the people of La Chamba is that the latter are home-based workers. In contrast to the overt exploitation of child labor in factory towns in the United States a century ago, in La Chamba it is less visible because children are working at home with their mothers. Although working in their own house is more benign than working in most factories, the underpayment of labor is similar.

The term "proletarian worker" suggests a person who is contracted to perform one link in a chain of production without connection to the final sale or use of the work. Industrialized proletarian handwork is standardized, commercial production of goods that may be done individually or with various individuals assigned to specialized stages of the process. With the changes brought by the capitalist expansion of recent decades, pottery making has been increasingly transformed into proletarian work that is essentially home-based manufacturing.

Although the role of crafts in non-industrialized countries is to produce goods needed in the community, after the rise of industrialism craft production has only rarely competed as a viable economic alternative to industry. In developing capitalist economies (India, Indonesia, the Philippines, Mexico, Peru, and so forth) the success of traditional handmade crafts has depended on selling them at low prices. Since the potters of La Chamba are part of the global model of consumer-oriented capitalism, they struggle with the problem of low returns for their work just as craftswomen in other countries do.

Constancy and Change in La Chamba Ceramics

In the prehispanic period in the Andes, the act of making crafts was imbued with cosmological significance, and many traditional potters of the Andes still work with values related to that cosmology (Duncan 1996, 333; Stone-Miller 1995, 14–16). However, the value drift in the definition of crafts during the global expansion of capitalism has led to their being understood primarily as commodities for the market. The young craftswomen of today understand crafts as a means of producing income rather than an act of mythological or cosmological significance.

As younger La Chamba potters have adopted the new ceramic styles and working patterns, a conservative-liberal tension has developed between them and the older potters. As each new style has appeared (first tableware and later fine ceramics), it has captured part of the market, leading to competition with preexisting styles. Although the innovators have revitalized local ceramics by expanding its economic possibilities, the older, more conservative potters have played a key cultural role in maintaining the traditional techniques, forms, and attitudes toward the craft.

The traditionalism of the older potters has provided a reference for the younger potters as they have created new forms and styles. While tradition has maintained the continuity of design through periods of change in the last century, innovators have stimulated the economic vitality that is necessary for the craft to survive. Since the La Chamba potters use prehispanic-indigenous styles and techniques of ceramics, they have kept open a window to the past and the unwritten heritage of that world. They form the slabs and roll the coils that they shape into vessels for the village, making ceramics that speak of cultural memory, of their daily domestic tasks, and of their lives.

The market economy has increased income for women potters but at the cost of long hours of work at wages that they would not accept for a regular job. To understand why women in La Chamba accept such low payment for their labor, it helps to know the history of the social-caste structure in which they live and the culture that they have developed to adapt to it. To be a rural mestizo laborer in Tolima means to be a member of a social and economic caste that is underpaid and has little or no opportunity for improved status. Understanding the indigenous origins of the potters of La Chamba is crucial to understanding their craft skill and their socioeconomic status today. Their indigenous ancestors challenged the Spanish more seriously than any other group in Colombia. Although they retained their independence from the Spanish longer than most other groups, they were eventually defeated in a genocidal military campaign that killed many and condemned others to lives of forced labor and slavery. The social history of Tolima describes how the rural society of the department, including La Chamba, came to exist.

2

Tolima

La Chamba's Place in Colombia

Geography, ethnicity, and history are important in explaining regional variations in culture and behavior in Colombia, and Tolima is a good example of the importance of these factors. Colombia is the northernmost country of the Andes and the connecting point to Central America, and it has been the traditional crossroads for migrations between the two Americas. New immigrating or invading groups have arrived in the north along the Caribbean coast and moved inland along one of the two large river valleys, the Magdalena and the Cauca. The two groups that have culturally shaped the present-day population of Tolima arrived by that route. First were the Pijao settlers who arrived a millennium ago; then came the Spanish officials, soldiers, and priests who arrived almost five hundred years ago (see Map 2.1).

While the inhabitants of northern Colombia have historically been the recipients of new influences from the Caribbean, groups in the southern regions of the country have been characterized by traditional cultures. That continues to be true, and the indigenous influences in Colombia today are the strongest in the central and southern areas, such as the upper Magdalena River Valley where Tolima is located. This is a region where the indigenous people strongly resisted the Spanish, a fact that has shaped the culture there and partially accounts for the unique character of the department.

Geography and Region

The chain of mountains traversing the country creates differences in altitude that produce a variety of climates and in turn affect agriculture, housing, work patterns, and socializing. The people who live on the valley floors and seacoasts adjust their lives to the year-round tropical heat, with temperatures ranging between twenty-five and thirty-five degrees centigrade. Those

Map 2.1. Map of Colombia. Colombia is located in the northwestern corner of South America and has both Atlantic and Pacific coasts. The country is divided by three chains of the Andes running north and south. Major rivers run through the valleys between these mountain chains, the Magdalena River in the eastern valley and the Cauca River in the western one.

Colombia

Colombians call their country *el país de bella flor,* meaning "the
country of the beautiful flower." A person sees a rose and delights in
its flower without being put off by the thorns that protect it. The
threat of the thorns is not ignored, but the color and delicacy of the
flower are emphasized. Colombia is a country of soaring Andean
peaks, rich riverine valleys, and luxurious vegetation of brilliant reds,
yellows, and greens. To live in this country is to be captivated by its
natural beauty, and by the eternal springlike climate of the mountain
towns and the rich colors of the vegetation.

Colombians also refer to their country as *el país del Sagrado
Corazón,* which means "the country of the Sacred Heart," and it is a
religious country. Rural and working-class houses usually have images
of Christ, the Virgin Mary, or saints on the walls, frequently color
prints torn from a magazine or newspaper. These images tend toward
dramatic scenes of life and death, and the image of the Sacred Heart
is a particular favorite because of its strong graphic representation of
the sacrifice of Christ. Inherent in these images is a reference to the
human violence that led not only to the killing of Christ but also to
the violence that forms part of the makeup of modern-day Colombia.

who live from one to two thousand meters on the intermediate mountain
slopes have a temperate lifestyle, with high temperatures ranging up to
twenty degrees centigrade all year. Those who live above two thousand
meters high in the mountains have a cool climate with temperatures of ten
to fifteen degrees centigrade. These contrasts in climate are reflected in the
crops, clothes, houses, and social organization of each region, so the cultural
differences between regions correlate strongly with the environmental ones.

The major geographical regions of the country are the Magdalena River
Valley (which is divided into upper and lower), the Cundinamarca-Boyacá
highland plateau, the southern highlands, the Cauca River Valley, Antioquia,
Santander, the Atlantic Coast, the Eastern Plains, the Amazon, Guajira, and
the Pacific Coast. The first seven regions listed have predominantly mestizo
populations, and the latter four have important indigenous groups.

Within these major ecological zones are hundreds of micro-ecological
niches having specialized local characteristics based on climate, vegetation,
and natural resources, and each geographical region has produced distinc-

tive cultural adaptations. Ecological zones range from cold mountain peaks to temperate hill country, tropical rain forests, and deserts. Three chains of the Andes divide the country along a north-south axis and contribute to sharp regional differences in local cultures. The two major rivers in Colombia are the Magdalena and the Cauca, and they originate in the cluster of mountains in southern Colombia called the Pasto Knot and flow north through the Andean valleys to empty into the Caribbean Sea. These two parallel river valleys have distinct histories, leading to regional cultural differences between their residents today.

La Chamba and Tolima

La Chamba is located in the upper reaches of the easternmost Andean valley, that of the Magdalena River (see Map 2.2). This valley is a rich agricultural area in the heartland of Colombia, and it is divided into the Departments of Tolima and Huila. Since the Magdalena River Valley is strategically located in the country, its control is crucial for the government and landed elite. It was one of the last regions conquered by the Spanish, and it has been a region of conflict ever since. The indigenous people of Tolima survived the war of Conquest, but they were subdued and became forced laborers for the Spanish.

Since cultural confrontations that terminate militarily rather than politically are never really solved, the seeds of antagonism have remained within Tolimense society to the present day. Within the last century that confrontation has re-emerged in the form of leftist resistance by the rural working class to the expansion of industrial agriculture by the landed elite. The potters of La Chamba work in this context of unresolved conflicts between the overlords (landowners of Spanish descent and capitalists) and the subjugated indigenous and mestizo workers and artisans. The *chambunos* (residents of La Chamba) forged their culture in this crucible of conflict and survival that began with the Spanish Conquest. It was hammered out between their reality as heirs of the indigenous Pijao heritage on one hand and their position under the socioeconomic control of Spanish descendants on the other. Since the Spanish primarily focused on controlling god, gold, and the government, they intervened very little in domestic activities such as craft making. That permitted the indigenous craft tradition to continue and even flourish in the upper Magdalena Valley, and La Chamba ceramics developed in that environment. By looking at the story of the indigenous inhabitants of Tolima, the Pijaos, their defeat by the Spanish, and the society that followed

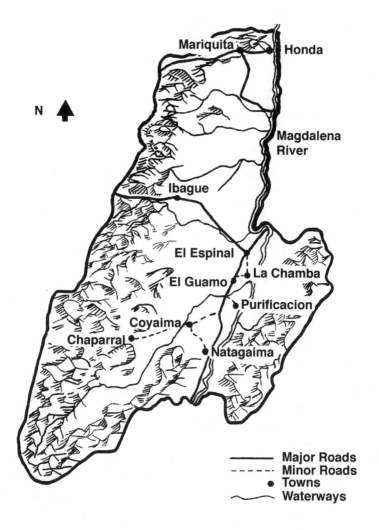

N

Mariquita Honda

Magdalena
River

Ibague

El Espinal

El Guamo La Chamba

Purificacion

Coyaima

Chaparral

Natagaima

———— Major Roads
- - - - - Minor Roads
● Towns
∼∼∼ Waterways

Map 2.2. Map of Tolima. The Department (or state) of Tolima is located in the upper Magdalena River Valley in south-central Colombia. Most of the department is fertile valley land.

that defeat, we can see the social and cultural context in which La Chamba came to exist.

The Pijaos and the Conquest of Tolima

The Pijao people occupied Tolima when the Spanish arrived. They were a Carib-language family group that had themselves invaded the region a few centuries earlier. They occupied the upper Magdalena River Valley, which extends from the rapids at Honda to its headwaters three hundred kilometers to the south. It is a vast grassy valley with rich agricultural lands bordered on the east and west by ranges of the Andes. These people called it "Tolima," meaning "land of the snows" in the Carib language (Ortega 1952, xv–xvi). The Pijaos, Coyaimas, and Natagaimas were the most important subdivisions of the Caribs mentioned by Fray Pedro Simón, the leading Spanish chronicler of these groups in the colonial period (1981, 6:446). Pijao seems to have become a general term the Spanish used to refer to any hostile indigenous group in this area since they did not distinguish one group from another with accuracy (Bolaños 1994, 23; Rappaport 1990, 38).

The Pijaos and the Panches living just to the north were village-dwelling agriculturalists who cultivated cotton, corn, yucca, sweet potatoes, and coca, and they hunted deer, guinea pigs, and birds for meat (Rojas de Perdomo 1985, 209). They were organized as independent chiefdoms with leadership based on military valor. The principal chief was a person who showed bravery in battle, and he was advised by a council of leaders also known for their military prowess. As many as seventy-two Pijao chiefs existed at the time of European contact, and each represented a different subgroup or band. With so many independent chiefdoms, shifting alliances seemed to have characterized their politics. During peacetime the chiefs had little authority and served primarily as spokespersons for the group, but during war they assumed greater authority as military commanders (Avellaneda 1995, 115; Rappaport 1990, 34–35). The Pijao and Panche soldiers were well organized and disciplined, and the Spanish likened them to European soldiers (Rojas de Perdomo 1985, 211).

Among the Pijaos the spiritual leader was the *mohán,* a shaman or healer, who could be either a man or woman. They made large spirit figures the size of a person in wood or stone, and they made others in wood or ceramics that were small enough to hold in the hand. Before battle the *mohán* supervised the offerings of lances, arrows, and stone weapons to the guardian spirits to obtain their blessing and read the ashes of certain plants to predict the outcome of battle. The Pijaos believed that the *mohán* could fly (Simón 1981, 6:81), a characteristic frequently ascribed to the shaman in indigenous groups in Colombia (Reichel-Dolmatoff 1988, 80–81).

Sebastián de Belalcázar, who founded Quito (1535) and Popayán and Cali (1536), first tried to enter Tolima in 1537 through Páez territory in the southern mountains. He encountered stiff resistance from the Páez and re-treated to Popayán after they killed twenty-six of his two hundred soldiers (Simón 1981, 5:233). However, the next year indigenous guides and allies successfully led Belalcázar and his men through the Andes to the Tolima side, avoiding conflict with the Páez. They reached the largest indigenous town in the region, Timaná, which had a population of five hundred inhabitants. Timaná was and is located in the mountains on the southern end of the upper Magdalena Valley near the ceremonial necropolis of San Agustín.

After a rest, Belalcázar and his men were led to the indigenous town of Neiva, located in Pijao territory in the Magdalena River Valley. The Pijaos seem not to have resisted the Spanish at that point, and Belalcázar claimed Neiva as a Spanish town (1538) and began the *repartimientos de los indios* (giving the rights to Indian labor and their lands) to the soldiers accompa-nying him (Simón 1981, 5:235). He left a small garrison of men to control Neiva and pushed on to Bogotá and the lands of the Muiscas in the central highlands, where he had heard there was much gold (ibid., 3:333ff). Belal-cázar did not play a significant role in later developments in Tolima, but one of the other early *conquistadores,* Gonzalo Jiménez de Quesada, did make an attempt to conquer the region. However, he and his men were overcome by illnesses after arriving in Tolima, and he called off the expedition and returned to Bogotá without making any significant impact on the local people (Henderson 1985, 28).

Once the Pijao understood the intentions of the Spanish to use them as forced labor and even to enslave them, they tried repeatedly to drive the Spanish from Neiva and Tolima, but they were not successful. The war for Tolima was fought over the next seventy-five years between the Pijao and the Spanish; four generations grew up with the expectation of carrying on the fight. There were hundreds of skirmishes and battles, and the stories of those encounters live on today in oral history. The *chambunos* tell a story, which will be described later, of Belalcázar and his men attacking their people and killing many (Lara 1972, 29).

In 1550, twelve years after Belalcázar first reached Tolima, the Spanish Crown authorized the establishment of a town at the Quindio Pass through the Cordillera Central. The purpose was to provide safe passage through that range of the Andes to the Cauca River Valley. A military mission was sent to establish the town and simultaneously to look for gold. The soldiers found an indigenous town near the entrance to the pass that was ruled by a chief named Ibagué, and they established their town there, naming it *San Bonifacio de Ibagué del Valle de las Lanzas* (Saint Boniface of Ibagué of the Valley of the Lances) (Henderson 1985, 28; Ortega 1952). The Spanish named the valley after the preferred weapon of war of the Pijao, the lance. There were an estimated eighteen thousand inhabitants in the area around Ibagué when the Spanish arrived in 1550. By 1600 Fray Pedro Simón (1981, 6:328) estimated the population of Tolima to be four hundred Spaniards and forty thousand Indians under Spanish control, a ratio of one to one hundred. There was also a large population of independent indigenous groups not under Spanish control, but he did not estimate the size of that population.

Although the Spanish found gold near Ibagué (Simón 1981, 4:294) and further south along the Saldaña River, it was not in the quantities that they had hoped. Later, Indian guides led them to silver deposits in the south near San Sebastián de La Plata and to gold and silver mines at Mariquita in northern Tolima. The latter eventually became the most important center of mining in this region during the colonial period (Henderson 1985, 29). In spite of these finds, Fray Pedro Simón complained that the Pijao were too preoccupied with fighting instead of being more productive in helping the Spanish find the precious metals that they so coveted (1981, 5:229).

The remainder of the sixteenth century was a period of conflict in the Upper Magdalena Valley as the Pijao, Panches, Páez, and Timaná people fought against the Spanish for control of the region. By the beginning of the seventeenth century the Spanish had defeated all of the groups except the Pijaos. At that point, the Spanish military controlled the towns of Neiva and Ibagué, which were inhabited by indigenous people who had accepted Spanish rule. However, the rural Pijao populations remained independent and beyond the reach of the Spanish military.

As the Pijaos attacked the Spanish in the towns, they inevitably fought with the Indian inhabitants who were collaborating with the foreigners. In 1569 they burned Neiva, in 1572 they attacked San Vicente de Páez, in 1577 they attacked La Plata, and in 1606 they attacked Ibagué. The latter attack seems to have been the last straw for the Spanish, who in 1607 launched the most concentrated military campaign yet mounted against the Pijaos. From 1550 to 1605 there had been forty-eight official Spanish military campaigns against the Pijao, virtually one per year. Fray Pedro Simón described twenty of those offensives as having been defeated or having suffered significant losses (1981, 6:328ff), and none of the other twenty-eight were able to dominate or control the Pijaos.

In 1605 the Crown and the Real Consejo de Indias (Royal Council for the Indies) named Juan de Borja as president of the Real Audiencia de Santafé (Royal High Court of Santafé in Bogotá) with the expressed charge of bringing the Pijaos under control. Juan de Borja was a military man and a *caballero del hábito de Santiago* (knight of the military order of Saint James). Saint James was the patron saint of Christians in battle, and his banners had led the Spanish against the Muslims in the wars of reconquest in Spain. With Borja the banners of Saint James led the Spanish in the battle against another infidel in the Americas, the Pijaos. In addition to protecting Spanish-controlled towns, like Ibagué, Borja's mission was to guarantee safe passage along the Camino Real del Peru (Royal Road to Peru), which passed through the Pijao territory in Tolima, leading to southern Colombia, Ecuador, and Peru. Since the Pijaos remained hostile to the Spanish, the threat to trade and communications along this important road was constant.

Borja arrived in Bogotá on October 2, 1605, and within a few months began the Spanish offensive. In 1607 his soldiers established Fort San Lorenzo on the Chaparral Mesa deep in the heart of Pijao territory. The fort was in easy reach of several of the hostile groups, including the Amoyá, Ambeima, Irico, Paloma, Marto, and Biuni (Simón 1981, 6:385). The Indians of the Amoyá province were the most populous, and they led the other groups in fighting. They were quite successful with guerrilla tactics against the Spanish (ibid., 6:389). From Fort San Lorenzo the Spanish started a war of attrition against the Pijaos that lasted for the next four years.

The Spanish brought formidable force against them with superior weapons, including guns, armor, horses, and Indian allies. Although the Spanish won the first battles, the war dragged on as the rebel Pijaos regrouped and fought again and again (Simón 1981, 6:400). The traditional enemies of the Pijaos were the Páez, who were located in the central range of the Andes in the south. They also put up a stiff resistance to the Spanish, and the two groups united against the Spanish and successfully held them off for many years.

This war was cruel and fierce on both sides (Rojas de Perdomo 1985, 216 and 340). Since the Pijao army did not have large military installations to attack, the Spanish attacked and destroyed villages and crops. Simultaneously, they justified their scorched-earth policy ideologically by using vilifying rhetoric against the Pijaos. For example, in his contemporary chronicle of the Conquest, Fray Pedro Simón condoned the attempted extermination of the Pijaos by demonizing them as infidels, cannibals, beasts, barbarians, and criminals lacking in human values (1981, 6:353, 376, 383, 434, 447). By denying the humanity of the Pijaos, the Spanish eliminated their moral responsibility for attacking and killing the civilian population of women, children, and older people. This was the same kind of genocidal abuse of civilian populations that Las Casas (1992) had denounced in other areas of the Americas one century earlier.

While Simón loudly attacked the Pijaos, he only dismissively reported that the Spanish also committed acts of barbarism, which included the cooking and eating of indigenous children (1981, 1:486). Borja (1922a; 1922b) himself justified the genocidal nature of his campaign against the Pijaos because of his demonized view of them and because of the Crown's directive to bring them under control. Nina de Friedemann (1995, 170) points out that the ethnocentrism of the Conquest did not allow questioning or reflection on the inhumane acts used by the Spanish to conquer the indigenous groups.

Borja invaded the Pijao territory on various fronts simultaneously. He gave orders to his men to destroy crops and confiscate harvests in order to starve the Pijaos into surrender if they could not be defeated militarily. The Pijaos were to "dejar la vida o la tierra" (give up their life or their land) (Simón 1981, 6:389). His logic was that if women and children starved to death, there would be fewer people to continue the struggle. The Spanish constantly patrolled the areas of the rebellious groups, raiding farms and destroying crops (ibid., 6:442).

Borja and Diego de Ospina inflicted a major defeat on the Pijaos in 1608 near Chaparral (Bedoya 1965, 51). Following that, the Pijao people living along the banks of the Magdalena River (the Natagaimas) and in the flatlands near Chaparral (the Coyaimas) came under the control of the Spanish. Some of them served as guides, advisors, and troops against the rebellious groups in the later stages of the conflict. Fray Pedro Simón praised these groups for having the wisdom and prudence to ally themselves with the Spanish (1981, 6:388–89), for receiving Christian teachings, and for paying tribute in gold to the Crown (ibid., 6:446).

Besides the search-and-destroy military tactics used against the civilian population, Borja also used attack dogs trained to kill people. Simón (1981, 6:435) witnessed incidences of captives being thrown alive to the dogs to be torn apart and eaten. One was a man named Chaguala who refused to convert to Christianity. After Chaguala asserted that he would rather go to the Pijao afterlife than the Spanish one, which he imagined to be cruel, Borja turned loose two dogs that began tearing him apart before the assembled observers. In a similar case, a group of Spanish soldiers tried to convert a ninety-year-old captive, and they also threw him to the dogs when he refused. Simón (ibid., 6:445) observed that the old man was carrying a small wooden *mohán* (shaman figure) in his hand, and that he held it until he died. These deaths by attack dogs were observed by peaceful Pijaos, and the stories must also have spread to the rebellious Pijao groups who were fighting the Spanish.

According to Simón, the Spanish finally defeated the Pijaos in 1611 (1981, 6:446). Although many factors led to that defeat, the final blow seems to have been the killing of the primary war chief, Calarcá, in a battle near Chaparral. He was killed by Chief Baltazar, a Coyaima fighting on the side of the Spanish (Henderson 1985, 28). Calarcá was a hero of the Pijao resistance and is still remembered today. Following four unrelenting years of battle, the death of many family members, and a devastated homeland, the Pijao will to fight ended with the loss of Calarcá. Within a year of that defeat, the Pijao political and military organization disintegrated. As happened with the Páez when they were defeated (Rappaport 1990, 39), many Pijaos probably joined other indigenous groups to lose their identity. However, the Spanish did not completely control the Pijaos even then, and small groups continued to carry out guerrilla raids against the Spanish sporadically until 1675 (Bolaños 1994, 24).

Pijaos also continued nonmilitary forms of resistance after their defeat by refusing to work for the Spanish and by escaping to remote areas outside of Spanish control. At the same time some of the Pijao allies, such as the Páez people, also left their traditional territories and migrated to areas where they could escape the Spanish forced-labor requirement (Bolaños 1994, 39). According to Fray Pedro Simón (1981, 6:446), the Natagaimas and Coyaimas remained intact after the war, and the people of the town of Natagaima today still consider themselves to be the most indigenous people in Tolima.

After subduing the Pijaos, the Spanish continued to exercise their mastery over them by using the forced-labor obligations of the *mita* (tribute labor) and the *encomienda* system (Spanish feudal estates) (Rojas de Perdomo 1985, 340). Forced labor frequently meant working in mines or other hazardous environments, where accidents and poor working conditions led to health problems and death for many. The Spanish also enslaved captured Indians, and they were working in the silver and gold mines of Tolima as early as 1550 (ibid., 217). Borja and Simón (1981, 6:446) both mention that many captured Pijaos became slaves after the war, and Simón specifically stated that he did not make a moral judgment against the Spanish who enslaved Pijaos. The normal practice was to give a sentence of ten years in slavery for resistance to the Crown, but in a letter to King Philip III in 1608, Borja (1922a, 115) argued for perpetual slavery for the Pijaos. He gave the examples of similar Spanish sentences levied against Muslims during the Christian-Muslim wars in Spain, against Africans, and against the Araucanos of Chile. Although the king seems not to have granted his request for perpetual slavery, many Pijaos did in fact remain slaves. The most famous slave-labor camp in Tolima during the colonial period was at the mines of Mariquita (Henderson 1985, 29), which later became a focal point for revolt.

An early-seventeenth-century map of the Magdalena River shows Spanish settlements with churches up to Honda, approximately one hundred kilometers north of La Chamba (Archivo General de Indias [hereafter AGI], Mapas y Planos, 196). However, no churches appear in the area of La Chamba, suggesting that there were no important Spanish settlements there. The Spanish did occupy towns farther south, leapfrogging over the Pijao territory. During the remainder of the seventeenth and eighteenth centuries, Tolima was a supplier of gold and silver, animals, and agricultural goods to Bogotá and the Crown. During that time the Crown divided the lands of Tolima into large land grants (*encomiendas*) and assigned them to Spanish citizens, which concentrated the land in the hands of a few landowners. A version of sharecropping developed that replaced the earlier forced-labor system. In the new system an indigenous family was given the right to clear and farm a plot of land in exchange for working certain days a week for the landowner. The area from the Magdalena River around La Chamba to the central range of the Andes on the west was given to Antonio Álvarez, a Spaniard who married a young woman of high standing in Bogotá (Lara 1972, 36). This distribution of lands to a Spanish feudal elite sealed the disempowered position of the indigenous-mestizo rural poor.

In 1781 many people in Tolima joined the Revolt of the Comuneros, freeing the slaves in the Mariquita mine and killing Crown officials in Neiva. But despite this rebellious outburst, 170 years after the conquest of the Pijaos, their descendants in Tolima remained a defeated feudal class. For example, the Spanish used prejorative terms such as "dogs" to refer to the indigenous-mestizo working class (Henderson 1985, 30). After the Spanish squashed the revolt, the people of Tolima slipped back into their subordinate status and remained largely silent participants in the Colombian national process for another century.

The conquest and enslavement, both actual and virtual, of the Pijaos established a cultural system in which Spanish overlords dominated the indigenous-mestizo inhabitants of Tolima (today Tolima and Huila). The caste separation between Spanish and Indian denied the descendants of the Pijaos access to political, economic, and social power. Their forced acculturation to the language, religion, political organization, and economics of the Spanish added the partial loss of traditional culture to their loss of land and independence. The indigenous populations of Tolima gradually built a cultural synthesis between their heritage and the Spanish one, making them cultural mestizos. In this process, they lost their identity as Pijaos and assumed their new identity as a landless rural caste of workers. In losing the war, they lost their political and economic independence, and in the new society that emerged they became the proletarian workers who survive by selling their labor.

Tolima in the Twentieth Century

In the last century, conflicts in Tolima have again been a powerful presence in Colombian politics, especially the Guerra de los Mil Días (The Thousand Days' War), La Violencia, the development of agrarian capitalism, the leftist organization of peasant groups, the land invasions of the 1970s, and the development of armed guerrilla groups. These events form the modern historical context of La Chamba.

The Guerra de los Mil Días, a civil war waged by Colombia's Liberal Party against the Conservative government, began in 1899 and lasted until 1902 (Santa 1988, 1463–83). Between eighty and a hundred thousand people were killed during the war, and much of the commerce, industry, and agriculture of the country was ruined (Henderson 1985, 51). The Liberals of Tolima enthusiastically supported this rebellion, and since Tolima is located in the middle of the country, much of the fighting occurred there. During this conflict the Liberals represented the interests of the indigenous people, working classes, and peasant farmers, and the Conservatives represented the landowners and the Catholic Church, following the basic social lines of the Conquest.

At the beginning of the twentieth century, Tolima included both the Departments of Tolima (north) and Huila (south), and powerful local *caciques* (chiefs or political bosses) controlled each area. Liberals controlled the area of Tolima, and Conservatives the Huila area, and they fought each other with heavy losses of life and property. After three years of indecisive war and economic exhaustion, the two groups signed a peace accord in 1902 without any resolution of the conflicts between them. In 1905 the central government divided Tolima into the current Departments of Tolima and Huila to cut down its importance and to reduce the power of the local *caciques*.

Fifty years later the two groups fought again in La Violencia, divided along the same lines. The political upheavals of La Violencia broke out in 1948 when Jorge Eliécer Gaitán, the leading Liberal candidate for the presidency of the country, was assassinated in Bogotá. In Tolima, the general outlines of this conflict followed those of the Guerra de los Mil Días, with indigenous and mestizo-descent *campesinos* fighting as Liberals and the Spanish-descent landowners fighting as Conservatives with support from the Church. Tolima became a primary battleground during La Violencia, and it had the second-highest violent death rate of all Departments during that period (Bergquist 1992, 71). The Conservatives in El Guamo, the township of La Chamba, were aggressive during La Violencia, toting guns to the town council meetings and importing explosives for use against the rural Liberal groups. They successfully used the threat of violence throughout this period to control the largely indigenous-mestizo rural population.

During La Violencia 361,800 people emigrated from Tolima to escape the terror. A total of 34,300 houses were burned, and 40,000 rural properties were abandoned, many of them permanently. This latter figure represents 42 percent of all rural properties in Tolima (Sánchez 1992, 105). Liberals in Tolima imprisoned and killed priests and invaded hacienda lands, and the oral tradition says that priests retaliated by offering absolution to their Conservative congregants for killing Liberals.

The houses of indigenous people were burned in Ortega and Natagaima (both former reservations to the south of La Chamba), and the Indians were expelled from the region by police and army units (Sánchez 1992, 89). People of Spanish descent took advantage of this exodus to illegally occupy lands owned by Indians, and they even hired armed gunmen to attack and harass the Indians to simplify the seizure of their lands. Central and southern Tolima became an outlaw's paradise as armed gangs formed in and around the towns of Rovira, Ortega, Natagaima, and Purificación. All of these towns have predominantly indigenous or mestizo populations (Henderson 1985, 189), and they are located near La Chamba. The social divisions between class and caste in the Guerra de los Mil Días and La Violencia in Tolima paralleled those of the Spanish Conquest, making clear that the divisions established at that time had never faded.

In 1953 the military under General Gustavo Rojas Pinilla took over the national government in an attempt to control the political violence. Although the worst excesses of La Violencia ended at this time, outbreaks of violence continued throughout the 1950s. Some analysts even believe that the "low-intensity civil war" of today in Colombia is a continuation of La Violencia. Besides gaining military control of the country, the Rojas government undertook several economic initiatives promising work in place of conflict. They built "urban centers" in many rural communities, providing schools, police stations, health centers, telephone offices, and other public services (Lara 1972, 45). They made financial incentives available to landowners in Tolima to increase rice and cotton production (Sánchez 1992, 105), stimulating the rise of the agrarian capitalism that had already begun to develop. The Rojas government wanted to move the land-based Tolima economy away from the existing low-productivity practices to more industrial agrarian practices.

Starting with the introduction of tractors, irrigation, and wage labor in the 1950s, large landowners in Tolima increasingly converted their operations from feudal share-cropping to industrial agriculture using hired laborers. They consolidated their lands into large fields planted with commercial crops. As landless peasants lost the option of share-cropping land, they had to migrate out of the area or become wage laborers on the industrial farms— in other words, an agricultural proletariat. Agrarian capitalism has continued to develop, and since the 1970s, 40 percent or more of the land in Tolima has been devoted to industrial agriculture, especially cotton, rice, sorghum, and sesame (Zamosc 1986, 133).

The expansion of urban industries at the same time meant that factory-made metal cooking pots were increasingly available throughout Colombia, reducing the demand in regional markets for the traditional clay pots. Potters responded by reorienting their work more to the urban markets in Bogotá and Girardot, working for these merchants on an order-by-order basis. As they shifted from selling their work in regional markets to working on orders from outside contractors, women potters became a rural craft proletariat, selling their labor for money like their husbands.

The increasing concentration of wealth into the hands of a few wealthy landowners exacerbated the tensions between the Spanish-descent elite and indigenous-mestizo caste. Only one-third of the peasant families in Tolima owned five hectares of land or more, while 57 percent were proletarianized or semi-proletarianized families with little or no land. Another 10 percent received land from the land-reform commission (Zamosc 1986, 151), which was established by the national government to redistribute land to rural landless people. However, this land was notorious for being marginal or unproductive land that would not support a family. In 1967, 40 percent of the land given to *campesinos* in El Guamo, Prado, Suárez, Purificación, and Chicoral was unused because of its poor quality or the insufficient size of the holdings (Henderson 1985, 234).

In the 1970s the conflicts over land inequities came to a head, and in 1971 two thousand people in Tolima invaded farming land along the Magdalena and Saldaña Rivers in the townships of Natagaima, Coyaima, Purificación, El Guamo (La Chamba), and El Espinal. All these townships are near La Chamba, and they have substantial indigenous and mestizo populations; the first two were prominent indigenous towns during the Conquest. These land invasions started in El Guamo (La Chamba) and were the most numerous in this township. After invading and occupying hacienda lands, the *campesinos* laid siege to the town hall in El Guamo and shut it down for several days as they tried to force the landowners to negotiate with them. Eventually the police broke the siege and forced the *campesinos* out of most of the lands that they had invaded, so that in the end little or no land changed hands. Most of the people involved in the land invasions had worked as tenant farmers or sharecroppers until the expansion of agrarian capitalism in the 1950s, when they became hired workers (Zamosc 1986, 81). Leftist resistance in the form of direct action became the response of the rural disenfranchised caste to the capitalist expansion of the landowners.

The Asociación Nacional de Usuarios Campesinos (ANUC, the National Association of Peasants) organized the land invasions of the 1970s. The ANUC also organized the peasant farmers and rural workers into a union to advocate for their rights. Other leftist groups saw the potential of organizing the disenfranchised rural caste in this area, and in the mid-1970s the Communist Party of Colombia renewed its efforts to organize the *campesinos* of Tolima (Pizarro 1992, 180). The Unión Revolucionario Socialista (Socialist Revolutionary Union) was also active in the area (Zamosc 1986, 141). The Fuerzas Armadas Revolucionarias Colombianas (FARC, or Revolutionary Armed Forces of Colombia), the most important armed guerrilla movement in Colombia, was formed in Tolima in the 1950s, after the Liberal forces were unable to break the Conservative domination during that period. In the 1980s the Unión Patriótica (Patriotic Union) was organized as a political party by the FARC to represent the interests of the disenfranchised, and it was very active in Tolima. After centuries of subjugation, the indigenous-mestizo people of Tolima were willing participants in leftist and radical organizations that advocated social change. By the 1990s these groups had lost much of their local support, probably because they produced few real changes in the socioeconomic structure of rural Tolima.

The people of La Chamba live and work in this context of unresolved conflicts, and the indigenous and mestizo people continue to form the rural working caste characterized by low wages and little or no ownership of land. As the Pijao fought against Spanish control in the sixteenth and seventeenth centuries, the indigenous and mestizo *campesinos* have fought repeatedly in the last century for economic and political enfranchisement. The mestizo culture formed out of this history defines Tolima today, including La Chamba.

Social Caste, Work, and Ceramics

In Tolima, as in Colombia as a whole, social caste correlates with economic level, skin color, ethnicity, circumstance of immigration to the country, and access to social change. The social caste structure was established by the experience of the Conquest, with the invading Spaniards at the top and the defeated indigenous people at the bottom. Members of the chiefly class of indigenous women (frequently called "princesses" today) became the wives of the early Spanish, and initially their mestizo children were socially accepted by the Spanish. Between 1550 and 1750 men were 90 percent of the immigrants to the Americas from Spain, with most of the Spanish women arriving only in the 1700s (Céspedes del Castillo 1992, 183). As the number of Spanish soldiers and fortune seekers grew, they took more and more Indian wives or mistresses of lower social status and the mestizo population grew rapidly. The hostility of the Spanish elite toward the mestizos also grew. As their numbers increased, mestizos repeatedly caused disruptions, claiming the rights and privileges of the Spanish (Colmenares 1970, 86–87). The overt exploitation of indigenous people by the Spanish under the *encomienda* system was the beginning of the social-caste system that has persisted until today.

A person's social caste determines multiple aspects of life, including access to education, marriage partners, employment opportunities, residence, and cultural activities. Members of Colombia's upper classes tend to be of European descent, a group consisting of two parts: the elite descendents of immigrants who arrived early in the colonial period, and immigrants who arrived later. The old immigrant elite are descendants of people who arrived during the first wave of Spanish immigration in the sixteenth and seventeenth centuries. They benefitted from the large grants of land made by the Spanish Crown, or they obtained land from the indigenous people by other means at little or no cost. Many of these families have retained their lands while some have used their capital to establish factories or engage in other capital-intensive ventures.

Almost half of the Spanish who came to the Americas during the initial Conquest came from the southern, Moorish-influenced area of Spain, especially Andalusia, and that figure holds true for most of the century following the Conquest (Gutiérrez Escudero 1992, 234–36). Although Ferdinand and Isabella conquered al-Andalus in 1492, the population of Andalusia remained primarily Moorish culturally throughout much of the sixteenth century, the period of the primary migration to the Americas from that region. The Andalusians brought with them the Muslim hacienda system as a socioeconomic structure and Muslim technologies, such as the Spanish-Moorish pottery-making system (Lister and Lister 1987, 270 and 279) used in the Colombian Departments of Boyacá, Nariño, and Cauca.

Within this European caste, people tend to reinforce each other socially, economically, and politically against the lower castes of color, the mestizos, mulattos, Indians, and Afro-Colombians. The Spanish used the city as an instrument of political and military domination over the rural indigenous populations, and the elites continue to cluster in the cities today. It is this European caste elite that sets the social and cultural standards to which the lower classes or castes are expected to conform.

An important value of the elite historically has been to avoid manual work, which was always assigned to the lower-caste people. The essence of the colonial system was the control of the manual work of the indigenous caste. That value continues to characterize Colombian society today, and it also filters down to mestizo people who aspire to the ideal status of not being manual workers. For example, a plumber or electrician in Bogotá may come to work in a business suit and tie, carrying his tools and overalls in a briefcase so that he will appear as a professional in the street and not a manual worker. The same "old immigrant" negative value toward manual work even affects

La Chamba potters, who see their work as "dirty" and undesirable, and prefer to do the non-manual or least-manual tasks associated with it, such as selling or burnishing. As a manual and "dirty" craft, pottery making is not an appropriate elite occupation, so potters are usually lower-status people of indigenous or mestizo descent.

Historically, the mestizos and mulattos have constituted the working and marginal social classes. Today these people tend to be the factory workers, farm workers, bus and truck drivers, school teachers, clerks, security guards, police, soldiers, plumbers, electricians, potters, and workers in hundreds of other positions. People of indigenous descent tend to live in economically marginal areas of the country in deserts, tropical rain forests, or remote mountain areas. These isolated populations have little participation in the larger national society.

Most village ceramics in Colombia are made by mestizos and indigenous people who fall into the caste of darker skinned, less educated people. Their place within the society is socially fixed with little opportunity for change, and their craft production is evaluated as that of marginalized, low-status workers. The ceramics of La Chamba may be quite sophisticated when compared with earthenware traditions cross culturally, but within Colombia it is not given social prestige comparable to the craft technique it represents.

The economic and political elites have used the social caste system to structure and control the expansion of capitalism in recent decades, and this group controls most of the capital resources of the country and most of the economic infrastructure. Petty capitalists, such as the middlemen who control the sales of crafts within the country, follow the top-down hierarchical style established by the elite capitalists. Just as the elite dominate the castes below them in the social hierarchy, petty capitalists dominate the potters, who are at the bottom of the economic chain. Although the potters of La Chamba have a finely finished product, they have virtually no possibility of challenging the economic hierarchy above them to gain professional respect or better economic rewards.

Conclusions

Tolima is a distillation of important factors in the make-up of Colombia: a destructive Conquest, caste separation between Spanish and indigenous-mestizo people, economic and political disempowerment of the poor, armed conflict, and capitalist expansion. The latter has brought new economic opportunities to the potters of La Chamba, but it also has brought new pressures and constraints that have led to changes in their work organization. To understand the region of Tolima and its conflicts is to understand the internal contradictions within Colombia itself, such as the wealthy land-owners versus the landless rural proletariat or the people of Spanish descent versus the indigenous-mestizo people. Just as the people of Tolima have resisted the Spanish-descended overlords through their history of revolts and land invasions, they have resisted Spanish culture by maintaining important elements of indigenous culture, especially in ceramics.

The ceramics tradition of La Chamba is a window through which we can focus on the cultural composition of Tolima society. There are hundreds of mestizo potters in Tolima and Huila who continue to use indigenous techniques, showing the deep rootedness of indigenous traditions. This is particularly apparent among the women potters of La Chamba, and this study examines their indigenous heritage in ceramics as well as the ways in which the expansion of the market economy has affected them.

3

The Community of La Chamba

La Chamba is an unincorporated village of one thousand inhabitants with a surrounding rural population of another thousand. It is such a small village in an isolated nook of Colombia that it would be forgotten if it were not for its craft tradition. It is seventeen kilometers down a rough dirt road from the nearest highway, and it is off the beaten track for tourism. Most Colombians do not know where it is located, although it is only 150 kilometers south of the national capital, Bogotá. The visual experience of arriving in La Chamba is little different from that of similar villages in this area, except for the Artesanías de Colombia center and the two stores that sell ceramics. The houses are loosely strung out along the dirt road, some of which are shaded by giant trees while others are exposed to the equatorial sun. The whitewash on the walls is in varying states of repair, and the village gives the appearance of an isolated town that is barely subsisting. In a brief visit to the village it may be difficult even to see the craft activity.

La Chamba is located in the broad valley of the Magdalena River, which is over a thousand kilometers long and bordered on both sides by chains of the Andes. Most of the valley is hot-weather country known for tropical fruits. The daily high temperatures range from twenty-five degrees centigrade in the higher, southern end of the river to thirty-five degrees in the lower, northern region near the Caribbean coast. There are two rainy seasons in the year (from February to May, and from October to December), during which the temperature drops slightly and minor flooding can occur. During the dry season (June to September) the temperatures are hotter, and the land becomes extremely dry.

Chamba means a wide, flat ditch or creek, and here the name probably refers to the confluence of three small waterways in the area of La Chamba, the Inga, Agua Dulce, and Regalada, which run through the village and empty into the Magdalena River. The daily high temperatures range between twenty-eight and thirty-two degrees centigrade most of the year, and the vegetation reflects the tropical climate; orange trees, palms, bananas, and broad, tall shade trees are common. People value these trees, which break the intensity of the noonday sun and also provide fruits.

The Magdalena River Valley

The Magdalena River flows from a height of 3,600 meters in the mountains of southern Colombia and empties into the Caribbean Sea near the city of Barranquilla. The Upper Magdalena Valley is the higher southern end of the river, and it is bounded by Honda, Tolima, on the lower end and the mountains near San Agustín, Huila, on the upper end. La Chamba is located in this upper end of the Magdalena Valley, some 600 kilometers inland from the coast. It is built on the riverine plain of the western bank of the Magdalena River, 350 meters above sea level. Since there is no bridge at La Chamba, the river can only be crossed by canoe. The current is swift at this point due to the drop of over 3,000 meters during the first 400 kilometers of its course, an average of 7.5 meters per kilometer. (See Map 2.1.)

Below Honda, where it becomes the Lower Magdalena, the river meanders through tropical lowlands for several hundred kilometers on its way to the coast. In the 560 kilometers of the lower half of the Magdalena, the drop is less than 350 meters, an average of less than one meter (63 cm) per kilometer. As the Magdalena River slows down and broadens, it becomes more appropriate for riverine navigation and commerce. Until the 1950s the river was still a major means of communication from Honda to the coastal port of Barranquilla, and paddle-wheel riverboats carried passengers and merchandise up and down the river.

The Upper Magdalena River Valley is characterized by a more indigenous population, and a wide range of crafts are produced there. However, near the Caribbean coast the population has more European and African influences, and crafts are produced in only a few communities. Of the entire Magdalena Valley, from its upper reaches in the southern mountains to its disappearance into the coastal estuaries of the Atlantic along the north coast, the area that produces the best ceramics is the Upper Magdalena, which includes the Departments of Tolima and Huila. Ceramics are made in a number of villages and towns along the Upper Magdalena, and clay deposits are found just under the surface in many places. So La Chamba is located in an area that is rich in crafts, and one that is also rich in clay deposits.

Environment and the Making of Ceramics

The physical environment determines for most communities whether there will be a local tradition of ceramics, and La Chamba is in an environment that favors ceramics making. Natural resources (especially clay and fuel) must be available in order to make ceramics, and La Chamba has both. In its rich alluvial deposits along the banks of the Magdalena River, there are three areas of clay deposits, which begin immediately below the topsoil and go to a depth of one meter or so. Across the Magdalena, in the foothills of the eastern chain of the Andes, there are other deposits of highly plastic clays rich in the red iron oxide used to make red slip, as well as deposits of white clay, which was formerly used to make slip for painting designs on the pots. Just as clay is required to make ceramics, a source of fuel is needed to fire the ceramics, and La Chamba has historically had a ready supply of firewood, although that has become more of a problem in recent years. Village ceramics communities also depend on access to markets to sell their production, so rivers or roads must be available to transport the pottery to market communities. La Chamba's location on the Magdalena River allowed its people to ship ceramics up and down the waterway.

Village ceramics communities also tend to exist in areas of marginal agriculture, which may result from the lack of fertile land or from the land's being concentrated in the hands of a few large landowners, as it is in La Chamba. Village ceramics becomes a viable economic choice when agriculture does not provide an acceptable standard of living. According to Dean Arnold (1985, 168), "as available land or the productivity of land for agriculture decreases per capita, people will increasingly turn to crafts like pottery." If they do not have any agricultural land, they will depend totally on ceramics; but if more economically secure work becomes available, potters will abandon the craft (ibid., 193). Most families in La Chamba use ceramics to supplement their income from agriculture.

Agriculture

The other component of La Chamba's economy is agriculture, and most of the arable land around the village is owned by a few large landowners, who use it for cattle ranching or large-scale commercial agriculture. The large farms plant commercial crops such as cotton, rice, *ajonjoli* (sesame), and sorghum, and the men of La Chamba work as day laborers on these farms. Historically, most of the men working as day laborers in commercial agriculture have also done small-scale farming in family gardens during their free time (Lara 1972, 87). The area of El Olvido located between the settlement and the river was divided into lots (mostly under four hectares) by the Junta de Acción Comunal (Community Action Council) in 1957 (ibid., 16), and this area has been used for garden farming by the people of the town.

The crops that are cultivated in the small household lots are yucca, tobacco, peanuts, bananas, plantains, pineapple, oranges, and guava, among others, and many households have one or more fruit trees in the yard of their house. People also cultivate herbs as condiments for cooking and as medicinal plants, of which coriander, cumin, garlic, and onion are common. Domesticated animals represent a way to invest and accumulate some capital, and if a family can afford it and has a place to keep them, they will have a cow for milk, a pig for meat, and hens for eggs. Many households also have a donkey as a work animal to carry sacks of clay, firewood, stalks of bananas, or other heavy loads, and some families who have more space may own a horse.

The Village of La Chamba

In the early 1900s, most of the houses were located along the banks of the Magdalena near the river landing, Chapetón (Lara 1972, 62), because that was the center of transportation and commerce. The sixty houses that made up the community were built in a dispersed indigenous pattern with land between each house for animals and crops. The building of the "centro urbano" in 1956, which included the school and the police station, led to gradual shifting of the concentration of the houses around the open field called the "plaza." Today houses are still built in an indigenous fashion along the roads and paths of the village, rather than being clustered in the contiguous Spanish style. (See Map 3.1.)

Traditionally, houses were built in the indigenous style with wattle and daub or adobe walls, thatched roofs, and beaten-earth floors, but new houses today are built with cement and brick building blocks, cement floors, and roofs of corrugated metal or composition materials. Many of the older indigenous-style houses still exist in the community (see Photograph 3.1). Houses tend to be small, with only one or two bedrooms, an all-purpose family room, and a kitchen. Bathrooms are normally separate from the house, and the kitchen is also frequently separate from the house. Although everyone has electricity, few have refrigerators, and most cook on wood or

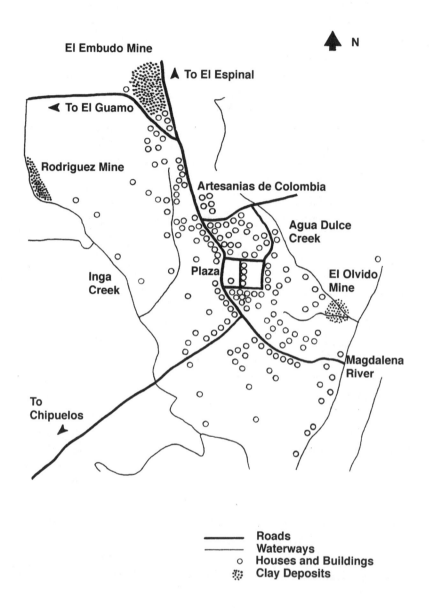

El Embudo Mine

N

To El Espinal

To El Guamo

Rodriguez Mine

Artesanias de Colombia

Agua Dulce
Creek

Inga
Creek

Plaza

El Olvido
Mine

Magdalena
River

To
Chipuelos

—————— Roads
—————— Waterways
o Houses and Buildings
Clay Deposits

Map 3.1. Map of La Chamba. The houses in La Chamba cluster around the one road that runs through the town to stop at Chapetón, the landing on the Magdalena River. The clay deposits are less than one kilometer from the houses of most potters.

Photo 3.1. A traditional house in La Chamba. The traditional house has adobe walls and a thatched roof. Both the adobe and the thatch aid in cooling the interior, which is important in this tropical environment. Saggars, cooking pots, and firewood for the kiln are stacked around the walls of the house.

charcoal stoves. Common floor plans include the square, the L-shaped house, and the shotgun-shaped house (one room contiguous with another in a straight line). The constructed area is normally from one to three hundred square meters.

There is a central grassy field called the plaza around which the public buildings are clustered, including the elementary and junior high schools, the church, the health center, the police station, and the telephone office. In the cool of the day the plaza is sometimes used by young men for soccer matches, and at other times people put their donkeys out to graze in the plaza, or young boys ride their bicycles back and forth across it. On average days, the streets of La Chamba are most active in the cool of the morning and during the hours from late afternoon to dusk. From midday to late afternoon, the women and children are inside in the shade of the houses, and this is their prime time to work on ceramics. By late afternoon the men arrive from the fields, and the children begin to come out to run errands and play.

In the village and its environs, people get around by walking or by bicycle. Almost every house has one or two bicycles, and some have a motorcycle. Transportation to other towns is by motorcycle, car, truck, or bus. While the research for this book was ongoing, there were three locally owned motorized vehicles, and all were used commercially: one bus, one car (used as a collective taxi), and a truck (used by a local middleman to ship ceramics to Bogotá). On normal weekdays, the bus makes the eighteen-kilometer trip to El Guamo in the early morning and another one around midday, and the return trips to La Chamba are approximately one hour later. La Chamba is administratively part of the El Guamo township, which means that all legal transactions have to be done there—from paying taxes to registering documents, including marriages, birth certificates, baptisms, and property sales. Since most transactions require official seals, people have to go to El Guamo regularly. The collective taxi makes daily trips to the neighboring town of El Espinal (sixteen kilometers), which has more stores and is the preferred place for shopping and entertainment. On market days in El Espinal and El Guamo, the bus and taxi make frequent round trips into town and back. In addition to the social and economic contacts with El Guamo and El Espinal, people also go to Girardot, the largest town in the area. It is also located on the banks of the Magdalena, just over twenty kilometers farther north from El Espinal.

Demography and Work

In 1987 a census of the nucleated area of the village was made as a part of this study, and 1,036 people were counted in 184 households, an average of 5.63 persons per household. This is almost twice the average rural household size in the highland pottery township of Ráquira, which is 3.16 persons (Duncan 1998, 51), and this larger household size correlates with the pattern of extended-family households in La Chamba.

The greatest concentration of La Chamba potters is in the nucleated village. This concentration is consistent with the fact that the township of El Guamo, where La Chamba is located, has the highest number of craftspeople (1,616) of all the townships located in the Upper Magdalena River Valley (Tolima and Huila). The next most important craft center in Tolima is Coyaima (520 craftspeople) which also has an important indigenous population (Artesanías de Colombia 1998, 212–15). The rural portion of the La Chamba population is largely engaged in agriculture, cattle raising, or fishing. These three rural occupations were more important in the 1800s and

Table 3.1. Increase in Ceramics Production in La Chamba, 1972–1987

	1972		1987		Increase	
	No.	%	No.	%	No.	%
Total households	178		184		6	3.37
Making ceramics	94	52.80	113	61.41	19	20.21
Contract burnishing	23	12.92	44	23.91	21	91.30
Buying/selling	12	6.74	13	7.06	1	8.33
Total	129	72.47	170	92.39	41	31.78

early 1900s, but commerce in ceramics has become equally important since the road was opened in the 1930s. Today, few households (only 3 percent) support themselves from their own farms, while 75 percent of the men work as day laborers in the industrial agricultural enterprises that surround La Chamba. Fishing is primarily a casual activity now, although there are a few men who fish and sell their catch regularly.

In recent decades ceramics has provided some income for most of the households in La Chamba, and many have also had income from agriculture or services. Only a few households depend exclusively on agriculture for their income. Another small group lives from service occupations, such as seamstress, tailor, carpenter, bricklayer, bus driver, boat operator, butcher, barber, electrician, and mender of fishnets.

Although 129 (72 percent) of the households in La Chamba reported work in ceramics in 1972 (Lara 1972, 84–85), in our study fifteen years later 170 (92 percent) reported work in ceramics (see Table 3.1). That was an increase of almost 32 percent, indicating the expanding role of ceramics in the economy of the community. There was a 20 percent increase in the number of people making ceramics, and a 91 percent increase in the number of people doing contract burnishing.

A complete census of the nucleated village and the surrounding rural zones was made by the Programa Ampliado de Inmunizaciones (Expanded Program of Vaccinations) of the Ministry of Health between September 1988 and February 1989. That census registered 2,050 persons in 312 house-holds with 38.8 percent under fifteen years of age, 49.9 percent between fifteen and forty-five years, and 11.3 percent over forty-five (Montoya de la Cruz 1990, 21). The age groupings drop approximately 10 percent for each fifteen years of age, and there are few people in the age range of sixty and above, indicating the community's high mortality rates and limited access to adequate health care.

Meal Preparation and Service

Since La Chamba is not a consumer-oriented community, the town's five family-owned shops sell little more than soft drinks, beer, rice, bread, dried grains, and a few other staples. There are also a couple of bakeries that provide fresh bread. A variety of fruits are grown in the family gardens, and they may also be purchased from local suppliers. Food that is not available in the village can be obtained in the weekend open air market in El Guamo.

Historically, meals have been cooked over an open wood fire. The hearth is made by placing three stones in a triangle on the ground, setting the cooking pot on them, and building a fire beneath it. Today cooking is done in the kitchen with a wood or charcoal-fired stove. Ceramic cooking pots were still used in some older households at the beginning of this research, but now almost everyone cooks in metal pots. The *olla* (traditional ceramic cooking pot) is still used by some to cook stew (*sancocho*), the meal most identified with this region of Colombia. *Sancocho* is a combination of potatoes, plantain, yucca, corn, pork, fish, and whatever else is available at the moment. Rice, potatoes, yucca, and meat are also individually cooked in similar pots. Normally, food is eaten from the *cazuela* (eating bowl), which is made locally, but on special occasions it is served in industrially made creamware plates or bowls. When we ate with local families, we were usually served on commercial creamware plates. The industrially made dinnerware has more prestige locally because it is associated with the city, and it is more expensive than the locally made tableware.

Public Services

La Chamba is an unincorporated village, and it has neither a mayor nor a town council, but it does have a small police station. It is administratively a part of the township of El Guamo, which in turn is controlled by the local landed elite. Public funds tend to be invested more in the infrastructure of El Guamo; there is little investment in the public services of La Chamba. Today the village does have the basic urban services, including electricity (since the 1950s) and running water (since the 1970s). Until running water was installed, local households got water from the river or one of forty shallow wells (*aljibes*). An average of five households used each one of these wells (Lara 1972, 13), and they were usually neighbors or extended family members. These wells were not hygienic and are no longer used, but hygiene is still a problem because of the lack of a proper sewage system.

There is a health center in the village, which is attended by a nurse who gives first aid and does paramedical procedures. A doctor comes one day a month to treat patients, but if immediate medical treatment is needed, the patient must hire the taxi to go to El Guamo, where more services are available. Most illnesses are treated at home using traditional herbal cures, and many people prefer these less expensive treatments to the costly medicines prescribed by medical doctors.

One telephone office serves this population of two thousand people, but it is only for long-distance calls to other towns. An average of four hundred calls are placed each month to Bogotá, but virtually none to other places, reflecting the pattern of migration to the capital and the centralization of economic and political affairs there. No one has a telephone in their house, and there are no public telephones in the town, except the one at the central office. The four hundred monthly telephone calls in La Chamba represent an average of approximately one call per household per month. If a person wants to make a call, they must go to the office, paying when the call is finished. To receive a call, a previous arrangement is made to call on a certain day and hour, and the person goes to the office at the appointed hour and waits for the call to arrive.

The Catholic Church never made significant inroads into everyday life in La Chamba, and that is consistent with the overall resistance of the community to Spanish cultural life. The Church was historically negative toward the indigenous culture in Tolima, and, in like manner, the people of La Chamba have not been very supportive of the Church. Anticlericalism is common, and it leads to a casual attitude toward organized religion. Although there is a church building in the village, it is usually empty and closed and no regular services are held there. A priest does come a few times a year to say Mass, and on occasion nuns come to hold services, but on most Sundays there are no activities. During the early 1970s a French priest, Father Hervé Bernés, gave Mass regularly in La Chamba on Sundays. He was a teacher in Bogotá, and he made the weekly trip to La Chamba as a voluntary gesture (Lara 1972, 77). There have been other periods when services were regularly held in the community.

However, religion is important for the rites of passage of birth and death, and *compadres* (godparents) are commonly chosen for all of the early life events of a child. The *compadrazgo* system in La Chamba represents a

synthesis between indigenous social bonds and the Christian religious practices introduced in the colonial period. A couple, who are family members
or friends, are chosen to be the *compadre* (godfather) and *comadre* (god-
mother) at the time of a child's baptism, and they are expected to be assistant
parents. They may correct a child for disciplinary reasons if necessary and
also help a child as a relative would. *Compadres* are also named for the
presentación (presentation of the child to the Virgin Mary), a local practice,
and the *confirmación*. *Compadres* may also be named for the newlyweds if
the wedding takes place in the Church. This *compadrazgo* system is common
in towns and rural areas in Colombia.

People who want to attend Mass go to one of the larger neighboring
towns, but for most people in La Chamba Sunday means the day the middlemen arrive to pick up their orders and pay for them. Women who have orders
to deliver that day are busy loading their production onto the truck of the
buyer, receiving payment, and negotiating the next order. After the business
is completed, they use the remainder of the day to visit with female relatives
and friends and to do domestic chores around the house. The young people
may also visit family or friends or the "Club Social," a local place for music
and dancing. Occasionally, there are school activities.

Family Organization

The family is the center of social life in La Chamba, and for the potters it is
also the center of their work lives. Both the nuclear and extended families are
important in different ways. Nuclear families consist of the parents and their
unmarried children, and in some cases related families cluster together to
form extended-family compounds. When a young couple establishes their
own household, they frequently settle near other relatives. Even if adult
children migrate out of La Chamba to find work, they are still responsible
when their parents become elderly. When the parents are widowed or can no
longer care for themselves properly, they go to live with the children.

The forming of a household frequently begins as a premarital liaison
between two young people, which may continue until the young woman
becomes pregnant. At that point they may agree to be legally married or to
live as common-law partners. The highest-status arrangement is to be married through the Church, and secular marriage through a notary is second
in importance. The nuns who work in the community continually encourage
people to marry in the Church, but many do not listen to their entreaties.
Although some people find marriage partners within La Chamba, especially

children of the original families, such as the Avilés, Prada, Céspedes, and Betancourt families (Lara 1972, 69), today many others are marrying outside of it.

Common-law marriage is the most frequent form of marriage, partly because of the marginal role of the Church and the absence of legal marriage outside of the Church in Colombia until recently. Interestingly enough, it is women who frequently prefer common-law marriage so that the husband will not have legal control over them in the case of separation. Since there was no divorce until the 1980s, married women who were separated continued to be legally under their husbands' control in matters of property, business, and children. Also, separated women could not easily establish new relationships with other men because they were still legally bound to their husbands. In the face of those obstacles, many women preferred common-law marriage to the legal variety. Women do have the right to keep and use the money they earn, and they frequently own their houses. The husband is expected to provide the food and other basic expenses for the household.

Kinship ties are important in the working relationships among the women potters. These relationships are characterized by frequent sharing and overlapping family obligations. If one potter receives a particularly large order, she may ask a female relative to help her by making part of it. Kilns are also commonly shared among family members, and materials may be shared. Women show their trust in each other through sharing and collaboration, adding to the solidarity of the matrilocal family organization.

Gender and Household Organization

The gender relationships between men and women in La Chamba are based on mutually exclusive areas of authority and responsibility. The economic independence of the woman and the strength of the matrilocal relationships guarantee a strong position for the woman. On the other hand, the cultural value of *machismo* favors men and gives them certain privileges that are practically inaccessible to women, such as legal rights over the children, freedom of mobility, and higher levels of education.

The gender-based division of labor defines men's work as a commodity that can be bought and sold in the community, but women's work is nonnegotiable, unpaid domestic labor. This means that women potters can function without a male partner because they can hire men to do the man's work around a workshop, such as firing the kiln or mining clay. In fact, this happens with considerable frequency in La Chamba because 27 percent of the families do not have a male partner in the household. However, men cannot function without a woman in the domestic economy of La Chamba, so if a wife dies, the man must remarry, move in with other family members, or find a female relative to do the woman's work for him. June Nash (1985, 70) recorded a similar situation among the potters of Amatenango, Mexico.

The house is the woman's domain. It is the place where she makes ceramics, organizes and supervises the children, and does the domestic chores of cooking and cleaning. Ninety percent of the potters do their ceramics work at home (Montoya de la Cruz 1990, 49). The woman has the primary authority over the children, but she rarely punishes them physically. The house is her office, where the intermediaries come to place and pick up orders for ceramics. The house is also her social club, where friends and other members of the family come to visit. She may go to a corner store to buy something for the next meal or to the telephone office to make a call to a son or daughter in another town, but her time outside of the house is limited. If she goes to the mine to dig clay or to the market in the next town, she will always be accompanied by a child, another relative, or her husband. Women are rarely alone.

Ceramics provide the women of La Chamba an opportunity to work and earn money, which gives them an independence that other rural women in Colombia do not have. Because work in ceramics is virtually guaranteed, many young women drop out of school early to begin learning the craft. They live at home until they marry, and then they usually live near the mother. Pottery making doubles the work that women do in the house, and they have little leisure time as a result. Socializing is done while women are working on the porch or patio of their house, especially during periods of burnishing. Men's authority within pottery-making households is diminished in comparison to strictly agricultural families because of the independence of the women in producing regular income to support themselves and their children.

The men's domain in La Chamba is the street corner, the local store, and the fields where they work. If men are healthy and of working age, they are rarely in the house unless it is also their place of business, such as a store or bakery. Men spend most of their days outside of the village doing farmwork; in the evening, they gather in men's groups at the village stores, where they stand talking and drinking soft drinks or beer. The events of the day are discussed as well as work prospects for the immediate future. Since most men work as day laborers, information on work is a hot topic. Men go home to eat and to sleep, but rarely do they spend an evening socializing with their wives and children. There are few community activities that bring men and women together outside of the family. A husband and wife are rarely seen together in public, and they spend most of their time apart in their own gender-specific worlds, with women living primarily within the house complex of the extended family and men spending most of their time outside of the house.

Gender and the Larger Social Sphere

While women's activities are concentrated in the social sphere of the extended family and men's activities are primarily in the work world outside of the house, the lives of men and women do overlap as *compadres* (godparents), *vecinos* (neighbors), and *chambunos* (residents of La Chamba). The *compadrazgo* practice creates an extensive system of social obligations and ties that run throughout the community. A husband and wife may have four to six (even up to eight) godparents each from childhood (baptism, presentation, and confirmation), so between the two of them they may have ten to twelve godparents. They in turn will choose *compadres* for each of their children. For a household with six children, which is common in La Chamba, they may name six godparents for each child through the course of their childhood, making a total of thirty-six godparents for the children. When those are added to the twelve the parents have, they can have a *compadre* network of forty-eight people. That network of social obligation cuts across extended-family groups, neighborhood groups, and occupational groups to provide social ties for the household throughout the community. Since *compadres* include both genders, this system requires men and women to collaborate with each other. Since *compadres* are really co-parents and the network extends throughout the community, children are always supervised, even when their immediate parents are not present.

Although many *vecinos* (neighbors) are extended-family members or *compadres,* not all are. By virtue of living near each other in a tropical environment where much of daily life is lived out of doors, people have repeated and frequent contacts with each other. Their children may play together, they may watch each other work from house to house, or the women may help each other with tasks. A frequent source of conflict between neighbors is their domestic animals, which may break into the other's lot and damage or destroy gardens or other property.

Contact with other residents of La Chamba occurs at the stores, in school meetings, during casual encounters in the street, or on the bus to the next town. Most people in La Chamba know each other, and most know the kind of pottery that each woman makes, the work of the man, their extended family identifications, and their children. Thus, the person in La Chamba lives in a society of ever-expanding social circles, from the nuclear family to the extended family, the *compadrazgo* network, *vecinos,* and finally the entire community.

Social Caste and Desires for Upward Mobility

The social-caste system in Colombia is highly regimented, and the rural poor at the bottom of the scale have few mechanisms to transcend its limits. Many see it as an impassable barrier, make no attempt to overcome it, and accept their position as low-paid, low-skilled workers. Some challenge the system by entering the path of armed resistance with guerrilla groups, but more commonly people look to education as a way out of their exploited positions at the bottom of the social system.

Formal education has been an agent for social change in La Chamba because it offers the basic literacy and arithmetic skills that are required to interact with the larger national society. These skills often lead young people to believe that they can have a better life outside of the community, and they migrate to the city looking for salaried employment in preference to the short-term contracts on which their parents depend as potters and day laborers. However, migration does not always lead to upward social mobility because the education available in La Chamba is minimal and does not prepare a young person to compete with the better-educated people from urban areas. Their caste identity as indigenous-mestizos from rural Tolima and their lack of education constitute a double disadvantage.

Five primary occupational tracks are open to young people from La Chamba. They are gender linked, and females have the narrowest choices. By the age of fifteen or so, they can become potters and remain in the community working with their mothers, or they can migrate to a city and work as maids until they marry, which generally happens by the early twenties. Most continue to live in the city after marriage. Neither option requires education beyond the five years of elementary school. Both alternatives for young women assume that they will marry (in either common-law or legal unions) and that the husband will be the primary provider. As a result, young women are not encouraged to study at the high school level, and most have dropped out of school by the end of the fifth grade, which is the end of elementary school in Colombia.

Young men have three basic occupational tracks open to them, the first being to go into agricultural work as day laborers, like their fathers. The second is to migrate to a city and work as unskilled laborers in any job that is available; many, for example, become construction workers, messengers, and guards. Those who are more fortunate may get a relatively secure job in a factory. These two tracks require only an elementary education, even though some complete additional years at the middle-school level (sixth to eighth grades). The third option is to leave La Chamba for better employment, which requires attending high school. The high school diploma opens the possibility of clerical employment, teaching, and technical or professional careers. In one special case, a talented young man (Eduardo Sandoval) even went to art school to study art and design after high school, but he was the only person we documented who studied at the university level. It is assumed locally that a decision to get a high school education is a decision to leave the community, and the people know that a high school education is necessary to deal with the larger Colombian society.

Young men frequently say that they will move to the city and get a job in *cualquier cosa* (anything), assuming that their willingness to work will be sufficient. Even though the salaries they earn in urban areas can dwarf those of their rural parents, the high cost of living in the city can reduce them to living in even more limited circumstances than their parents in La Chamba. Those who aspire to low-level professional or white collar positions do not always complete enough education for those jobs. Any economic crisis within the household, resulting from an illness or other misfortune, can cause the student to drop out of school and work to help the family. As a result, only a few young people are successful in their ambition for upward mobility.

At the beginning of this study three of the children of the Silva-Prada household were in their teenage years and were making decisions about education and future work. Martín at fourteen had already indicated that he planned to leave La Chamba to complete high school and go to college to become a teacher. He had received the tentative offer of a scholarship to attend a high school in Ibagué, and he was waiting for it to be finalized so that he could go there to study. His older brother, Aurelio, who was fifteen, had finished primary school but did not want to study further, even though his father offered to pay for his high school education. He was doing day labor in agriculture when he could get jobs, and the rest of the time he helped his mother burnish ceramics. The two smallest boys, Jimmy, age ten, and Jairo, eight, were too young to have occupational plans.

Maritza, who was thirteen, had just completed primary school and decided not to study further because she did not like school. She said that having to do performances in front of the public for school functions and having to sell raffle tickets in the community to raise money for the school were especially embarrassing, so she decided to quit. Besides not liking school, she wanted to begin earning her own money, so she took the three-month course on ceramics offered by Artesanías de Colombia to learn "fine ceramics" forms. These are nontraditional forms that her mother, aunts, and cousins did not make, so knowing how to do them gave her a special niche within the extended family. For each of these young people, education was the filter that kept them in the community or gave them opportunities to leave.

The culture of formal education in La Chamba reinforces the social order of low-skilled individuals who will become low-paid manual workers within the economy. In the first place, most families do not expect children to study beyond primary school, and do not encourage them to have educational ambitions. Second, the schools reinforce the social skills of negotiating and interacting with others but place far less emphasis on content skills. Third, the large landowners around La Chamba need a pool of low-skilled manual laborers who are willing to work on a day-by-day basis. The only workers who will accept those terms are people with minimal educations and no other alternatives for employment. The inadequate formal education residents receive in the public schools guarantees future generations of uneducated, unskilled workers who will have to work for the minimal wages required for the industrial farms to be profitable.

Young people in La Chamba may have horizontal mobility to move to another town or to the city, but there is little opportunity for vertical social or occupational mobility. If a young person wants to stay in the community as a farmer or ceramist, it is assumed that the only academic skills he or she will need are basic reading, writing, and arithmetic. Much of the business conducted in the community is by oral agreement, so there is very little paperwork. This custom means that the accuracy of oral memory is most important, but this is learned in the community and not in school. People learn to do complex calculations of prices, firing costs, and production schedules in their heads, allowing experience to refine the accuracy of memory. So formal education is not especially important for this work.

Schools in La Chamba

In 1956 the present primary school was built, and it has functioned regularly since 1959 with the complete five years of primary school and enough teachers (five) for most of the children in the community to attend. In the 1970s a middle school was built, adding three more years of education. In 1998 the Ministry of Education approved the offering of the full high school diploma for La Chamba, but by the time of this writing it was still not being offered. Today, eight years of primary and middle school are taught, and funding is expected for the high school program. In 1972 the primary school had 206 students, and in 1988 it had 240 students, an increase of 16.5 percent in sixteen years. In 1988 there were more boys (130, or 54 percent) than girls (110, or 46 percent) in the primary school, but there were more girls (27, or 66 percent) than boys (14, or 34 percent) in the middle school. This indicates that boys are dropping out at faster rates than girls after elementary school.

Many people in La Chamba consider the schools to be an intrusion by the larger society into the local community, a foreign system imposed from the national offices of the remote Ministry of Education in Bogotá. In fact, formal education is relatively recent in the history of La Chamba, and it is not encouraged in many families. There is no local control over the schools. The curriculum is established in the national capital, and teachers are hired and paid through the national offices in Bogotá. Parents complain that the teachers lack a sense of responsibility to the school and that they regularly cut the classes short so that they can leave early for the day. These conditions are fairly common in rural Colombia (Hanson 1986, 36), and as a result 80 percent of the adult population in the country has a primary education or less (Psacharopoulos and Loxley 1985, 63).

In the elementary school there are few desks, and several children share each one. (See Photograph 3.2.) The classrooms consist of cement walls and floors, and a chalkboard hangs on one wall. There are no maps or visual teaching aids, and the meager salaries of the teachers are not sufficient to permit them to buy aids themselves, although they do provide their own chalk. Most children study with no textbooks because their families are too poor to buy them, and each student carefully guards his or her paper, pencil, and other materials. The *Asociación Padres de Familia* (Parents Association) does projects to improve the physical plant. In 1989, forty-six parents were members of the *Asociación,* and they built a multi-use ball court and fenced in the school.

Teachers orient the classes toward participation and interaction. They use the Escuela Nueva (new school) approach to pedagogy, which implies participatory teaching, and students are encouraged to play active roles, commenting, questioning, giving reports, and organizing group activities. Even though the physical plant is minimal, the students do in fact participate

Photo 3.2. Children in school. Space is limited, children share desks, and materials are few. In such a crowded situation children develop excellent social skills, and they form friendships with their peers that are important in this small community.

actively, which teaches them to form ideas, express themselves, and actively negotiate with each other, in the process developing excellent interpersonal skills.

Since the schools are crowded, there are morning sessions from 7:00 A.M. to 12:00 noon for one set of students, and afternoon sessions from 1:00 P.M. to 6:00 P.M. for the other students. Many teachers in the morning session live in El Guamo and come to La Chamba on the public bus, which arrives at 8:00 A.M. and returns at 11:00 A.M. So, in fact, the teachers hold classes for only three hours instead of five because of the bus schedule. The shorter hours mean that they cannot teach all of the material set in the curriculum. The teachers explain that they have to leave early because the salary (slightly more than U.S. $100 per month) is not sufficient to live on, and they have to teach at other schools in El Guamo during the afternoon hours to increase their incomes to an acceptable level. The teachers who have the afternoon schedule are more scrupulous in completing the five hours assigned to them because they do not have to travel to another school afterwards.

Admission to the elementary school is uncertain because there are usually more children ready to enter than there are spaces available in the first grade. As a result, some students are delayed one year in starting school. Sixty students are admitted in the first year, and there is usually a 10 percent loss rate over the first three years. So the number attending drops to fifty or so for the second and third years. Since students are required to attend only three years, the number drops after that to approximately forty students in the fourth year, and thirty or thirty-five in the fifth year. Only half of the students complete primary school out of the group that started the first grade. That retention level is high for rural Colombia because on a national level only 18 percent of rural students complete primary school (Hanson 1986, 36).

After the fifth and final year of elementary school, many students are in their early teens, a result of having begun school late or having missed or failed some years. By that age they are considered old enough to begin working, and many parents do not see the value of education beyond the primary level. Although there were thirty-five students in the last year of primary school in 1987, only twenty-one (60 percent) went on to the first year of middle school. In 1988 only fifteen continued on to middle school (Montoya de la Cruz 1990, 65). That represents only one-third of the students who actually start primary school. This is consistent with statistics nationwide, where 69 percent of craftspeople have an elementary education or less (Artesanías de Colombia 1998, 23).

The middle school offers three grades, but the enrollments are small: forty-six students in the three grades in 1987, forty-one in 1988, and forty-six in 1989. It is common for students to be at least sixteen years old (and some eighteen) when they complete the eighth year, the last in middle school. Of the sixty students who enter the first year of primary school, only ten (17 percent) study to the eighth year; the other fifty have already dropped out of school and started to work. No more than two or three (5 percent) actually complete high school.

Most of the middle school students (79 percent of the boys and 67 percent of the girls) report doing some income-related work outside of the school in either crafts, agriculture, or construction. Most assist their mothers in ceramics, including 43 percent of the boys and 59 percent of the girls. At that age they are old enough to do adult jobs, and most choose to begin working and earning money rather than spend three more years in high school. (See Table 3.2.)

Until recently, if a student wanted to study at the high school level, he or

Table 3.2. Gender, Age, and Work among Middle School Children

Grade	Age	Number	Male				Female		
			HW	C	AG	CO	HW	C	AG
6th	11	2					1	1	
	12	5	1				2	2	
	13	4	1	1	1		1		
	14	1		1					
	15	3				1			2
7th	11	4			1			3	
	12	1		1					
	14	3			1		2		
	15	1			1				
	16	3					1	2	
	17	4	1				1	2	
8th	15	7		1				6	
	16	1		1					
	17	1		1					
	18	1					1		
Total		41	3	6	4	1	9	16	2

Source: Montoya de la Cruz 1990, 68

HW = Housework; C = Ceramics; AG = Agriculture; CO = Construction

she had to move to another town where it was offered, or commute daily to El Guamo. Few households in La Chamba had the money to pay the food and lodging for a child to live in another town to go to high school, so the only real option was to commute. It also cost too much for some students to pay for the bus or collective taxi each day, so they commuted the thirty-six kilometers round trip by bicycle. That eliminated most girls from going to high school, but by 1998 that was changing with the approval of the full high school program for La Chamba.

School attendance is not compulsory, and it tends to be irregular. If there is no space in the school for a child to enter or if the family needs the child to work, he or she may stay home the entire year and not study. During peak planting and harvest periods in La Chamba, many children work in the fields and may miss as much as two months of classes at a time, and even during regular periods of classes, attendance may be lax with students missing classes for no other reason than not wanting to go.

In addition to the regular schools, other classes have been offered to the community in the past. In 1969 nuns of the Order of María Inmaculada opened a convent in La Chamba, and in 1970 they set up adult literacy classes at night in a building donated to them by the Bavaria Brewing Company of Bogotá. In 1971–72 116 students attended classes there (Lara 1972, 47), but attendance declined soon afterward, which led to the closing of the night school and to the nuns leaving La Chamba. In the 1980s the Instituto Colombiano de Bienestar Familiar (Colombian Institute of Family Welfare) set up a nursery school in the old convent, which was loaned to it by the Order, and four local employees cared for preschool-aged children.

Learning the Work Ethic

Being an industrious worker is highly valued in La Chamba, and mothers are expected to train their children to work well. Showing her concern about work, Anatilde Prada said, "The children of today do not know how to work, and it is difficult to make them work as hard as I did as a child." She said that her older children, who have left home, are all working well, and the two older boys at home work satisfactorily, but her primary concern is her youngest daughter, Maritza. According to Anatilde, she is lazy, slow, and sloppy in her work. Although she already knows all of the steps in making and firing ceramics, her pieces are irregular, and they are difficult to sell. Anatilde says that when Maritza applies the slip, it ends up on her dress, in her hair, and on the floor, a complete mess! She can only burnish twelve bowls a day when she should be doing eighteen.

Anatilde knows that Maritza must become completely proficient in all aspects of the production because it is her future. She expects Maritza to work full-time in ceramics and to take care of her in her old age. Anatilde explained that when she was a child, she lived with her grandmother and had to work hard every day. Water had to be brought to the house from the river, over one kilometer away. Between six and eight o'clock in the morning, she made several trips to the river, bringing all of the water needed in the house for the day. She also helped collect firewood for cooking and did other household chores. But with electricity, water, and gas readily available today, she said there are not many chores for the children to do, and they do not learn to work hard. In spite of her comments, her children regularly worked three to four hours a day after school, beginning at ten years of age. By age fourteen or fifteen they dropped out of school to work full time. So the children of La Chamba do have a strong commitment to work. The fact that mothers refer to the work ethic frequently in their conversations is an indication of its importance in the community.

Conclusions

La Chamba is a small village located in the tropical lowlands of a rich agricultural valley. Large Spanish land grants concentrated most of the good agricultural land in the hands of a few people during the colonial period and that situation has continued until today, with the result that most men are marginal workers in an agrarian capitalist system. The household organization is supplemented by a complex network of social ties, including *compadrazgo* and neighborhood linkages. The social class system is interwoven with marginal educational opportunities to limit the possibilities for upward mobility for the young. This circumstance keeps part of each generation in La Chamba, continuing the ceramic tradition for which it is famous.

4

The History of La Chamba Ceramics

The origins of village ceramics in Colombia are lost in the mists of an unwritten past, and it is only through oral tradition, archaeology, and the chronicles of the Conquest that we can glimpse the early history. However, the information that does exist provides a continuum of vivid sketches that allow us to glimpse the outlines of the last five hundred years. From prehispanic times to the present, Colombia has been a country of ceramics. Village-made planters or pots frequently sit near the entrance of Colombian houses, quietly symbolizing the rootedness of the culture in the earth and the craft traditions that are quintessentially Colombian. In the living rooms of most educated people, ceramics from the prehispanic period are set alongside European or Oriental porcelains, representing the many cultural influences in this country.

The village ceramics of today evolved during the colonial period as indigenous and European styles of pottery merged, one aspect of the mixing of peoples that led to the mestizo culture of Colombia. Ceramics are a good indicator of the social, political, and economic changes that have occurred in the country. In fact, the history of ceramics in Colombia is as much an indicator of social and cultural history as is the history of wars and presidents.

Prehispanic Ceramics: Continuity and Change

The prehispanic groups that existed at the time of contact define a baseline against which the traditional pottery of contemporary indigenous and mestizo groups can be compared. For example, the relationships between the prehispanic Muisca and contemporary Ráquira ceramics can be traced directly (Cardale 1989, 57), as can those between the prehispanic Tairona and the contemporary Kogi (Chaves 1985b, 61–62). A study of design continuity in other areas of Colombia also suggests cultural links between prehispanic and contemporary groups, such as the Nariño culture and the Inga (Duncan 1992a, 133–34) and the Sinú and potters in Córdoba on the Atlantic Coast (Chaves 1985a, 78). Connections between the prehispanic potters of Tolima and the contemporary potters of La Chamba are described in this study. Cooking pots and other traditional pottery made in mestizo areas of Colombia, such as La Chamba, are so closely linked to the prehispanic-indigenous ceramics as to be considered an extension of it. Although Spanish influences interrupted the cultural continuity with the indigenous past, they did not break it. Women potters today throughout Colombia continue to preserve that native heritage in their work.

The Spanish destroyed the high tradition of prehispanic art ceramics after the Conquest because of its links with indigenous religion and political power. However, the low tradition of narrative and playful figures and functional pottery did survive in everyday usage. In spite of the Conquest, Colombia has preserved a dynamic and creative tradition of village ceramics that reflects a history measured in millennia. In this long history there were many invasions and conquests between indigenous groups before the Spaniards arrived. The latter did not erase indigenous history; rather they added yet another cultural layer on top of the earlier ones. However, the purging of prehispanic culture carried out by the Spanish military, clergy, and agents of the Crown during the Conquest did suppress the political and religious identities of indigenous peoples.

Two victims of this cultural purging were surface painting of cosmological concepts on pottery (Cardale 1989, 57; Duncan 1992b, 14–17) and the making of precolumbian ceramic icons of shamans (mohán) and mythical beings (Duncan 1993, 24–25). The various prehispanic cultures of Colombia were divided between those that painted pottery surfaces, and those that did not. The Carib-speaking people of Tolima did surface painting on ceramics, using abstract, geometric signs that had cosmological and religious significance. Although this painting tradition has been lost in La Chamba, people remember that ceramics were painted in the village in the past. Some isolated indigenous groups in Colombia still use these motifs in their craft design. When potters stopped making the prehispanic ceramic figures of chiefs and shamans, they started making Spanish-inspired figures of horses and chickens in their place, transforming the tradition of figure making.

In the prehispanic-indigenous cultures, mythology and ritual are the primary iconographic factors in art. When the Spanish suppressed the traditional religious systems, the cultural roots that nourished that art dried up. Nina S. de Friedemann (1993, 151) suggests that the commerce and tourism of recent decades, driven by a fascination with the exotic, are as destructive to the traditional symbolic values of village ceramics as was the suppression of "pagan" elements during the Spanish colonial period. The loss of prehispanic symbolism, and the knowledge that supported it, converted the posthispanic ceramics of Tolima into domestic functional ware. This loss of conceptual content robbed Tolima ceramics of its esthetic projections. Today the people of La Chamba still make ceramic forms based on precolumbian shapes, although they have also adopted some Spanish ones. Local oral tradition also confirms this continuity with the prehispanic past because *chambunos* say that pottery has been made here since the "time of the Indians"—that is, the Pijaos.

Tribal Ceramics: Pottery of Carib-Speaking Peoples

Various Carib language groups occupied this area when the Spanish arrived, including the Pijaos and the Panches among others. The Pijaos were located in the area immediately around La Chamba, and the Panches occupied the territory to the north (Rojas de Perdomo 1985, 217), including sites near El Espinal, only sixteen kilometers from La Chamba. Potters who live in that same area today in the *vereda* (rural district) of Montalva make ceramics similar in design to the Pijao-Panche pottery (Montoya de la Cruz 1990, 27). The Pijaos occupied the Upper Magdalena River Valley from Fusagasugá, Cundinamarca, in the north, to Garzón, Huila, in the south (Rivet 1943, 55). They also lived along the Luisa River in the *veredas* of Rincón y Santo and Chipuelos (Montoya de la Cruz 1990, 26), both of which border La Chamba. Farmers in the region still unearth their ceramics occasionally. The Colombian anthropologists Gerardo and Alicia Reichel-Dolmatoff (1945, 507) also documented biological and cultural characteristics of the Pijaos among contemporary people near La Chamba, showing the continued presence of Pijao descendants in the region.

Prehispanic ceramics showing influences from the Cauca River Valley are also found in some areas near La Chamba (Reichel-Dolmatoff 1965, 107), but they seem to predate the historic Pijao occupation. These ceramics include round bulbous pottery shapes of animals, as well as other shapes representing fruits. They are frequently painted with red slip, and are sometimes decorated with painted scrolls, spirals, and diamond shapes. Calima and Quimbaya-like gold ornaments have also been found in the area (ibid.,

109). However, at the time of the contact with the Spanish, the cultural influence of the Cauca Valley groups was not apparent among the Pijaos along the Magdalena (ibid., 101). Figurative ceramics found in the area also portray gabled houses with open-sided walls (ibid., 109), showing what was probably the architecture of these groups.

They also had a prolific production of cooking and water pots, which varied in technical skill and style from group to group. From some sites there are reports of forms that were delicately worked, and from other sites come reports of more rustic wares, which probably reflects the varying skills of local potters. Red slip was commonly used to decorate the pottery of these groups. One vessel shape made by these groups had a spherical body with a wide mouth, and it is similar to the cooking pot of today. A taller ovoid pot was also made, which sometimes had a human figure modeled on its neck. Ceramic spindle whorls, used for spinning cotton, were also made, and ceramic funerary urns have been reported for several sites (Rojas de Perdomo 1985, 214–15, 227).

Survivals from the Pijao language also appear in the local place names, including "Chamba," which means creek or drainage, "Guamo," which is the name of a large fruit tree, and *mohán*, which means shaman (Bedoya 1950, 25, 30, 35). The word *chamba* also exists in Spanish but with other meanings, and only in Colombia does *chamba* mean creek (Cuyas 1962, 161). This suggests that the Pijao (Carib language) meaning was incorporated into Colombian Spanish. The myth of the *mohán* is another indication of the cultural heritage from the Pijaos, and the figure of the *mohán* is one of the few ceramic figurines made in the community today. According to the myth, the *mohán* is an old man who can be seen sitting on the river bank, smoking a cigar. A riverman who tries to approach the *mohán* will be caught by the river currents and drowned. This myth describes typical powers of a shaman (Tovar 1958, 32) and suggests a memory of the mythology of the prehispanic group.

Other parallels between Pijao practices and contemporary La Chamba culture include similar ceramic techniques and forms. For example, the round and ovoid shapes of the precolumbian period are the basic shapes made today in La Chamba. Red slip was used by the Pijaos, and today all pots are painted with it. White slip was also used by the Pijaos for decorative drawings (Lara 1972, 32), and it was used until recent decades in La Chamba. Finally, the water bottle made in La Chamba is similar to one made by the Pijaos. These coincidences in mythical beliefs and ceramics suggest cultural continuities between the prehispanic Pijao and the people of La Chamba today.

Colonial Ceramics: Early and Middle Colonial Periods (1537–1740)

The Conquest was a cultural earthquake that transformed the independent and autonomous indigenous culture into a subject one. The resistance of the Pijaos to the Spanish Conquest in the area of present-day La Chamba was formidable, and that may partially explain the continuing resistance to the Spanish culture and the strength of the indigenous cultural tradition today. As mentioned earlier, oral tradition in La Chamba says that one of the principal leaders of the Conquest, Sebastián de Belalcázar, attacked the Pijaos at Chapetón, the river landing of La Chamba, in his desire to obtain gold from the local people. In the bloody battle that followed, many Indian families were killed (Lara 1972, 29). The name of the river landing, *chapetón,* means Spaniard, which suggests that the river landing was the place where the indigenous people met the Spanish. There is little information about the cultural and artistic events of the early and middle colonial periods in the Pijao area.

Late Colonial Period in La Chamba (1740–1810)

In 1746, near the end of the colonial period, an official reference is made to the area of La Chamba as belonging to a large hacienda given by the Spanish Crown in a land grant to Antonio Álvarez. The Álvarez hacienda extended from the central range of the Andes to the Magdalena River, fifty kilometers to the east, and ownership was passed down through the same family line for the next 150 years (Lara 1972, 36). Shortly after this, in 1772, the names of La Chamba and Chapetón, the river landing, appear in the official records when a royal official, Francisco Vargas, traveled through the region and visited them (Villegas 1986, 37).

The history of La Chamba for the last two hundred years has been one of large haciendas and of workers who cleared and farmed the land and made pots, baskets, and other craft objects for everyday use. During the 1700s and most of the 1800s, the hacienda owners used a feudal system in which the rights to a plot of land were granted to a worker for three harvests, with the condition that he would clear the land and cultivate it. At the end of the grant period, the land reverted to the owner, who then used it as pasture land for cattle. In exchange for permission to use the land, the worker had to dedicate a specific number of days each month to work for the owner of the hacienda.

The worker and his family lived on the plot temporarily granted by the hacienda owner and practiced subsistence agriculture, which created a dispersed residential pattern. Similar feudal arrangements were made on haciendas throughout the Andes, whereby indigenous people worked for free in exchange for the right to use a plot of land.

Although the workers who originally cleared the hacienda lands were primarily of indigenous origin, *mestizaje* did occur, either genetically, through intermarriage and concubinage, or culturally, as Indians acculturated to Spanish practices. Although the present-day population is considered mestizo, it has pronounced Indian physical and cultural features. This is in spite of the fact that during the first 150 years of the colonial period, the indigenous populations in Colombia declined continuously. In part, this decline resulted from the genocidal practices of the Spanish in military actions and in part from the forced labor imposed on indigenous communities, in which lives were sacrificed in favor of productivity. However, there may have been other reasons for the decline in the officially registered Indian population that involve strategies of indigenous resistance to the Spanish, four of which can be identified as follows.

First, a de facto genocide resulted from the forced migration of conscripted laborers to work in mines, which frequently ended in death, and from the high mortality rates that followed the introduction of European diseases. Second was the tendency of indigenous people to migrate out of areas controlled by the Spanish to avoid the obligations of paying tribute and the forced-labor requirements, which meant that they disappeared from Spanish records. Since Spanish control was concentrated in a few towns, indigenous people could avoid it by moving to remote rural areas (Colmenares 1970, 70). Third was the growing number of mixed blood (*mestizo*) children resulting from unions between Spanish men and Indian women. With this process of *mestizaje* the Indian population shrank and the mestizo population grew. Fourth, indigenous people who learned Spanish, became Christians, and adopted Spanish dress could blend in with the mestizo population and lose their status as Indians. All of these factors probably contributed to the decline in a population that was defined as "Indian" by the Spanish.

In spite of this trend of *mestizaje,* the people of La Chamba were still considered Indian in the late 1800s. An event in 1876 demonstrates their continuing antagonism toward the Spanish. Doña Marcelina Leal, the grandmother of one of Lara's informants, built a chapel in the area of the present-day village, and a Spanish priest came to offer Mass in it. He attempted to establish friendly relations with the indigenous people living in the area (Lara 1972, 29), but his mission met with no success because of the community's continuing negative attitudes toward the Spanish. So we know that as late as the 1870s the people of La Chamba were still identified as being Indian, and they were culturally resisting the Spanish.

Early Provincial Ceramics: Republican Period (1810–1903)

Throughout the early Republican years of the 1800s, the production of unglazed earthenware continued intact in the Colombian countryside, and it was documented in the paintings and watercolors of a group of local and foreign artists who were dedicated to painting rural and small-town life of the time. One of these was Edward Walhouse Mark, the vice-consul for Great Britain in Santa Marta (1843–46) and later in Bogotá (1846–56). He did an excellent series of watercolors documenting landscapes, architecture, people, and customs of the period (Banco de la República 1963).

Various travel logs written by foreigners in the last century also mention ceramics, but never with the visual detail afforded by the artists. For example, Carl Gosselman (1981, 36), writing in 1825, mentioned the use of several large earthenware amphoras for water in the dining room of a house in Cartagena. He also speaks of Afro-Colombian women carrying water jars on their heads to the river to collect water in Santa Marta (ibid., 45), and mentions the production of large, wheel thrown *tinajas* (water jars) and *ollas* (cooking pots) in Mompós, located in the Lower Magdalena River Valley (ibid., 115). Alfred Hettner (1976, 84) and Augusto LeMoyne (1945, 126) also refer to the prevalence of functional ceramics in their descriptions of Colombian town life in the nineteenth century.

Oral tradition gives some information about the people living in La Chamba in the 1800s. Don Julio Betancourt, one of Carmen Lara's informants (1972, 33–34), who was born in 1885, knew from accounts when he was small that the *chambunos* were making ceramics in the early 1800s. Throughout the nineteenth century, La Chamba men were dedicated primarily to agriculture while the women made crafts. The home-based production of crafts was oriented toward the needs of the household and the immediate community, including ceramics, baskets woven with palm leaves, candles from animal fat, soap, sewing, bread, and other products. The dispersed residential pattern of the last century and the economy of self-sufficiency encouraged women to practice several crafts rather than specializing in one. The isolation of the area from the large urban centers prevented large-scale craft production during this period.

Ceramics were for domestic, utilitarian use, especially for cooking and storing food and drink. The traditional cooking pot, the water storage jar, and the water bottle (*múcura*) date from this time, and the precolumbian, indigenous-style serving bowl (*cazuela*) was the dinnerware for rural households of the 1800s in this area. As is done today, banana leaves and gourds may also have been used to serve food. The ceramics of La Chamba today are still based on designs consistent with their use in the rural lifestyle of Tolima in recent centuries.

By the early 1800s, there was systematic commerce up and down the Magdalena River in long, covered cargo boats called *champanes*. These boats and the way of life that surrounded them were amply documented by the English watercolorist Mark, mentioned earlier. Although he did not record scenes from La Chamba itself, he did paint scenes of the river and of people near the village, including El Guamo and Honda, both only a few kilometers away (Banco de la República 1963, 166, 260). His watercolors show that earthenware ceramics were common in the *champanes* and the communities along the shore, and they show unglazed earthenware similar to that still produced by the traditional country potters of the region. A number of scenes record people getting water from the river in earthenware jugs, which they carry on their shoulders in indigenous fashion (ibid., 246, 258) (see Figure 4.1). Views of house interiors show the jugs being used for storage (ibid., 242, 252).

Mark also shows barrels of goods being loaded and unloaded from the boats at river landings very similar to Chapetón, the river landing of La Chamba (Banco de la República 1963, 52, 64, 74) (see Figure 4.2). The oral history of La Chamba records that these boats stopped at Chapetón to buy crafts and agricultural products, and the boatmen sold meat, potatoes, and other products needed locally. Men from La Chamba also worked on these boats, taking loads upriver to the towns of Purificación and Neiva, the capital of the neighboring state. This was the beginning of the regional marketing system that is still in use today. These boats seem to have been used until the early 1900s (Lara 1972, 37).

Late Provincial Ceramics (1903–1930)

During the early twentieth century, the community was gradually reorganized from a dispersed settlement to a more nucleated one, and a simulta-

Figure 4.1.
*Aguador de
Guaduas* (Water
Carrier from
Guaduas). Edward
Walhouse Mark
painted this man
in 1846 carrying
water from the
Magdalena River
in Guaduas, a
town north of La
Chamba. People in
La Chamba
carried water pots
on their shoulders
in a similar
fashion until
recently. From a
watercolor by
Mark, reproduced
with the permis-
sion of the Banco
de la República,
Bogotá.

neous expansion of the market for ceramics occurred at the regional level.
By the beginning of this period, people were living primarily along the river
bank near the landing at Chapetón. Most men were doing sharecropping,
and some also traveled selling the ceramics of their women relatives. Mean-
while women worked as home-based craft producers, with increasing specialization in ceramics. The men also engaged in garden farming for the
household's subsistence needs, and they did fishing.

In 1903 most of the remaining lands (15,000 hectares) of the old Álvarez
hacienda were sold, and only the area of the village of La Chamba was
retained by the descendants of the hacienda owners. In 1907 they also began
to sell the area of the village itself, and plots up to five hectares in size were
bought by thirteen local families. These land sales are the first official record

Figure 4.2. A *champán* at the river landing. *Champanes* were flat-bottomed river boats that were the primary means of transporting heavy cargo up and down the Magdalena River in the 1800s, and they regularly came to La Chamba. Barrels and ceramic pots filled with goods were shipped this way, along with other cargo and passengers. From an 1840s watercolor by Edward Walhouse Mark. Reproduced with the permission of the Banco de la República, Bogotá.

of the village in its current location. The families who bought those original plots are still present in the community: the Betancourt, Céspedes, Rodríguez, Torrijos, Méndez, Ramírez, and Avilés families (Lara 1972, 58). Before buying the house plots, these families apparently lived on them as workers for the hacienda.

By this time, men from La Chamba were making flat-bottomed barges and taking products downriver to pottery merchants in Girardot, and occasionally as far as Honda and Puerto Berrío (Lara 1972, 38). From this time period to the 1960s, the Girardot pottery merchants were the primary market for La Chamba potters. The barges were built with a simple technology of tying together the trunks of lightweight trees with organic fibers, making them organically disposable. The barges carried mostly ceramics but could also take pigs, bananas, or other agricultural products, and they were directed by one or two men, using paddles and push poles. After the trip they were abandoned to decay in the river because the current is too swift to propel barges back upstream by hand, and the men returned home overland.

This river commerce was strong for the first three decades of the twentieth century and continued well into the 1960s. On a cycle of approximately every three weeks, twenty to thirty barges would leave La Chamba for the trip downstream to sell the ceramic and agricultural produce of the town. The men would be gone for one week, more or less, and would return to begin accumulating merchandise and building the raft for the next trip. The women used the three-week cycle to make, dry, and fire the next shipment of ceramics. The importance of farming declined during this period as the people, both men and women, turned their attention to craft production and sales. When the first road was built into the community in the 1930s, the river commerce declined rapidly. There is still one man in the community, Juan Sandoval, who makes barge trips downriver in the traditional manner. He said that he continued the practice because he loved the river, and that he had been doing it since he was a child. The disposable barge, which costs almost nothing to build, is a low-cost alternative to a truck, which he did not have the capital to buy. But he is the last one to ship by barge, and now all other goods are shipped out by truck. The better-financed middlemen from neighboring cities, who can afford trucks, have taken over the role of the men of La Chamba in transporting the goods of the village to market.

By 1920 there were sixty households in the community, half of which were dedicated to making ceramics. The other half were agriculturalists, and some of them still practiced other traditional crafts, such as weaving palm mats (Lara 1972, 37). The commercial success of ceramics stimulated a process of immigration to the community from neighboring areas, which led to population growth around the nucleated settlement.

Urban Market Ceramics: Mid-Twentieth Century (1930–1968)

The mid-twentieth century brought important changes to La Chamba: the first road was built into the community; a school was established; the community grew to two hundred households; it entered the national craft market; and the first government services were provided, tying the village more closely to the larger national society. The growth in the population continued the process begun in the early part of the century as people moved into La Chamba from neighboring rural areas. A kinsman or kinswoman who had a series of crop failures, whose house burned, or who lost a spouse would migrate into the nucleated village, where greater security was to be found. The period of La Violencia in the late 1940s and early 1950s also brought people from the less protected rural areas to the village. Finally, the building of the "urban center" by the Rojas administration in 1955 meant that La Chamba was one of the few rural centers in the area with a health center, police station, and school, and these also attracted immigrants.

Immigration stabilized in the late 1950s, and during the 1960s a process of emigration from the community began as rural laborers were drawn into the workforce of Colombia's growing cities. The population has remained stable from that point to the present. In comparison with previous periods, the production of ceramics grew quickly during the mid-twentieth century, and specialization became more common. Each woman began to specialize in certain forms and in specific sizes, with some dedicated to making traditional ware (pots, water storage jars, or water bottles) and others to tableware (eating bowls and casseroles).

The first one-room school was established in 1930, but only the first three years of elementary school were offered. National public education had been established by law in 1903, and the Ministry of Education was created at that time. However, it was not until the Liberal Party won the elections of 1930 that public education was expanded throughout the country, and the school in La Chamba was a part of that national effort to bring education to more people. The complete five years of elementary education were offered in the cities, but only three years were offered in rural areas (Hanson 1986, 29–30), such as La Chamba.

The first teacher in the La Chamba school was Evelia Ramírez from El Espinal (Lara 1972, 42). Both boys and girls could attend the school, although they went in different shifts. Ramírez taught ceramics as one of the courses. She came to have an important role in the community, organizing weekly extracurricular activities, called *fiestas de familia* or family parties, which included dances, theatrical presentations, and harvest festivals (ibid., 43). This period in the 1930s is remembered as one of community good will.

In 1937 Evelia Ramírez helped promote and direct the building of the first road into La Chamba, and she is remembered as a dynamic figure, mounted on a white horse, directing the road construction workers. The road connected La Chamba to El Espinal, the next town to the north, which in turn is connected to major regional and national highways. The new road brought La Chamba potters into more direct contact with external markets, and they quickly began to respond to the broader commercial possibilities.

After the building of the road, merchants from Girardot and other urban areas began coming to the community to ask for new types of ware, such as covered casseroles and cups and saucers, pieces that came to be called "tableware" or *loza,* leading to a major change in the design of La Chamba ceramics. This new ceramics style was made for table use and serving, whereas the traditional pottery was for cooking and storing food. According to oral history, the practice of reduction, the process used to turn the pieces black, began with the introduction of tableware. Although the traditional cooking pots are always fired red, tableware may be red or black, the two colors now identified with La Chamba ceramics.

One of Evelia Ramírez's students was Ana María Cabezas, who learned ceramics and went on to play a crucial role in La Chamba ceramics for the next fifty years. In 1941 the state government organized a statewide competition of craft ceramics, promising to establish a school of ceramics in the town of the winner. Ana María Cabezas, then thirteen years old, won the competition, and the school was finally established in La Chamba in 1944. Enrique Cárdenas was sent to teach in the new ceramics school, where he taught for one and one-half years. He trained students to make pieces by hand building with slabs and coils, concentrating on pitchers and flower vases. He occasionally decorated the finished surfaces with paint but did not burnish nor glaze pieces. Although Ana María Cabezas had won the prize that led to the school being established, she did not study in it because she was sixteen when it began, and she was already working as a potter. During this period the other traditional crafts were declining and disappearing in La Chamba.

In 1944 Ana María Cabezas won another regional prize with a red and black tableware set, and in 1945 she won a prize in an international exhibit of popular art held in the National Library in Bogotá. In the latter exhibit, both she and her students sent work, which included tableware and figurative pieces. The latter included fruits and animals, and they also incorporated precolumbian themes (a supernatural figure and a serpent) from the Catío, Pijao, and Quimbaya groups (Lara 1972, 44). Cabezas won the prize again, and forty years later she proudly showed us the diploma given to her by the Ministry of Education verifying the prize.

In 1945, at the age of seventeen, Cabezas was named director and professor of the ceramics school, a post she held until 1957. Her trajectory is important because she was a pioneer who helped redefine the concept of ceramics in the community. She is respected and acclaimed locally for having developed and introduced the idea of "fine ceramics" (discussed in chapter 8) and for having trained many of the ceramists of the younger generation.

In 1949 Gilma Barreto, another ceramist from La Chamba, was named as a second teacher at the school, and she taught there most of the next three decades. Although conflicts arose between the two teachers, they worked together until 1957, when Ana María Cabezas resigned.

The school had a decisive influence on the development of ceramics in La Chamba. Carmen Lara suggests that the school led the student ceramists to adopt the techniques and forms of urban tableware taught by the two teachers and enrich the traditional country pottery made in the community (1972, 44). More sophisticated techniques were introduced into the production process, and ceramists began to be aware of the need to select clay according to the style of ceramics to be made. The school trained students to use slip and to burnish the surfaces to partially seal them. New designs were also taught at the school, which contributed to the emergence of the new tableware style of serving trays, platters, and bowls that the urban merchants were requesting. Precolumbian decorative styles were studied from photographs and drawings in books and from precolumbian pots discovered in neighboring rural areas. The ceramics school taught young women the basic skills of La Chamba–style ceramics. This permitted the students to train themselves more quickly than was possible through the traditional apprenticeship with a mother or aunt.

In 1956 a Junta de Accion Comunal (Community Action Council) was organized to stimulate the development of the village, but La Chamba remained an unincorporated community, attached to the larger neighboring town of El Guamo. In the same decade local *hacendados* (large landowners) started the cultivation of rice on an industrial level using tractors and hiring local workers as day laborers. This significantly expanded wage employment opportunities for men, and they increasingly began to work in industrial agriculture instead of transporting pottery for their wives or working as sharecroppers. By that time, the more wealthy pottery merchants in Girardot had bought trucks, which virtually eliminated the role of La Chamba men in transporting pottery to market by river. During this period, electricity was brought to the village, local stores were established to sell ceramics, and a guest house opened.

The demand for La Chamba ceramics expanded as urban interest in national crafts increased in the middle decades of the century. La Chamba tableware came to be regarded as the finest representative of authentic crafts, and a restaurant serving traditional Colombian food, such as *ajiaco,* was expected to serve it in La Chamba pottery. This is an interesting paradox because *ajiaco* is not made nor eaten in La Chamba; rather, it is a typical dish of the colder mountain valleys and plateaus of central Colombia. But this is ceramics used for cultural symbolism, and elements are combined for their abstract meanings rather than because they are historically correct.

Fine Ceramics and Figures: Late Twentieth Century (1968 to present)

The Colombian economy has been stimulated by the international capitalist expansion of recent decades, and it has affected both the agricultural work and ceramics production of people in La Chamba. As the large landowners surrounding La Chamba shifted their land from sharecropping to commercial crops in the 1950s and La Chamba men became day laborers on the big farms, their income became less predictable, and older men often were not hired. In reaction women have increased their production in ceramics to supplement and stabilize family incomes, as predicted by other studies (Arnold 1985, 179; Carrillo 1997, 197).

The market expansion of recent decades has also led to increased orders from middlemen in Bogotá and other cities, which has dovetailed with the increased production. The tourist and national markets for La Chamba pottery became important during this period, and these new markets replaced the regional indigenous ones. The commodity production of tableware continued to grow, and the new "fine ceramics" style of carefully modeled pieces was developed.

The national government started a series of initiatives to support the development of crafts as a household-based industry. In 1966 Artesanías de Colombia began actively marketing La Chamba ceramics, providing an alternative to the traditional marketing system controlled by a few merchants in the nearby town of Girardot. Artesanías de Colombia has not only sold La Chamba pottery nationally, but it has also exported it internationally. In 1968, SENA (Servicio Nacional de Aprendizaje, or National Learning Service) established a craft education center in the town, which essentially replaced the moribund state school of ceramics. The craft education center offered elementary education to craftspeople, as well as courses in ceramics design and production techniques. A second major governmental effort to stimulate local craft production was the establishment of a craft marketing center in 1970 by Artesanías de Colombia and the opening of a guest house to promote tourism.

The opening of the Centro Artesanías de Colombia in the town focused attention on the community as a marketing venue. Essentially, it completed the ongoing process of breaking the monopoly of the Girardot merchants, and it stimulated independent middlemen to come to La Chamba to buy directly at the center or from potters themselves. Although this competition brought more openness to the local market, many potters continued selling to their established clients in Girardot (Lara 1972, 20).

Over the last three decades, governmental support for La Chamba crafts has had less impact than anticipated. SENA abandoned its national policy toward the support of crafts, and the La Chamba center was closed before it had much effect. Craft-oriented tourism never developed as had been expected, and the guest house had to be closed. Although Artesanías de Colombia built a beautiful marketing center, designed by a major national architect and constructed with local, tropical materials, sales from the center never paid for the costs of its maintenance, and the budget appropriations from the national offices dwindled over the years. Within a decade the physical structure and the marketing effort was only a shadow of what they had been, and by the mid-1990s Artesanías de Colombia was discussing plans to reduce their operation and sell the center.

By the 1980s the center had primarily come to serve young, marginal craftswomen who did not yet have established clients for their work. In the effort to support this group, the Center backed the organization of a craft cooperative, which used part of the building to sell the work of its members. The center also supported the re-initiation of classes in ceramics with Ana María Cabezas as the teacher. As a public service, the center installed electric kilns to fire the work of those young potters, who did not have easy access to one of the community kilns. From the late 1960s to the late 1980s, the center supported the marketing of La Chamba ware, but by the 1990s middlemen had taken over the local market almost completely.

The Artesanías de Colombia program did not have the success in La Chamba that it had in the other major Colombian village ceramics town, Ráquira (Duncan 1998). The intervention in both towns was based on three programs: the introduction of complex technology such as mass-production techniques (using, for example, potter's wheels and molds), as well as training programs and marketing. The organization was especially successful with the first two programs in Ráquira, where men began making ceramics and adopted wheels, plaster molds, glazes, and advanced kiln design, and they also took the classes to learn these new techniques. In contrast, complex technology was not introduced to, nor borrowed by, the women potters of La Chamba. Their classes emphasized the coiling and hand-modeling techniques that the potters of the community had always used, but offered no new techniques, which suggests that the planners at Artesanías de Colombia did not think that mass-production techniques were appropriate for these women potters. The demands of gender ideology (see chapter 5), work organization (see chapter 6), and domestic economy (see chapter 11) have also served to thwart the freedom of women to choose technologies that would increase their productivity. The third program of Artesanías de Colombia, marketing, was never as successful in either town as the middleman system and, as a result, became increasingly marginal. With no significant contribution to make in La Chamba, the center slowly declined in importance.

Ceramics as Cultural History

Ceramics is material culture, and the history of culture in a community helps to define the visual and technical qualities of the ceramics made there. Social factors such as gender, generation, and ethnicity also influence the visual styles and working patterns used by local potters to produce their particular kinds of wares. Local ceramics traditions are forged in this crucible of history and social factors, as each new generation learns the existing ceramic culture and adapts it to new historical circumstances.

Knowledge of both cosmology and history may be needed to understand design elements and motifs in crafts. In the Andes, ceramics, basketry, and weaving are integral elements in the warp and woof of gender behavior and ethnicity. They provide social identity and an economic base, and constitute a medium for creative expression. Crafts are critical components in the iconography of people, and they preserve a record of the crucible of cultural influences in which societies are forged.

The craft traditions of the Andes, including Colombia, Ecuador, Bolivia, and Peru, are the strongest and most dynamic of South America because of their indigenous roots. Since precolumbian times, crafts have played a major role in the cultural identity of Andean groups, and today heraldic motifs and community colors continue to identify the handwoven clothing of many of the traditional peoples in the Andes. In ceramics the color or shape of a pot identifies the region and the community in which it was made. Even the individual maker can be identified by the position of a handle or a particular angle in the profile. Social and individual identities are linked to visual expression and become part of the essence of being.

Craft is one of the expressions of human material culture, which produces objects with visual values that may please, intrigue, or challenge the viewer. Material culture (arts, crafts, clothing, technology), linguistic expression (legends, myths, song texts, discourses, books), performances (ritual, theater, music), and other behaviors reflect the values, thoughts, and social relations of the makers. The art and craft of ceramics reflect important characteristics of the cultural process in Colombian mestizo society, especially ethnicity, gender, and generation.

La Chamba ceramics exist in a state of flux as people develop their own styles and working techniques. Essentially, a potter behaves in terms of his or her own particular perspective on the shared social, environmental, and cultural context. In the same way, each ceramist in La Chamba works with a learned heritage of ceramics, and each will use the cultural core of assumptions about form, texture, color, line, and other technical concerns to make decisions about the crafting of their vessels. The creation of styles of ceramics and the decision to work in one style rather than another are cultural decisions that entail technical and esthetic judgments on issues such as the weight, balance, texture, and color of a pot. The history of Colombian village ceramics provides a baseline of cultural content against which the development of the society can be measured.

Historical differences between social groups lead to differences in the ceramic information that is available to each and also to differences in ethnic-linked technologies and attitudes toward the craft. In La Chamba, for example, the military and cultural resistance of the Pijaos to the Spanish correlates with the absence of Spanish technology and work attitudes in ceramics. After historical events are consolidated within the culture of a group, they provide reference points for later generations. In La Chamba, the violent experience of the Conquest, the cultural resistance to Spanish culture during the colonial period, and exposure to twentieth-century capitalism have been major factors shaping contemporary craftmaking.

The major social influences on the work of La Chamba potters are their distinctive cultural background, generation, and social class. These variables affect family organization, the community, work patterns, technology, and design itself. The cultural background of La Chamba potters is indigenous, as can be seen in their ceramics. Generation also affects the working patterns and design styles in La Chamba, with the older adults making traditional cooking and storage pots, those in middle age making tableware for urban markets, and the younger adults making innovative and experimental "fine ceramics," some of which will become popular and form the new traditions of the future.

The potters of La Chamba, like all village potters in Colombia, are marginalized within the overall class structure of the country, and they do not have the social prestige to demand higher prices for their work. Social class structures their design traditions, patterns of work organization, and economic potential within Colombian society. As rural people who are mestizos and peasant farmers or artisans, they have little opportunity to alter their social standing.

La Chamba and Its Future

Village earthenware pottery is the everyday experience of millions of people in the world in villages like La Chamba. With ten millennia of continuity in human societies, earthenware pottery is one of the oldest extant crafts that is still produced today. However, in the last century its functional role has changed dramatically with the introduction of new materials for cooking and food-storage containers, the expanded accessibility of piped-water systems, and changes in food preservation, such as canning and refrigeration.

La Chamba pottery has gone through a number of changes during the twentieth century as its potters have reacted to the influence of the marketplace, although those changes have been consistent with local craft traditions. The tableware forms introduced in the 1940s and 1950s and the fine-ceramics forms introduced in the 1980s involve the same basic forms and working techniques as the traditional cooking pottery. Ceramics are made by women working within enduring social parameters: it is a low-investment handwork operation that can be adapted to their domestic responsibilities. As market demand for La Chamba ceramics has grown, so has the number of women making ceramics. Rather than adopt mass-production techniques, women have simply increased their hours of work, and they have recruited household members to help them.

Although earthenware pottery is no longer technically needed for cooking, carrying water, or storing foods, the production of traditional pottery continues to be important in La Chamba and in Colombia. Today traditional pottery may be used in households in tropical regions to cool water, or it may be found as an art object in the visually sophisticated apartment of an artist or architect alongside other art objects from around the world. These seeming incongruities make up the particular mosaic of tradition and modernity that characterizes Latin America.

La Chamba is a small tropical village that at first glance seems to be like any other. Its rustic country façade and relaxed pace belie the productive energy that exists here. Although the official efforts at development have produced little apparent result, the women potters of La Chamba maintain a lively entrepreneurial tradition on their own. The people of La Chamba are not wealthy, but they maintain their ceramics tradition with a pride and creativity that has brought them to the forefront of Colombian craft design. However, the exodus from La Chamba has reached the point that the local population is barely replacing itself. Many young people go to the city in search of easier and better-paying work. Their migration raises the question whether La Chamba ceramics can maintain its role as a creative and dynamic center in the national craft scene for another generation.

5

Women Potters and Female-Focused Household Work

Since women are home-based workers, they are at a disadvantage in the competitive labor world of capitalism. Gender ideology defines them as the home-based partner in the household who cares for the children and prepares food for the man. Being limited to the home was not a problem in the traditional agricultural system because women and men had equally important roles in maintaining their subsistence lifestyle. However, after the emergence of agrarian capitalism in the 1950s, labor became primarily evaluated in terms of wages, and the home-based role of women was undervalued. In response to that women potters began orienting their production more to subcontracted orders. To the extent possible they have maintained the female-focused household work groups that are characteristic of La Chamba.

Mothers, Sisters, Housewives, and Potters

The gender ideology for women in La Chamba defines them first as mothers and sisters, then as housewives, and then as potters. As mothers and sisters they carry out their family roles raising their children and collaborating within the sisterhood of their matrilocal extended families. As mothers La Chamba women focus on the skills and behaviors of their daughters, and some may even be said to be obsessive with them. They supervise their daughters' skills in family relationships, household tasks, and ceramics making. They support and care for their sons also, but sons have more leeway, and mothers are less directive of their behaviors. Many women live out their entire lives within the sisterhood of the matrilocal extended family, which is their everyday community within the overall community of La Chamba. Although the clan and lineage organization that might have existed in their indigenous past has been lost, the non-Spanish matrifocal family continues to function as a family unit.

Women are the managers of the household. They obtain the daily food and prepare it; they care for the house and clean it; and they provide for the needs of their husbands and children. They need a continual flow of money for everyday necessities such as food, and to pay for the other needs of the family such as clothing, education, and health care. Since La Chamba men do not always have a steady income, women are pushed to explore additional sources of income, leading to their role as potters.

Following the indigenous tradition of pottery making in the Americas, pottery is defined as a woman's occupation in La Chamba. As children, girls and boys accompany their mothers daily, learning to mine clay, prepare it, make pots, and fire them. However, at adolescence boys and girls divide. While girls may continue making pots, boys are not expected to do so. After adolescence, men rarely touch moist clay (see the discussion of humoral theory in Chapter 10), and women become the potters.

The Culture of Women's Ceramics

Matrilocal residency and women's cooperative groups are characteristic of the La Chamba system of making ceramics. Women make the ceramics and oversee every step in the production process from mining the clay and preparing it for working to making pots, burnishing them, supervising firings, and selling the finished pots. The women's cultural complex of ceramics pervades the Upper Magdalena River Valley and can be found in other regions of the country, but La Chamba is the most prominent example. Women should be considered bi-vocational because they combine ceramics production with their household tasks; in this research no woman was ever documented working as a full-time potter to the exclusion of domestic work. In half the households of La Chamba, women's income from pottery supplements that of the husband, but in the 27 percent of the households headed by women, the household depends completely on ceramics for income. Women produce some income in 80 percent of the households, and most require their children to help with production.

In La Chamba women tend to set up cooperative household-based work groups. These are primarily organized around the nuclear family, but they can expand to include collaboration between members of the matrilocal, extended family, especially mothers, sisters, aunts, women cousins, and nieces. Husbands, sons, brothers, and fathers are also incorporated into this cooperative group as secondary collaborators. Labor is not a commodity in the domestic economy of La Chamba but rather a form of collaboration.

Women's ceramics are characterized by shared tasks, and women actively recruit family members to share the work. For example, women relatives may assist each other in the production of pieces to fill orders, and children and older relatives may help by burnishing pieces. Occasionally a mother and daughter may collaborate on a pot, with the mother building the basic pot with traditional techniques and the daughter finishing it by modeling additions to it. Studying indigenous potters in Chiapas, Mexico, June Nash (1985, 70) concluded that men organized themselves mechanically and women organized themselves organically, following Durkheim's terminology. In making this distinction, Nash refers to men performing similar tasks side by side, each one working independently, while women tend to work in interdependent stages with each woman doing the tasks that she performs best. The potters of La Chamba also work in this "organic" interdependent pattern of cooperating to produce ceramics.

Women and Work

Work that is exclusively performed by women includes domestic making of pots and preparation of clay, while men's work is primarily in agriculture. Although gender relations are basically symmetrical between women and men in the nuclear family, there is a vertical integration of generations among women that leads to a matrilocal focus among extended families.

In indigenous-mestizo villages like La Chamba, women tend to be conservative in their work styles, which is reflected by their maintenance of the prehispanic-indigenous techniques of making ceramics. Even though the mass-production techniques in ceramics used by men in other towns in Colombia are more economically efficient, the indigenous system used by the potters of La Chamba is well adapted to the domestic cycle of work culturally expected of women. Ceramics making also gives women more economic independence within the nuclear family. The matrilocal extended family in La Chamba gives women more freedom of action than does the male-headed nuclear family found in other regions of Colombia, and the women of La Chamba have used their freedom to become some of the most innovative women potters in the country, creating new vessel and figurative forms and new design styles.

Even though pottery making offers them economic independence, women consider it a dirty and difficult occupation, and not working in ceramics has greater prestige. If a woman does not work, it indicates that the household is well-to-do and that her income is not needed. The opinion among women is that if it is necessary to work in ceramics, it is preferable to do the relatively clean and easy task of burnishing. Least desirable, but most common, is to take responsibility for the complete production cycle, which more than half of the adult women do out of economic necessity. As is the case for many women potters in Latin America, there are almost no other alternatives for them to earn money in the cash-starved village economies (Hendry 1992, 111).

Observing potters in indigenous pottery communities in Mexico and Peru, Arnold (1985, 101) explained the predominant role of women as the result of the need to supplement the household's income from marginal agriculture. He identified six reasons why it was structurally more appropriate for women to make pottery than men in a subsistence farming economy: (1) it is easily compatible with caring for children; (2) it can be made at home; (3) it does not use dangerous materials or machinery and does not present any danger to the household; (4) it does not require great concentration and is compatible with the interruptions implied in child care; (5) it can be interspersed with other household chores; (6) the day-to-day attention required by pottery has the same rhythm as the domestic schedule. Since food and subsistence are guaranteed by farming, women can take the economic risk of making pottery that may or may not sell (ibid., 102). In La Chamba both men and women consider pottery making to be a women's occupation and not an appropriate occupation for men. Ideology and functional constraints thus combine to reinforce pottery making as a women's occupation, and women grow up with the expectation of becoming potters.

Men and Work

Although husbands are not regularly involved in the production of ceramics in most La Chamba families, in eighty-seven (77 percent) of the households surveyed for this study in 1987, men helped in an average of 1.7 male tasks. Each male task represents a minor time commitment, so men's help is limited. Even firing, which is considered a man's job, is actually done by husbands in less than half the households. Frequently, an older son or brother actually helps the woman.

Men assist their wives, mothers, and sisters in ceramics production by firing the kiln (46 percent of the households) and mining the clay (46 percent). Twenty-seven percent of the women are widowed or separated from their husbands, and many hire men to fire their pots. Those who cannot get a man to fire their work may resort to selling it unfired to local middlemen, who in turn fire and sell it. Some women do fire their own work. Slightly more than one-third (34 percent) of the men gather firewood for the kiln. Older men, who no longer work in agriculture, assist their wives by burnishing pots (32 percent). But they were uncomfortable when we observed them burnishing because that is work for women and children. Men making pottery is even more rare, and in this research we observed only one man making pots, which embarrassed him greatly. He was an unmarried man who lived and worked with his mother and sister. There was one other young man who made hand-modeled figures, but he migrated out of the community to live in Bogotá. Rarely do men learn to make ceramics, and rarely do they admit to knowing what they do know.

Of the 135 adult men in the community, 107 (79 percent) work in agriculture, with 103 of those working as day laborers on the big commercial farms that surround La Chamba. The other four are independent farmers who plant their own fields, a figure that has declined from fifteen independent farmers in 1972 (Lara 1972, 16). Fifteen (11 percent) men are owners of stores or provide a service (such as police work), and thirteen (10 percent) buy and sell ceramics as middlemen. Selling is the task in which men are least involved, and the fact that women sell their own work in 83 percent of the cases is an indication of their economic independence.

Demography of Ceramics Making

Women make ceramics in 113 (61 percent) of the 184 households in La Chamba, and in 157 (85 percent) of the houses people either make, burnish, or sell ceramics. A total of 162 women are potters in La Chamba, which is an average of 1.4 potters in households where ceramics are made. This means that half of the households have one woman making pottery and half have two, usually a mother and daughter. A total of 340 people work in some aspect of ceramics, representing one-third of the village population.

Polishing the slip painted surface after it dries (called burnishing) is the slowest operation, and it requires more time to burnish some of the pieces than it does to make them. Most potters burnish their own work, or household members do it for them. However, nearly one-quarter of the women do not have family members who can help them, or they decide not to burnish their own ware because they can actually earn more money per hour by making pots and contracting out the burnishing. They contract one of the forty-four women who work exclusively as contract burnishers to burnish for them. The women who do only burnishing earn half the income of those who make ceramics, but most potters consider them to be in a better position because the work is clean and easy. If a woman can afford only to burnish or not to work for wages at all, it is a sign that her husband has a good income.

Women and children do most of the burnishing, but four older men, who no longer work in agriculture, burnish on a regular basis, and twenty-four men do burnishing occasionally. The normal pattern of household work is that the mother makes the ware, and she and her children burnish it. Other adult women in the house, such as a grandmother, an aunt, or an older daughter, are probably also potters or at least do burnishing.

Of the 113 households where ceramics are made, sixty-two (55 percent) have their own kiln. Women without a kiln may sell their production to someone else, who fires and sells it; indeed, some local men make a business of buying, firing, and selling the production of women who do not have a kiln. Younger women frequently fire their ware in the kilns of neighbors or family members, and some fire their work in the electric kilns of Artesanías de Colombia.

Headship and Gender in the Family Life Cycle

When a husband is present in a household, he is recognized as its formal head because of gender ideology and because of his greater income. Although the wife will not be considered head of the household as long as the husband lives there, she does make many of the daily decisions about household activities. As a result, men and women in La Chamba share authority within the household, similar to the indigenous patterns in Ecuador (Hamilton 1998, 26f) and Panama (Tice 1995, 175). La Chamba women are the social and cultural pillars of the household, and they are usually an important, if not the primary, economic support for it. The fact that most marriages are common-law unions, combined with the tendency toward matrilocal residence, imposes strict limits on the authority of the man in the household. During the years in which men are most productive economically (twenty to fifty or fifty-five years old), they tend to be absent from the household during most daylight hours, always working, visiting, or drinking with friends. A male who is regularly in the house is either a child, an old man, disabled, or not carrying out his male role. As a result, the time commitment of men to the household tends to be marginal during their early and middle adult years.

The percentage of households headed by women in La Chamba is high in comparison with other rural mestizo communities in Colombia. In our survey, 27 percent were headed by women, and in a later census of the village and rural areas 30 percent of the households were headed by women without male partners (Montoya de la Cruz 1990, 46). In comparison, fewer than 5 percent of the women in Ráquira, a mestizo pottery community in the highlands, live in a household without a male head (Duncan 1998, 58), which indicates the importance of women in La Chamba social organization.

The high percentage of woman-headed households in La Chamba indicates the economic independence of women. Forty-four of the women household heads (89 percent) earn their income from ceramics; 85 percent of them make or burnish ceramics, and 4 percent buy and sell ceramics. Only two (4 percent) women heads of household live from something other than ceramics, and they are seamstresses. Making ceramics is the most viable source of income for most women in the town. The income for households headed by women is far less than those headed by men. Without a man there is one less income, and that is compounded by the fact that women earn less. So, in a household headed by a woman, the income may be one-third to one-half of the income when a man is present, which pushes those families deep into poverty.

The number of woman-headed households in La Chamba is consistent with the findings of Tice among the Kuna craftswomen in Panama, where women also have considerable economic independence. In three communities she studied, she found 25 percent, 31 percent, and 36 percent of the households headed by women (1995, 171). Also coinciding with the information from La Chamba, she found that independent nuclear families tended to be headed by men, but that nuclear families within extended or compounded families were more frequently headed by women. In fact, among the Kuna, the majority of nuclear families within extended families were headed by women, ranging from 54 to 80 percent in the three different communities Tice studied (ibid., 173).

In La Chamba a husband is usually present in the household during a woman's child-bearing years, when his earning power is the greatest and she is economically dependent because of the small children. During this period, the man's role as the head of the household is the strongest of any period in the life cycle, and the woman may spend much of her time pregnant and confined to the house doing domestic tasks. The large number of pregnancies in La Chamba (commonly between eight and ten), and the household obligations that result from having many small children at the same time, keep women in a dependent position, which strengthens the men's importance as the sole breadwinners. Men are more frequently the head of the

Table 5.1. Family Size and Headship

Family size	Male head No.	%	Female head No.	%	Total No.	%
1–3	38	59.37	26	40.63	64	100
4–6	45	73.77	16	26.23	61	100
7–9	48	87.27	7	12.73	55	100
10 or more	4	100.00	0	.00	4	100
Total	135	73.37	49	26.63	184	100

family as the number of people in the household increases, ranging from 59 percent of small families to 74 percent of medium-sized families and 88 percent of large families (See Table 5.1). The larger the number of children in the household, the greater is the dependence of the woman on the man's income.

When men are the head of the household, they frequently take a strong, macho role with little regard for their wives' concerns or interests. This seemed to be a problem particularly when men in their thirties or forties married women in their late teens or early twenties. We observed a number of cases in which women complained bitterly of men being harsh and repressive in the marriage relationship, and in some cases we documented husbands using the threat of physical abuse to control their wives. However, in the middle adult years, the relationship tends to be more symmetrical as women acquire more economic independence and more authority as the mother of the children. In later years, the roles reverse as women assume more and more important roles in the household, and men become economically dependent on them. By the time men are fifty to fifty-five years old, many can no longer compete effectively as day laborers in agriculture, and some begin to help their wives in ceramics. As the earning power and influence of men in household decisions diminish, the earning power and influence of women increase, an indication that gender power correlates with earnings. As a result, women are in a stronger position within the household in their middle and later years.

Because of higher rates of male mortality and abandonment of the family, women begin to assume the headship of families in midlife. When this occurs the household is usually smaller, partly because there is no man in the house and partly because only the younger children remain. As a result, women usually head a smaller household than do men; in fact, they are head of 40 percent of the smallest households but only 12 percent of the largest ones. The distribution of household sizes forms a balanced continuum, with approximately one-third being small, one-third medium-sized, and one-third large.

The Household and Work

The nuclear and extended families are both important social groupings in La Chamba, and together they constitute the basis of the social organization of the community. The nuclear family is the basic unit in ceramic production, and it frequently works within the context of the extended family. The custom of the youngest daughter continuing to live at home as an adult to take care of her parents in their old age creates a modified nuclear family. Usually the surviving parent is the mother; fewer men survive as aged members of the society. Thus the mother-daughter bond continues throughout life.

Women have a preference for matrilineal extended families because of the collaboration they permit with their mothers and sisters. Women who do not have sisters and whose mother has already died do not have a matrilineal support group, and some women who have migrated into the community also lack extended-family support. If the man can afford it and can convince his woman partner, he will have a house at some distance from her relatives. Men have a preference for the neolocal nuclear family, which affords them more authority. However, if the young couple depends on her making ceramics as an integral part of their income, she will need to be near her family for assistance with mining clay, child care, and firings, and she may also depend on using the family kiln. Thus the tension between stand-alone nuclear families and the extended family is also frequently a tension between economics and gender. For this reason, the residence pattern (matrilocal or patrilocal) is negotiated between the husband and wife and depends on the relative contributions of each to the household income.

The Sandoval-Valdés Nuclear Family

Juan Sandoval and María Isabel Valdés de Sandoval live near Chapetón. Their house is located up a dirt walkway, one hundred meters or so from the river landing. Lidia Inés, their adult daughter, lives with them. She works with her mother making ceramics, and she will continue living with her parents and caring for them in their older years. Their son, Eduardo, has migrated to Bogotá, but he visits the family regularly.

The Sandovals were born and raised in La Chamba, and they are one of the more traditional families in the village. They still live along the river, which historically was the center of the community. Their traditional, country-style house is immaculately clean, like the finishing of their ceramics. María and Lidia Inés make ceramics on the floor or on ankle-high tables in the indigenous fashion, rather than on waist-high tables in the Spanish fashion. They make tableware, including *cazuelas* (eating-size serving bowls), platters, and large fish-shaped serving bowls. Their pieces are carefully finished and burnished. Eduardo, the son in Bogotá, makes figurative forms (discussed in chapter 9), and his pieces are also known for the exquisite polish of the finished surfaces. The father, Juan Sandoval, is engaged in the traditional-style river transportation, taking agricultural products down the river on homemade barges, as discussed in chapter 4.

As a nuclear family, the Sandovals are an example of the small-family pattern; they have a minimal extended family and few remaining children in the community. They live in a wooded area set apart from most houses, which isolates them from close continual interaction with other families. Juan Sandoval is a strong figure in the household, and the family lives in that location because it is near his work. The mother-daughter bond is strong, but Eduardo also has strong ties to the family (see Photograph 5.1).

The Sandoval nuclear family, a small household with a strong male head, is representative of one kind of family in La Chamba. There are probably as many versions of household organization as there are families in La Chamba, but most vary between the small nuclear family, like the Sandovals, and the larger extended family, like the Prada family, who live along one side of the "plaza" in the new urban center of La Chamba.

Extended Family and Work

The extended family usually comprises a cluster of women relatives and their respective nuclear families. The members are bound together by the physical proximity of their houses, in addition to their pattern of sharing and collaboration. Although husbands have authority within the nuclear family, they have marginal roles within the extended family. If a husband is not present, the male role in the nuclear family is carried out by an adult son or a brother of the woman. He will be responsible for the male tasks of firing the kiln, providing income from agricultural work, and disciplining the children. A woman who chooses to have children and not marry can do so, and she can function normally within the extended family group. Whatever she needs a man to do can be done by a brother or other male relative.

Photo 5.1.
Sandoval family
firing. Eduardo and
Lidia Inés Sandoval
fire pieces at their
parents' house next
to the Magdalena
River. The eastern
range of the Andes
can be seen in the
distance. The kiln is
out of the frame,
and they have
dragged these
saggars filled with
small pieces out of
the kiln to do
reduction, a process
that will turn the
pieces black.

People tend to work together within the extended family, and it is common for clusters of women family members to share working spaces and kilns, freely loan supplies, care for children, and help with firings, amongst other things. Among the women potters of La Chamba, 76 percent work with their own women relatives; if they work with a man, in 85 percent of the cases he is a relative. (See Table 5.2.) La Chamba women work very little with people outside of their own families, and in fact work groups tend to be female-focused family groups. The one-quarter of the women co-workers who are not family members are mostly burnishers, and they are contract workers who are usually not from La Chamba and do not know how to make ceramics. The six nonfamily men who were reported as working with

Table 5.2. Family Membership and Gender among Co-Workers

	Men		Women		Total	
Relationship	No.	%	No.	%	No.	%
Family	34	85	197	75.19	231	76.49
Nonfamily	6	15	65	24.81	71	23.51
Total	40	100	262	100.00	302	100.00

Source: G. Rojas 1984, 2–3

potters do kiln firings on a paid basis. However, women also buy slip clay and wood for the firings from men.

Matrilocal residential clusters are formed as older sisters, and occasionally their daughters, establish their households near their parents' home. This matrilocal residential cluster normally is organized around a kiln, which is the property of one member, but it is loaned to everyone in the family. Most of the daily social interaction occurs between the members of the extended family. Tracy Ehlers (1990, 53) reports similar clusters of women working together in weaving communities in Guatemala, which are also female-focused family businesses. The addition of a daughter as a worker in a matrilocal work group either expands the existing production of the women or permits them to diversify into other products that no one in the group was making before.

The Prada Extended Family

An example of the extended family in La Chamba is the Prada family, which lives in the center of the village. It is organized around two older sisters, both widows, and their daughters, who are married now and have built their houses next door to each other. Five houses make up this group, and two kilns are shared between them. This study focuses primarily on the Wenseslada Prada half of the extended family.

Wenseslada Prada and her two younger daughters, Clara and Aura, live in the largest house in the family compound. Clara, who is twenty-four years old, is a single parent with four children, but Aura, who is twenty-two years old, does not have children or an ongoing relationship with a man. Their unmarried twenty-seven-year-old brother, Jairo, lives with them, but he does not work in agriculture or have any regular employment. He sees agriculture as a dirty job that he does not like, but he does not have the education or training for a clerical or technical job. Not being married, he is not obligated to work regularly. Wenseslada Prada and her two younger daughters make the income for the household from their ceramics, and he assists them with firing their production. The mother makes traditional pottery, and Clara and Aura make tableware.

In the three houses on the east side of Wenseslada's house live her sister and two of that sister's married daughters. Wenseslada's daughter Anatilde and her family live on the west side of her house. So the Prada extended family cluster is composed of the two older sisters, their unmarried children, and the families of their married daughters. Wenseslada and her sister own the two kilns in the Prada compound, and the entire extended family has the right to fire their work in either one.

The Silva-Prada Branch of the Family

Anatilde Prada married Aurelio Silva, and they are known as the Silva-Prada branch of the family. When the couple married, she became Anatilde Prada de Silva. In Colombia, as in other Spanish-speaking countries, women retain their maiden family name throughout their lives and add on their husband's last name. In La Chamba, however, women commonly introduce themselves with the name of their birth family, so she would introduce herself as Anatilde Prada. In contrast, women in patriarchal communities in Colombia more frequently introduce themselves with their husband's last name—that is, Anatilde Silva. In referring to the nuclear family the last name of both the husband and wife is normally used, the first being that of the father and the second that of the mother. This family is made up of the two parents, the five children at home, who are between the ages of eight and fifteen years old, and the three older children who have already left home, who range in age from seventeen to twenty-two.

The father, Aurelio Silva, is forty-seven years old, and he works as a day laborer on the large commercial farms that surround the town. The mother, Anatilde Prada, is forty years old. Between the ages of eighteen and thirty-two, she had ten children, two of whom died. The number of births and deaths she reported are common figures for La Chamba, and she is happy to have eight children, although she worries that their household barely has enough money to survive.

The three older children come to visit whenever they can. The one who comes most frequently is the oldest son, who is unmarried and does unskilled manual work in Bogotá. He always comes during vacations and long week-ends. The two older daughters are married and come less frequently because of their own household obligations. This pattern of emigration of the older children is normal, and most households have relatives in El Espinal, Ibagué (the state capital), or Bogotá.

The children living at home are Aurelio, Martín, Maritza, Jimmy, and Jairo. Aurelio (fifteen years old) has dropped out of school, lives at home, and is beginning to work as a day laborer in agriculture. When he cannot get jobs, he helps his mother burnish her production. Martín (fourteen years old) is in middle school, lives at home, and aspires to go to high school and study to become a teacher. Maritza (thirteen years old) lives at home and dropped out of school at the end of primary school. At the present Maritza makes eating bowls like her mother, does burnishing, and helps with the firing. Her domestic chores include helping her mother cook, wash clothes, and clean the house. Until she is married, the money that she earns will go for household expenses, but some of it will always be left for her own personal expenses, such as buying new clothes. Jimmy and Jairo are the smallest children, aged ten and eight.

Given the special relationship between mothers and daughters, Anatilde expects more from her daughter, Maritza, than from any of the sons. Indeed, she expects Maritza to be her own principal collaborator for the rest of her life. The Silva-Prada family is located in the middle of the local socioeconomic hierarchy, and although they are not wealthy, they do provide reasonably well for themselves. They live from the income of their work, but have no surplus to protect themselves from illness or other unforeseen problems. They own their house and another one-acre plot where they have fruit trees. The average house plot in La Chamba is twenty by thirty meters (Montoya de la Cruz 1990, 20), and the Silva-Prada plot is approximately that size. Since their house occupies most of the lot, there is no space to build a kiln, and Anatilde has to fire her work elsewhere. She does have a bamboo platform in the front yard where she puts finished work so that it will dry in the sun.

The house is built of concrete block walls, zinc-coated corrugated metal roofing, and a cement floor. The furniture consists of the parents' bed and wardrobe, two beds for the children, a table with four chairs, a television, and one bench. There is a two-burner gas stove and a table in the kitchen, and the bathroom and laundry area are built separately at the back of the house. Summing up their lifestyle, Anatilde said, "We make just enough money to eat, send the children to school and buy clothes. We can't afford to get sick or miss work because then we couldn't buy food."

The Maker of *Cazuelas*

Anatilde Prada de Silva makes *cazuelas* (soup bowls) on the shaded back porch of her house to fill an order from the intermediary who buys her work. She makes three to four dozen per day, depending on the orders. When there is a rush, she and the children work all day Saturday to speed up the process. First, she wedges the clay on a clean place on the ground where she has spread finely powdered clay. As she wedges, she sprinkles more dry clay powder on top of the moist clay and kneads it to a doughlike state. She wedges the clay into a log-sized lump that weighs approximately twenty kilos, and with that she will be able to work most of the day.

Anatilde Prada sits on the floor in the indigenous style of working used by all of the potters in the community. She is so accustomed to working on the floor that she also frequently sits there to watch television or talk. She places the log of prepared clay in her work area, together with a bowl of water, her scraping and cutting tools, and the bowls that she uses as molds. She stretches her left leg out straight, folds her right foot back under it, and pulls her dress up above her knees to keep it from getting dirty.

She slices a slab of clay off the end of the log and pounds it flat on the floor, evening it out and eliminating any air pockets it might contain. When the clay is the right thickness, she lays it over the mold and compresses it into the shape of a bowl. She carefully scrapes the sides, trimming and smoothing the edges and walls until she is satisfied that the bowl is perfectly shaped. Then she sets it aside to firm up a little while she begins the next one. The process has taken her five minutes. She continues to work, and the line of bowls beside her begins to grow. Later, when the bowls are leatherhard, she adds one small knob handle on each side of the bowl at the rim.

Anatilde specializes in making the *cazuela*, or eating bowl. She lays a slab of clay over an upside-down *cazuela*, which functions as a hump mold (see Photograph 5.2). The newly formed pieces are slightly larger than they should be, but they shrink to the proper size as they dry. She is proud of her work and says that her pieces are uniform in size and shape and always finished perfectly. She has a steady group of clients who contract her work,

Photo 5.2. Making *cazuelas*. Anatilde Prada de Silva makes *cazuelas* (soup-like bowl) while she sits on the floor of the porch of her house. The bowls are initially dried on the porch, but afterwards they are moved indoors because of the possibility of rain. Before the firing they will be given a final drying in the sun on a bamboo rack in front of her house.

and she says it is because she is especially careful with the quality of the finishing of her pieces.

Maritza and the two oldest sons help Anatilde burnish her production, all working together as a group, usually sitting on the back porch of the house or in the living room watching afternoon soap operas on television. Anatilde occasionally directs one of the children to bring something needed for the work or to run an errand. Maritza can burnish twelve bowls a day; her older brothers do eighteen; and Anatilde does eighteen to twenty-four. The two smaller boys are not expected to help much, but the ten-year-old does burnish a few pieces. The smallest one, Jairo, does not like burnishing, so he is given other chores, such as gathering the dried donkey dung that is used in the firing process and breaking up the clumps of recently mined clay to prepare them for soaking.

While Anatilde and her children sit together burnishing, they talk among themselves, catching up on family and community gossip, or they chat with a neighbor or friend who drops by. Occasionally they take a break and go out to see who is passing on the street, make a short visit to the grand-

Burnishing

After lunch Anatilde Prada and her three older children each pick out their favorite burnishing stone from the small box of tumbled, semiprecious stones that the family keeps for this purpose. They sit on the porch to burnish bowls made the day before while Anatilde completes making her quota of *cazuelas* for the day. When she finishes, a little before three o'clock, she leaves the bowls to firm up on the patio floor and begins to burnish along with the children.

After the burnishing is completed, the bowls are placed outside to finish drying before they are fired. They rest in the sun on a long bamboo table in front of the house. Jimmy, the youngest son, is sent out to gather dried donkey dung, to be used for the firing. When he returns with the bag of dung, he leaves it at one end of the front porch.

At three o'clock a popular Colombian soap opera comes on the television, and everyone brings the bowls on which they are working into the living room and sits down to work and watch the program. Anatilde goes to the kitchen and puts water on to boil to begin making the *sancocho* stew for dinner. She does not let the children watch television all of the time they are burnishing because they become distracted with the programs and do not work as fast; and sometimes they are not careful with their finishing, and she has to touch the pieces up afterwards. But this interlude keeps them from getting too bored while they work, and she too enjoys the program.

When the program ends at four o'clock, they turn off the television but continue working in the living room because it is the coolest room in the late afternoon. Also, from there they can watch the street better. Jairo goes outside and uses a wooden club to pulverize dried clumps of clay, which will be moistened later in preparation for the next day. By half past five they have almost finished the three dozen bowls that Anatilde made yesterday, and she leaves the boys to continue burnishing while she and Maritza go to the kitchen to finish the dinner. She sends the younger boys out on other errands, including buying bread for the evening meal. Once Aurelio Silva, the husband, arrives, she serves the steaming bowls of *sancocho*. The boys sit around the patio eating while their father sits at the table. Later Anatilde and Maritza come out with their food, and everyone eats and talks about the day's work.

mother's house, or do some household chore. There is a rhythm to the work of making bowls and burnishing them, and everyone knows the routine from years of experience. This means that much of what they do is assumed and unspoken, a work pattern that June Nash also observed among Mayan women potters (1985, 49).

Life Cycle and the Productivity of the Woman Ceramist

The productivity of the ceramist in La Chamba varies according to each stage of her life, her ceramic skill, and the number of people who work with her in burnishing and firing. The four stages in the life cycle of women potters are apprenticeship, young adulthood, maturity, and the elder period.

Apprenticeship

The first stage is the apprenticeship, which most women do with their mothers although some learn with an aunt or grandmother. During this stage, the young woman is expected to learn every aspect of the craft of ceramics, including mining, preparing the claybody, making pieces, preparing and applying slip, burnishing, and firing. The productivity of daughter apprentices is notoriously low, and during this period her work may be sold along with that of her mother since she does not yet have her own clients. The apprenticeship may last as long as ten years, from her early teens until she is married, which is usually no later than the early twenties.

Young Adulthood

The early adult stage begins as the potter marries and establishes her own household. During this period, her work is affected by the number of children she has and the amount of time their care requires. By this time, the young ceramist has defined the style (tableware or "fine ceramics") in which she works and the specific forms in which she specializes, such as eating bowls, pitchers, or casseroles. Unless the young potter can sell her work through her mother, she will have to sell it on consignment through the local intermediaries or the local stores. During this time of her life, the woman usually has some time to experiment with new ideas and to master the needed skills. Productivity at this point is greater than it was as an apprentice, but not as great as it will be when she is a mature ceramist. This period lasts another ten years or so, from the time of marriage until the woman is in her mid-thirties and has children who are old enough to help her.

The Mature Potter

In mature adulthood, the woman ceramist reaches the peak of her productivity, and this begins in her mid-thirties and lasts about twenty years, until her mid-fifties. By this time, the ceramist is highly skilled, has established a reputation for the kind of work that she does, has teenage children who can help her, and has established clients who buy her production. Each of these elements is important, but the central one is the work of her children. The more children she has who can burnish her production, the more she can produce.

The Elder Potter

By the time women are in their mid-fifties, they have honed their skills to perfection, and they are practiced in the style they make. They have established their reputation with middlemen, but they have few if any helpers. This stage of work lasts until the end of the woman's working life, which can be another twenty years. By the beginning of this stage women are at the peak of their earning ability, they are proficient potters, and they have well-established clients. Women usually continue making ceramics as long as they are physically able to do so, or until they die. The concept of retirement does not exist, and they do not have a retirement plan to support them even if they wanted to retire. As a result, they continue making ceramics as long as they can produce the income. When they can no longer work, one of the children usually assumes responsibility for them. The production of women during this final period gradually diminishes as they slow down physically and as the last of their children marry and leave home. Since men usually stop doing paid agricultural work by their mid fifties, they may replace the children in burnishing their wives' ceramics. Even during their late sixties and early seventies, many women can still produce a load of work a week or more.

Conclusions

Gender, family, and work in La Chamba are inseparable. The women of this community have kept a traditional craft alive to produce income for their households in the expanding money-based economy. Although profits are minimal for each individual ceramist, they combine their income with that of a husband or daughter to produce at least a subsistence-level income. However, the underlying threat to this system is the poverty implicit in the current economic structure of crafts. Women who have grown up making ceramics value the craft and continue to work in it, but many of their daughters are not willing to accept the below-subsistence-level income that goes with being a potter. The poverty that drives those daughters from the community erodes the future workforce of this craft.

6

Work Organization for the Home-Based Potter

Cross culturally, home-based workers are usually women (Wilkinson-Weber 1997, 54; Mies 1986, 112; Feldman 1991, 44), and their work is structured to complement their parallel roles as wives and mothers. Their work organization usually takes on the characteristics of the women's culture of their particular society. In La Chamba that means that women work in household groups, either in nuclear families with children and a husband, or in larger extended families with grandmothers, mothers, sisters, aunts, and cousins. La Chamba women usually work with each other in collaborative interdependent networks, and they organize their work so that it is minimally intrusive on the physical space of their houses.

Crafts and Home-Based Women Workers

The global expansion of capitalism in recent decades has led to a change in the role of women's work in many societies. This has been particularly true in the home-based crafts, such as pottery and weaving. These two crafts have largely been defined cross culturally as women's work (Murdock and Provost 1973, 211–12 and Bradley 1989, 117), because the rhythm of craft work permits women to combine income-producing work with domestic tasks. One reason given by La Chamba potters for working in ceramics is that they can earn money, care for children and even incorporate them into the work, and simultaneously do cooking and other household tasks. Home-based crafts are an important source of income for many Latin American households, and this is particularly true where there is a large indigenous population (Tice 1995, 12) or mestizo one, such as La Chamba.

Much of women's work in Latin America has historically been "invisible" because men are the primary breadwinners, and women's income is considered supplemental. Latin America also has one of the lowest formally recognized employment rates for women in the world. Women's workforce participation rates in various world areas are: Africa, 23 percent; Asia, 28 percent; Latin America, 15 percent; and the Middle East, 11 percent (Moghadam 1997, 104). Both Latin America and the Middle East have strong traditions of the woman staying in the home, which limits their work to home-based activities that are rarely recorded in official statistics. In Latin America, women's wage work has been historically associated with indigenous women or women of African descent; "Spanish" women were not expected to work (Safa 1996, 150). This attitude is changing among the professional classes as more and more women study at the university and enter the managerial, health care, communications, and education professions.

Women's work is also less visible because patriarchal families tend to appropriate the labor of their women members (Safa 1996, 87). This occurs in crafts communities when men sell their wives' production and keep the money themselves, which means that they own the woman's work. This invisibility contributes to women's labor being undervalued economically and being remunerated at rates less than the minimum wage for men (Deere 1990, 286). The work of the poor, rural craftswoman is usually subsistence-level production, whether it is domestic housework or commercial craftwork (Mies 1986, 49). She works for the household, essentially as an anonymous worker (McKee 1997, 24–25).

In Latin America the work of indigenous or mestizo women is frequently undervalued because Indian culture has a low social status. The women potters of La Chamba have that problem, and they are underpaid at half the legal minimum wage, and sometimes less. That underpayment is justified because they are seen as poor, rural (that is, of indigenous descent) workers whose labor is not valuable. Their remuneration is based not only on market principles but also on the evaluation of their ethnicity and social caste. The home-based contracting system has become the capitalist version of the exploitation of the indigenous workers that has existed in this area since the Spanish Conquest.

Women and Work Culture

Home-based women workers usually see themselves first as family members and secondly as workers (Rangel and Sorj 1996, 93; Wilkinson-Weber 1997, 51). Their attitudes toward income and work conditions and their identity as workers depend on their roles within the household. Studying home-based seamstresses in Brazil, Alice Rangel de Paiva Abreu and Bila Sorj (1996, 94) suggested that women, in contrast to men, found it more difficult to establish an identity separate from their family roles. They suggest that this is particularly true for home-based women workers. Where their identity is closely tied to their family roles, they evaluate work and income as household issues more than as personal issues.

Women develop active strategies to realize their potential for productive work in spite of the economic and gender subordination implied in their assignment to the domestic sphere (Rangel and Sorj 1996, 94). The combination of craft production and domestic work leads to double or segmented workdays in which women typically combine their income-producing work and home-maintenance work simultaneously (cooking and weaving) or in segmented stages (cook, make pots, cook, burnish pots, and so forth). These become double workdays because women frequently work twelve or more hours per day to complete both sets of work.

Gender and Production in La Chamba

The potter's workshop in La Chamba is a household affair, with a woman working with her children and occasionally receiving help from her husband. Her work begins early in the morning and continues throughout the day, with irregular interruptions to deal with household obligations; to cooperate with her mother, sister, or aunt; prepare meals; attend to children's problems; or solve other household and family issues. The women potters of La Chamba do not define themselves by their vocation of ceramics. They see themselves as mothers and wives who work in ceramics to earn income for household needs, and their activities around the workshop reflect that attitude.

The 113 households in La Chamba where ceramics are made can be organized into a status hierarchy using such criteria as market valuation, level of investment, amount of technical versus manual work, esthetic quality, and income. The makers of the oldest style (cooking pots) are oriented toward volume of production and put less emphasis on the esthetic or craft quality of what they make, and they have the lowest socioeconomic status. Women who make tableware have a middle status that can reflect good income, but the volume of production makes their work hard. In contrast, the makers of figures and "fine" one-off vessels have a higher status because of the creativity and quality of their pieces and the higher prices they receive per piece.

The production process is adapted to the cycle of domestic responsibilities of the woman, and it is designed so that it will not significantly disrupt the household. Although the signs of ceramics making are ever present, they are relegated to corners and porches so that the normal flow of household life continues unimpeded. Most women work on a shaded porch because it is cool and it permits them to watch what is going on in the yard, at the neighboring houses, or in the street. (See Photograph 6.1.) Following the indigenous housing pattern, there are no walls around the houses, in contrast to the enclosed patios of Spanish architecture. As a result, people can see each other from one house to another, and the porch or patio are favorite visiting places, easily accessible to family or friends who drop by to chat. A few families, especially those whose children have left home, have extra rooms in their house, and the woman may use one of them as a ceramics workshop.

The making of ceramics in La Chamba requires no specialized equipment and occupies little space in the house, relying on the manual skill of the woman rather than the technical efficiency of equipment. Neither the Spanish-style pottery wheel nor plaster molds are used in La Chamba, even though both are faster production techniques. A primary reason for the absence of these techniques is their inconsistency with the entire system of living and production in the village. Both the wheel and molds require space and investment, and they are more associated with a studio or small-industry type of production system (Duncan 1998, 146–56). The women of La Chamba maintain a delicate balance between work for income and their

Photo 6.1. Drying clay and platters. Clay is drying in the foreground, and a bamboo drying rack holds platters for their final drying before firing. The kiosk in the background has a table and chairs, and it is the family gathering place.

domestic responsibilities, and mechanizing production with the use of the wheel or production molds would shift this balance toward the former, a choice that the ceramists of La Chamba have rejected up to now.

Making Ceramics

All pots start from a slab of clay, which is pounded out on the floor between the woman's outstretched legs. First she sprinkles a light layer of sand on the floor and places a ball of clay in the center. Then she uses her fist and open palm to pound the clay into a pancake-like slab (*plancha*) two centimeters thick and approximately forty centimeters in diameter (the size of a large pizza). The potter smoothes out the slab as much as possible and skillfully flips it with two hands over the ceramic pot used as a mold to form the rounded bottom. The clay slab picks up sand from the floor, but it is later painted with slip to produce a smooth surface.

The potter sprinkles sand on the mold before laying the slab on to ensure that the clay does not stick to it. She presses the slab so that it takes the shape of the mold and pinches off the excess irregular line of clay that forms along the edge. (See Photograph 6.2). Then she uses a gourd scraper (*totuma*) and

Photo 6.2. Making a cooking pot. Doña Julia Avilés is shown here working in her workshop, a small building behind her house. She squatted on the ground in indigenous fashion and worked for long hours. She has just laid a slab over the hump mold to form the base of the pot. She uses the sand on the floor to keep the clay slabs from sticking to the mold.

The Maker of Cooking Pots

Doña Julia Avilés is a small woman, wrinkled from six decades of life but wound tight with energy. She is one of the older potters in La Chamba, and her house is on the Magdalena River near Chapetón. Her husband, Don Roberto Avilés, is too old to farm, and he helps her by burnishing and firing the cooking pots she makes. Their house is small, with only a living room and two sleeping rooms, and it is shaded by the overarching branches of tall tropical trees. On the front porch sits a large red earthenware water pot. A drinking glass is placed on a ledge next to it.

Their one-room kitchen is built next to the river, separate from the house. Like their house and workshop, it has bright, white-washed walls that contrast with the opaque greens and browns of the tropical vegetation that surrounds the house and seems to engulf it. The couple cook on a wood fire set into an adobe ledge that also serves as a cabinet; everything in the kitchen is smoked from the fire. They eat on a rough-hewn table, and they store dried beans, corn, rice, and yucca in small pots made by Doña Julia, which sit on the table and the cabinet. A window in the kitchen looks through the trees to the river, which flows quietly less than one hundred meters away. The pottery kiln is located nearby on the same side of the house.

Their workshop is another small building directly behind the house. There Doña Julia sits on the cement floor and pounds out a slab of clay to put over the upside-down pot mold to start the bottom of a cooking pot. Don Roberto sits nearby in a straight chair burnishing yesterday's production. She works on two or three molds at a time, so that as one slab is firming up, she can be preparing others. The volume of her production depends on the size of the order she is working on. If there is no rush, she will make only five or six pots a day, but during a rush, she produces eight or more pots per day. At the slower pace it takes two weeks to have a kiln load, but she can make enough pieces to fill the kiln in one week if necessary.

The couple work without talking much, lapsing into long silences. Sometimes the sound of the work itself is the only communication. Periodically, the silence is broken as Doña Julia pounds a slab into shape; the only other sound is the music of the birds outside in the tropical canopy. After a slab has been on the mold for thirty minutes or so, it is ready to be removed. She adds coils to build the shoulder, neck, and rim of the piece. As the pot is finished, it is placed along the back wall of their workroom, so that it can firm up slowly. Since the room has neither electricity nor windows, the pair sit near the door to have light. As the day progresses and the new work gradually fills the room, the air inside becomes heavy with humidity and the musky smell of damp clay. When the pots of the day's production are firm enough to be handled, they are painted with red slip or liquid clay, and the next day Don Roberto burnishes them with a fine river stone.

water to scrape and smooth out the surface of the clay. The mold with its draped slab are placed outside of the studio door so that the slab will firm up quickly in the sun and open air.

In an hour or so, depending on the weather, the bottom of the new pot can be firm enough to come off the mold. This is called the leatherhard stage. At this point the slab has the contour of an open bowl, and various shapes can be built off it. It is essentially the rounded bottom of the pot-to-be with the upper edge being the stomach or shoulder of the pot. The potter builds up the wall, neck, and mouth with coils. For this phase, the bottom molded portion is placed on a rounded shard or bowl, which functions as an unpivoted wheel, so that the piece can be turned as the potter works on it.

The potter sits on the floor with the pot between her feet, and she turns it either by foot or by hand as she lays on the coils, building the wall higher. She rolls out thick coils between her two hands, letting the coil hang down until she has an even coil thirty-five to forty centimeters long and five centimeters in diameter. She lays the coil onto the rim and pinches it into place, making a weld with the existing wall, and she compacts the thickness of the wall to one centimeter. (See Photograph 6.3.) Work on the upper half of the pot, which slopes inward, is done slowly to allow the new coils to firm up. The final coil makes the short neck, and its upper edge is smoothed out into the lip. Once the form is complete, the surface is cleaned with a gourd or plastic scraper, and the pot is left to firm up before being painted with slip, which is liquid clay.

If the pot to be made has a sharp inward slant at the shoulder, such as

Photo 6.3. Adding a coil to a pot. Doña Julia is laying on a coil to complete the upper profile of a pot. She will pinch the coil into place, fusing it with the existing wall and smoothing it out with wet corncobs and gourd scrapers.

the *tinaja*, or water pot, and some covered pots, a slightly different process is used to start the coils. When the upper edge of the pot-to-be is at the leatherhard stage of firmness, the potter tears the edge into a series of slits five centimeters long and five centimeters apart and bends the resulting tabs inward to form a distinct curve. With pressure from her fingers and a corncob, she fuses the overlapping slits and molds the clay inward to close in the shape. Then she uses the same coiling process to close the pot to the neck and mouth.

Larger pieces that may be worked further are covered with a plastic bag or sheet to slow the drying process and to ensure that the piece dries uniformly. It permits the potter to come back later and work further on the piece. Handles are modeled into place, and any figurative elements in fine ceramics are added by hand modeling. The combined steps of molding, coiling, and modeling are an indigenous technique found in various places in the Americas (Hendry 1992, 66; Lackey 1982, 78).

Slip Painting

While the new pot is still leatherhard, the potter adds finishing touches and paints it with red iron slip or *barniz,* which is liquified clay prepared by the potters. To make slip, clay is soaked until it reaches a completely liquid state, and then it is passed through a cloth to remove thick particles, producing a smooth liquid of a consistency similar to thick cream. A small quantity is always kept ready for use in the house. On traditional pottery it may be applied directly by hand, but on the tableware and fine ceramics it is applied with a brush or cloth. Fine ceramics are given three or more applications to insure the uniformity of the finish.

The purpose of the slip is to give the desired color, a smooth finish, and a partially sealed surface. La Chamba slip is always the color of red iron oxide, the dominant mineral in local clays. The smooth, iron-red finish produced by the slip is highly valued and preferred to the coarse texture and beige color of the claybody. La Chamba ceramics are identified with the surface quality produced by the slip, and almost all of the local production is covered with slip, which produces a surface similar to that of Greek and Roman pottery. Following a similar principle to the one used in Greek pottery, La Chamba potters turn the slip-painted surface to a dense black color through reduction, a technique described in chapter 10.

Burnishing

When the *barniz* is dry to the touch, the pot can be burnished with a smooth river stone or a tumbled semiprecious stone. Burnishing is the polishing of the surface of a pot or bowl by rubbing a hard, smooth stone over it with pressure in a systematic pattern. This is the point in the work cycle where everyone helps, including men, children, and older adults, and if possible it is done in a group, so talk can relieve the tedium of burnishing. Although husbands of working age were never documented helping their wives do burnishing, older husbands and unmarried sons do help in one-quarter of the houses, according to our survey. (See Photograph 6.4.) Louana Lackey

Photo 6.4. Burnishing. After he became too old to work in agriculture, Don Roberto Avilés began helping his wife, Doña Julia, by burnishing her pots. The two work closely together; she makes the pieces, and he burnishes and fires them.

(1982, 111) also found in Acatlán, Mexico, that the women potters preferred to do the burnishing in a group. In contrast to La Chamba, they wait until there are enough pieces for a kiln load, then they paint the surface with a cloth dipped in *tinta* (slip) and immediately burnish them.

Burnishing is practical in that it strengthens the wall of the pot. According to Dean Arnold (1993, 99), burnishing the outside wall increases wall strength by 13 percent and burnishing the inside wall augments strength by 21 percent while burnishing both gives the same strength (21 percent). In La Chamba it is most important to burnish the outside wall, which is painted with slip, because of the esthetic appeal of the polished surface, but the inner wall is also burnished to help seal it.

When a child is five or six years old, the mother begins to teach him or her to burnish. However, what the child can do at that age is more a matter of accompanying the mother than working. By the time a child is ten to twelve years old, he or she is expected to begin burnishing pots on a daily basis, but there is a difference in expectations according to the child's position in the birth order. Older children have to start working at an earlier age because the mother does not have anyone else to help her. In contrast, the younger children may start working at a later age, particularly if older siblings are still working.

The complete surface is burnished up to three times, each at an angle different from the previous one. The polishing stone is moistened with saliva so it will slide over the surface more easily. If a hard particle tears the surface, it is removed, and the tear is repaired by a local application of slip. People burnish while sitting down, and they hold the pot in their lap. Most burnish with their right hands and support the inside wall of the pot with their left. During the dry season, pieces will dry in two or three days, and smaller pieces may dry from one day to the next. Before burnishing they are normally left in the shade of a porch so that they dry slowly, but after burnishing they may be placed in the direct sun on bamboo drying platforms to hasten the drying.

Rules for Work and Kinship

In La Chamba household members are expected to collaborate on an unpaid basis with the pottery maker of the house. Since pottery is considered a domestic craft, much like the woman's household duties of washing clothes and cooking, it is not viewed as a commercial enterprise. Nor is helping the mother or sister make pottery seen as an economic exchange but rather as a family obligation. Sons, daughters, husbands, brothers, sisters, and grandchildren will help as needed, but their labor is not a commodity to be paid for. However, their help will be reciprocated when appropriate. When workers are hired in La Chamba, they are always nonrelatives, and frequently they are people who are not from the community. The one ceramics job for which women are normally hired is to burnish pots, and men are frequently paid to bring firewood and the special clay for making slip. We were told that men were sometimes hired to fire kilns, but we did not see that among the multiple firings that we observed involving twelve different households.

Labor Allocation, Time Distribution, and Work

A description of the daily organization of the clay work of a home-based potter in La Chamba indicates the interweaving of domestic and craft work for the woman worker. In this process the woman directs the work of the children, allocating their labor, to reach a common household production goal. The workday for women is punctuated by the ceramics tasks, including mining and preparing the clay, making pieces, and burnishing them. Women mine clay once or twice a week depending on their rate of work. Large quantities are never mined because the women limit their mined load to what they can lift onto a donkey and what they will need for the next two or three days of work; they do not store prepared clay.

La Chamba women normally make and burnish ceramics Monday through Friday and have everything prepared to fire on Saturday. However, if they have an order that requires more than one week to complete, Saturday may become an additional day to make pots. If a woman has to go to El Guamo to market or for other reasons, she may miss one of the normal workdays. Her orders may vary from small ones of fifteen dozen bowls, which can be completed in one week, to fifty or sixty dozen, which require a month to complete. A woman with teenaged children at home to do the burnishing can work at a faster rate than is possible otherwise. Without children or other assistants, she has to contract people to do the burnishing, giving up much of the profit, or slow down the rate of production as she does the burnishing herself.

The mother is the director of the household-labor enterprise. She also performs over eighty hours of work herself each week, including both ceramics and domestic tasks. Her work includes approximately forty hours per week on ceramics and another forty hours devoted to domestic responsibilities. She works from sunrise to early evening, usually twelve hours per day. Sunday is dedicated primarily to domestic work, marketing, and at least once a month to delivering an order of ceramics and negotiating the next order.

Anatilde Prada's work is equally divided between ceramics production and household and parenting responsibilities. She also assigns, directs, and supervises the 64 hours of ceramics work contributed weekly by her three older children who live at home. Most of the children's work consists of burnishing ceramics (60 hours), the production task for which their mother has the greatest need for assistance. Aurelio, Jr., and Maritza also assist their mother in preparing the pots for firing and odd jobs that account for another 4 hours. Some of the other common odd jobs done for the mother are listed here:

Task	Who does it
1. Accompany mother to mine clay	Younger boys
2. Bring and return the donkey	Any child, especially boys
3. Pulverize clay	Older boys, also young ones
4. Borrow food from relatives	Daughter or younger boys
5. Gather donkey dung	Younger boys
6. Minor food purchases	Any child, especially younger boys
7. Check kiln scheduling with other relatives	Daughter, older boys
8. Move bowls for drying, storage, and firing	Daughter, older boys

Maritza, the thirteen-year-old daughter, has the heaviest workload with thirty-eight hours (twenty-two in ceramics and sixteen in domestic tasks), which she was doing as well as attending school throughout the early part of this research. In addition to working half of each school day burnishing bowls, she was responsible for preparing food, washing clothes, and doing other odd jobs. Her mother expected her to work the heavier schedule of the women while her teenage brothers did more of the men's work outside of the house. After she dropped out of school, she started a work schedule similar to that of her mother.

Anatilde Prada plans, schedules, and leads the two-track work responsibilities simultaneously, both ceramics production and domestic coordination. She is the director of a small, master-artisan business enterprise, and has the executive responsibilities and the work hours associated with it. In addition to providing the mothering and child rearing that are required, she is also the executive officer. The result is a heavy workload that is the equivalent of two full-time jobs (see Table 11.2).

Interdependence in Women's Work Patterns

La Chamba women maximize their work potential by organizing the ceramics production process as a household team effort, a strategy that emphasizes cooperative work. This cooperative approach to work is even spread out to the extended family as women share information, orders, tools, and kilns between households. Although the household work team is directed by the mother, she is also the primary worker, and her household collaborators are, in fact, helping her complete an order for delivery to a middleman. Although she has higher status as a mother, in the household work circle she is actually the lead worker, even working harder than the children or husband who collaborate with her.

Lynn Stephen (1993, 44) found that Zapotec women weavers also characterized their work as a team effort involving husbands and children. Although the household works as a team, the women are responsible for production decisions, such as the allocation of children's labor, the timing of the weaving production, the number of pieces to be produced, and the negotiation of the selling price. Like La Chamba women, the Zapotec weavers plan, organize, and allocate the work of their household members, but it is the coordination of a cooperative effort rather than an authoritarian control of work.

Lisa Leghorn and Katherine Parker (1981, 256 and 281) suggest that men tend to organize their work around a hierarchy based on control, but that women tend to create cooperative groups emphasizing skill and networks of support. Research on men potters in other areas of Colombia confirm their suggestion; the men commonly organize hierarchical pottery workshops with a master potter at the top who directs workers, including wives and children (Duncan 1998, 78), a marked contrast with the cooperative work groups of the La Chamba women.

Not only is the work in La Chamba frequently organized around a cooperative household work group, it may even be organized in interdependent steps as two women work together on different stages of the work, either mining or preparing clay, making a pot, or firing. Working in interdependent stages was described among Mayan women potters by June Nash (1985, 70) in what she called "segmentation of pottery production." She said that this type of cooperation permits "specialization within a domestic production group," and that it is especially characteristic of women's work. This cooperative, interdependent organization permits the women to break down the work associated with ceramics into tasks that are appropriate for the skill and strength level of each member of the household work team.

The Unobtrusiveness of La Chamba Ceramics

The women of La Chamba tend to organize their ceramics work so that it does not interfere with the normal flow of daily life. This is in keeping with their view of themselves primarily as mothers and wives and only secondarily as potters. Once the work is completed for the day and the pieces in progress are stored, a visitor might not realize that the house is actually a ceramics workshop. Ceramics making is brought into the house during the day, but once the work is over, all of the materials are removed to the back or sides of the houses to be as little intrusive as possible.

Bags of clay to be pulverized are stored on one side of the house, and pots in which clay is soaking in preparation for use are also usually located along the side of the house out of view. A small pot containing slip may also be there. Clay is prepared only as it is needed, so there is no surplus to occupy space. Finished pieces that have yet to be fired must be stored inside to be protected from the rain, but they may be kept in a separate room devoted to that purpose. These rooms are heavy with the humidity of the drying pots, and the smell is usually dank and musky.

Since La Chamba women work on contract, they usually deliver their production as soon as it is completed. In fact, women normally fire their last round of production on the Saturday before the middleman comes on Sunday. As a result, they have little inventory to store, and stacks of finished fired pottery are rarely seen around the household workshops.

Another unobtrusive aspect of their ceramics production is the lack of dust and the general cleanliness of the household workshops. Women who make larger pieces, such as cooking pots or the large, one-of-a-kind pieces in "fine" ceramics, work outside of the house, sometimes in a separate studio building behind the house and sometimes in an open-walled, covered patio where they are protected from the sun and rain. Women who make the smaller *cazuelas* (bowls), like Anatilde Prada, work inside their houses and carefully clean up afterwards. Because of the smaller size of the pieces they make, *cazuela* makers require less space.

The fact that the climate is warm all year round permits them to do all of the dusty and dirty work outside, such as pulverizing the clay and mixing it into a claybody. The fact that they work with small quantities of clay at a time also means that little dust is generated. The clay is soaked in old cooking pots, so the water dampens the dust. When the damp clay is taken out of the soaking pots, it is wedged outside, frequently on a hardened place in the ground, until it is ready to use. Surfaces may be scraped while they are leatherhard, but they are rarely, if ever, scraped when dry, so no dust is produced. The end result is a relatively clean ceramics-making operation that permits the women to maintain a clean house while working at one of the dirtiest occupations in the world.

Low Productivity and High-Quality Finishing

La Chamba's production is more labor intensive than that of other pottery communities, such as Ráquira, where men are potters. Although the productivity per person is lower in La Chamba, the quality of the finishing of each piece is higher. Artesanías de Colombia made a study of the monthly production of eighty-seven workshops in La Chamba and recorded that 71,098 pieces were made, an average of 817 pieces per workshop (Rojas 1984). That gives an average of 204 pieces per week per workshop, a rate of production that corresponds closely to the 180 to 200 pieces per week that we documented in this study. The fact that a potter can make more than 200 pieces per day (instead of a week) on a potter's wheel indicates how slow the manual production is in La Chamba.

The two primary reasons for the slow production among La Chamba potters are the forming techniques and burnishing. The techniques used for making ceramics include the use of ceramic hump molds, coiling, and hand building. With each one of these processes considerable hand finishing is required to complete a piece, which reduces the total number of pieces that can be made. However, the advantage of the La Chamba production system is that it maintains the art-and-craft quality of hand-made ceramics. There are slight irregularities from one piece to another of the same series, and the ceramist's hand and eye work together to produce forms that can become exquisite.

Although slower techniques are used to form La Chamba ceramics, the real production bottleneck is in the burnishing of each piece. For example, the burnishing of a *cazuela* requires ten to fifteen minutes, more than twice as long as it takes to make the same bowl. This means that a person can only burnish five to six bowls in an hour. Of course, the trade-off is the fine quality of La Chamba ceramics, a point of special pride among the local people. It is the quality of the finishing that has led to the wide acceptance of La Chamba tableware and fine ceramics in the markets of Colombia. The buying public requires fine finishing for pieces like those from La Chamba that are to be displayed in the house or used as tableware.

Work and the Home-Based Potter

Like home-based women artisans in many parts of the world (Annis 1987; Ehlers 1990; Mies 1982; Tice 1995; Wilkinson-Weber 1997), the potters of

La Chamba work double shifts to provide income for their households and care for their children. Home-based crafts allow them to do this, but it is a demanding life, and many women of the younger generation question the demanding pace. However, the women in La Chamba have no other alternatives to provide income for their households, and the insecurity and irregularity of their husbands' incomes makes their own contributions necessary. This economic situation pressures women to continue producing ceramics for the well-being of their families.

7

Provincial Style

Cooking Pots and Bowls

La Chamba ceramics have always been functional, and they are made according to clearly defined principles of design and quality, especially in terms of form, texture, and color. As one of the older ceramic traditions in Colombia, La Chamba has incorporated elements of design from precolumbian, Spanish, and contemporary periods. As a provincial craft, this is a medium that emphasizes technique and repetition of forms over individual innovation, but it also reflects the creativity and esthetics of the group. La Chamba ceramics represent not only the esthetic principles of this community but also those of the Colombian society, and this contributes to their commercial popularity.

The Provincial Style

The traditional pottery (*ollas*) of La Chamba, including cooking pots, water jars, and bowls, make up the Provincial style. It can be traced back to the nineteenth century and probably reflects the Pijao-influenced ceramics of earlier periods. Tolima has been a provincial agricultural zone from the Spanish colonial period to the present, and the local pottery style was adapted to rural life in a nonindustrial, agricultural society. It provided containers for cooking over open fires, storing agricultural produce, carrying water from the river, and eating. This was functional ware for domestic use, and it was bartered or sold to family members and neighbors within limited local trading circles. Today potters still make some of these forms, but they sell them through middlemen to national and international markets.

Ceramics in La Chamba are part of the prehispanic-indigenous-mestizo tradition of ceramics making in Tolima and Huila, characterized by coiling, modeling, and hand building. The shapes of the pots, the forming process, the kiln, and the firing procedures in communities such as Campo La Vega, Claros, and Acevedo are similar to those of La Chamba. Most of the pottery made in these communities has been functional earthenware used daily by households for their food and water.

The Provincial style in La Chamba is similar in visual style, working patterns, and marketing to pottery found in agricultural communities in many other parts of the world. Pottery is an important cultural solution to a common need of containers for cooking, storing, and serving food, and it also has unique advantages in carrying and cooling water (Arnold 1985, 144). Clay is especially important for making containers in arid areas of the world where other materials, such as wood, are scarce. Its widespread availability, the ease of shaping it, and its hardness and durability once fired have made clay a popular material in preindustrial societies.

Colombian village ceramics have roots in two earthenware traditions: the prehispanic one from the Americas, and the Iberian one. The latter in turn is closely intertwined with the Berber-Moroccan earthenware complex (Lister and Lister 1987, 259, 270, 279). In both prehispanic and Berber earthenware (Jereb 1995, 115), women are the primary makers of pots, and they make them primarily for domestic use to be traded locally. This tradition does not require highly specialized production skills nor capitalistic markets to maximize returns. The indigenous earthenware tradition is well adapted to subsistence-level living in self-sufficient and largely self-contained agricultural communities. In areas where wood, skins, metal, and other materials for making food and water containers are in short supply, ceramics are sufficiently flexible to satisfy most cultural needs for bowls, pots, or plates.

Although earthenware cooking and water pots were a constant in human societies for thousands of years, this has changed in the last century with the advent of new foods, new materials for food and water containers, new cooking techniques, and new economic expectations on the part of potters. In Latin America, village pottery traditions have gone through a period of dynamic changes with the introduction of new forms, technologies, and competition in urban and international markets.

The Cooking Pot and the Bowl

The cooking pot and the bowl are the two central forms in the La Chamba design system, and in general these two forms correspond to the prehispanic heritage in Colombia. In La Chamba, as in most of the country, water was traditionally stored in prehispanic-indigenous-type water pots, or *tinajas,* rather than the Spanish-type amphoras, and food was prepared in prehispanic-type cooking pots. Probably as a result of this association with food, the cooking pot, or *olla,* is the most powerful icon of traditional ceramics in Colombia, and its iconographic significance indicates the importance of indigenous values within the mestizo culture of Colombia. The image of the cooking pot stimulates the emotions of home and hearth associated with home cooking. The *olla* is associated with the idea of family, and this is true as much for urban professional households as it is for rural agricultural ones. *La olla* is a feminine word, and the cooking pot is considered to have a feminine quality, in part because it is associated with nourishment and nurturing and in part because of its round, curving lines.

There is also a negative side to the iconography, revealed in a popular saying, *estamos en la olla*—literally, "we are in the pot," meaning "our goose is cooked." Although many good things come from the cooking pot, it is a cauldron in which things are boiled, and this phrase means that we are in trouble. It can be applied when there is no money to pay the bills, or no time left to complete an assignment due at the university. It can also be used if someone does something wrong and has been discovered. Indigenous cosmology is essentially dualistic, with all things having both positive and negative aspects. Thus the iconography of the *olla* of indigenous origin has an essentially dualistic interpretation, which includes both good and bad, the delight of cooked food and the desire not to find yourself in trouble.

The bowl is the other important pottery form in the precolumbian-indigenous tradition, and it includes the larger serving bowl (*cacerola*) and the smaller eating bowl (*cazuela*). It is normally found along with the cooking pot in every major ceramics region, and Colombian village ceramics are identified with this complex of the cooking pot and bowl pottery. The indigenous cultures of Colombia form part of the bowl-eating traditions of the Pacific-rim peoples, in which the various courses of a meal are served in separate bowls. In Colombia that means soup, main course, and dessert. The *cazuela,* the eating bowl for which La Chamba is well known, is a cultural icon like the cooking pot, and it communicates the idea of traditional cuisine.

Form and Function

The shape of La Chamba pots and bowls is spherical, similar to those in the earthenware traditions in most of the world. In functional terms, the circle is a strong form that eliminates the stress points that occur with angles. This is particularly important for the cooking vessels, which go through thermal shock on a daily basis, heating and cooling rapidly. Ample volume is preferred by La Chamba potters, and each shape is bulbous so that the pieces are sufficiently open to receive liquid or solid food. In this pottery tradition, the form of water jars follows the lines of the human body because they have been historically used to carry water from the well or river to the house. These pots had to fit comfortably on people's hips, shoulders, or backs, where the weight (twenty to thirty kilos) of a full pot of water would be carried. Since most households had to make several trips per day to bring water, this was a major concern. Dean Arnold (1993, 121, 122, 124) studied water carrying in Peru, Guatemala, and Mexico, and found a direct relationship between how women carry water (on the hip, head, or back) and the shape of the pot. Since women tend to carry water pots on their hips, most pots for water have a profile made to fit the curve of the hip. A neck is added that is long enough to fit the crook of the woman's arm holding the pot in place on her hip. The shapes of other pots and bowls are also adapted to specific uses in cooking, storing, drinking, or serving food.

1. Carrying water. Before water was piped into the houses, women carried water from the river or neighborhood wells (*aljibes*) in medium-sized pots (*ollas*), and an even larger pot (the *tinaja*) was used to store the water at the house. During this research, many households still stored drinking water in these large ceramic pots because it kept the water cool even on the hottest days. The water bottle, or *múcura*, is a small container for carrying water by hand, and it holds two to four liters. It is used to carry the smaller amounts of water that a person would consume during the course of a day. The *múcura* is carried by hand, and the user drinks directly from the spout. It has a long narrow neck designed to prevent spillage.

2. Cooking. Cooking is done in enclosed, spherical pots or open, concave toasting pans. The *olla*, which is an enclosed cooking pot, is used for cooking stews, making rice, and cooking vegetables. It has a full, round, bulbous shape that provides good volume, and an enclosed mouth with a lip that prevents the contents from boiling over. The *olla* may also be used in the kitchen for storing dry foods. The toasting pan (*tostador*) is a rounded disk-like pan used for the toasting of food over an open fire.

3. Serving. Food is usually served in a bowl, whether it is a stew or dry food like rice and fish; traditionally, plates were not made in

La Chamba. In recent years some potters have experimented with making plates for sale to buyers in Bogotá and other cities, but these experiments have not generally been successful. The bowl continues to be the form identified with La Chamba.

As the nurturers within their households, the women ceramists of La Chamba are the providers of food and drink, and they make the cooking, serving, and food-storage pots that they themselves will use. These are spherical pots with ample curves that guarantee adequate volume for the food as well as structural strength for the pot. These shapes have clean lines based on the circle and the curve.

Visual Values in Ceramics

When the people of La Chamba evaluate ceramics, they look at texture, shape, and color, which are the autochthonous visual elements of this design system (Duncan 1985c, 4).

1. Texture. Different textures used in the surface treatment of ceramics include: the natural surface of the claybody; a smooth finish resulting from a simple application of the local slip; and a polished finish resulting from a special slip and intense burnishing. The natural fired surface is a rough texture, almost like sandpaper, because of the quantity of temper in the claybody. Sometimes this texture is accentuated by scraping the surface to produce a more heavily pitted effect, which contrasts with areas of highly polished finish. The natural surface is used for the porous filter element in a water filter that is made by some of the younger women, and occasionally others use it to decorate experimental pieces. The claybody contains a high degree of montmorillonite, a mineral that resists surface luster even when burnished (Kruckman and Milligan, 1978, 57), and it has to be painted with a slip to achieve a surface that can be burnished.

   The second type of surface is the simple burnished one that is the most common, and it consists of one burnishing of a single coat of slip. This is an easy and fast finish that is used on less expensive ware such as the common cooking pot or water-storage pot. The rough, natural surface can be covered this way, and the burnished slip produces a semi-sealed surface. This finish is preferred over the natural surface, but it is used primarily as a functional requirement. The third type of surface is the highly polished finish. This is the most valued texture, and it is most prized when the application of the slip is completely uniform and when it is so polished that it gives a shiny reflection of light. Although the satin polished finish is somewhat more sealed, its real value for the La Chamba potters is its visual uniformity and satin-like quality, which is achieved by using the finest slip available (Litto 1976, 125; Villegas and Villegas 1992, 72).

2. Shape. The esthetic value of form in La Chamba is based on traditional design principles having roots in precolumbian ceramics. The spherical shape of La Chamba pots communicates the idea of fullness and completeness, and these pots are symbols of well-being because of their association with food and drink. In La Chamba houses, large water-storage pots are frequently placed near a door, which creates a visual focal point as the iron red sphere contrasts with the white-washed walls. In other houses two, three, or four pots may be placed in a row outside soaking clay, and they produce a rhythm of color and form that is visually striking. In the kitchens, pots are used to store grains or any other dried food. *Chambunos* place their pots where they can be seen and visually appreciated as well as used.

3. Color. The traditional color of La Chamba ceramics is a medium tone earthenware red, and that continues to be the color that people appreciate the most today. Considerable effort is spent to achieve purer and more perfect versions of this color. Earthenware red is the only color used for traditional ceramics, and it is also used for the new fine ceramics. An ebony black color, produced by reduction, is used on tableware, and it is highly valued by the urban buyers of La Chamba ware (Litto 1976, 125; Villegas and Villegas 1992, 72).

La Chamba is famous in Colombia for its blackware, a trait that distinguishes it from other village ceramics traditions in the country. However, blackware does occur in most of the other major prehispanic-indigenous regions throughout the Americas. During the prehispanic period, blackware was made by the Chimú and Inca in Peru (Lucena 1990, 51; Stone-Miller 1995, 174–75) and by Nariño and Tairona potters in Colombia (Labbé 1986, 14–15 and 192–93), and there are Indian groups in the Colombian Amazon today that produce blackware (Chaves 1985a, 70). In North America, blackware was popularized by María Martínez of San Ildefonso Pueblo, and it has become a recognized Pueblo style (Haberland 1986, 125). The ceramists of Oaxaca in Mexico are also famous for producing beautiful blackware, frequently similar to that produced in La Chamba. Blackware has long formed a part of the indigenous repertoire of ceramics techniques throughout North and South America.

Color mistakes occur with the blackware, especially when an improperly managed reduction process leaves areas that are partially oxidized and remain reddish. People say that the resulting crazy quiltwork of red and black makes one dizzy, so they do not sell such pieces. Potters also have color problems with redware; particularly unacceptable are the yellowish stains that bleed through the red slip from El Olvido.

The potters of La Chamba are critical of the visual qualities of their own production and of that of their neighbors, evaluating it in terms of texture, shape, and color. Within the community, the ceramists recognize a status hierarchy among themselves as to who makes better pieces, and the prestige of a ceramist is based on the visual quality of her pieces as well as the quantity of her sales.

The Repertoire of La Chamba Forms

The repertoire of forms currently being made in the village includes twenty-nine distinct shapes, each of which can have stylistic variations introduced by the individual craftswoman. (See Table 7.1.) Each of these shapes is made in a number of different sizes, leading to an even wider variety in the forms produced in the community. For example, one form, the standard cooking pot, comes in ten sizes, and the eating bowl comes in four sizes. Many pots or bowls may also be altered by adding handles or lids; or two, three, or four bowls may be combined to make a compartmentalized serving bowl for sauces or snacks. So there are many variations of the twenty-nine basic forms. The eating bowl (*cazuela*) is included under the "Tableware" column because it is made and used today as tableware, but it is a traditional form along with the cooking pot.

Twenty-six of the forms are made by fewer than 10 percent of the potters in the community. Among the 162 women potters surveyed, each one made an average of two forms. This represents a considerable degree of specialization, but it is consistent with the small number of forms made by the rural women potters in Ráquira, who usually make just one to three forms (Duncan 1998, 156).

Three forms stand out as the dominant ones made in the community: the *cazuela* is made by most of the potters, and serving platters and cooking pots

Table 7.1. Repertoire of La Chamba Ceramic Forms

Provincial pottery			Tableware			Fine ceramics		
Forms	No.[a]	%[b]	Forms	No.[a]	%[b]	Forms	No.[a]	%[b]
Cooking	38	23.46	Soup bowl	107	66.05	Water filters	9	5.56
Toasting	12	7.41	Platter	58	35.81	Planters	5	3.09
Water	9	5.56	Water pitchers	12	7.41	Piggy banks	4	2.47
Molds	1	0.62	Plates	15	9.26	Fish bowl	4	2.47
			Sauce bowl	12	7.41	Candle holders	4	2.47
			Serving spoons	4	2.47	Flower vases	4	2.47
			Cups, saucers	3	1.85	Hen casseroles	2	1.24
			Ashtrays	3	1.85	Other forms	7	4.32
			Butter dishes	1	0.62			
			Charcoal burners	2	1.24			
			Casseroles	7	4.32			
Total[c]	60	18.58		224	69.35		39	12.07

[a] Number of potters making the form out of 162 surveyed.

[b] Percentage of potters making the form out of 162 surveyed.

[c] The 162 potters reported making an average of 2 forms each for a total of 323 reports of forms made.

are next in popularity. Over two-thirds of the women, primarily in middle adult years but including some younger women, indicated that they made some form of tableware, making that the most important style in the community in the 1980s and 1990s. The volume of tableware orders is so great that orders of fifty dozen or more of *cazuelas* are made to a single ceramist at a time. Traditional pottery is made primarily by women of the older generation, and it is primarily sold in nearby regional markets. Few potters are working in the new "fine ceramics" style, and they are almost exclusively younger women. The fact that the evolution of styles has been a generational phenomenon shows the craft is not static and that change is an essential part of its survival. The new style of fine ceramics will probably become the traditional ceramics of the future, and other new styles can be expected to emerge.

Description of Traditional Forms (*Ollas*)

The Provincial style in La Chamba includes the cooking pot, toasting pan, eating bowl, water-storage pot, and water bottle, and the basic shape for this pottery is the sphere. The water bottle is a sphere with a spout; the cooking pot is an ovoidal sphere open on the top; and the storage pot is a sphere open at the top. (See Figure 7.1.) These shapes are derived from the heritage of prehispanic-indigenous functional wares. Like all of La Chamba pottery, these pieces are painted with red slip (red clay and water mixed to the consistency of cream), and the surface is burnished once, more or less quickly, in contrast to the two or three burnishings of the newer styles. The surface of the lightly burnished traditional pots can be irregular in color, and it is usually opaque, in contrast to the bright satin sheen of "fine" ceramics.

Cooking pots are characterized by porous, partially sealed surfaces, and

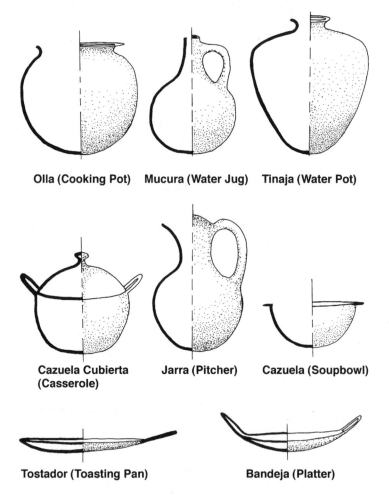

Olla (Cooking Pot)   Mucura (Water Jug)   Tinaja (Water Pot)

Cazuela Cubierta
(Casserole)   Jarra (Pitcher)   Cazuela (Soupbowl)

Tostador (Toasting Pan)   Bandeja (Platter)

Figure 7.1. La Chamba ceramic forms. The *olla, múcura, tinaja, cazuela,* and *tostador* are traditional forms of provincial ceramics in La Chamba, and the *cazuela cubierta, jarra,* and *bandeja* are newer forms that were developed as tableware.

the insides of these pieces are lightly burnished but with no slip to seal the inside. As a result, they absorb part of the liquid or food they contain, which "cures" the pot, giving the food cooked in it a special flavor that is valued by many people. The pottery water containers are also valued for this porous quality because it helps cool the water.

1. The cooking pot, *olla*. The cooking pot is a sphere that is stretched upward into an ovoid shape with a wide mouth, a barely perceivable shoulder, and a rounded base. (See Figure 7.1 and Photograph 1.1.) The wide mouth facilitates filling the pot, stirring the contents, and dishing out the food. The rounded base was originally designed to allow the pot to be balanced on three stones above an open fire, and the shape has continued even though it is rarely used over open fires today. This pot can also be used for storage, especially the larger versions of it. Ten sizes are known, but today only seven are made. Although each size has a specific measurement and mold from which it is made, a craftswoman can alter the pot slightly to make it larger than its standard size. The smallest pots are measured according to the amount of rice that can be cooked in them. The smaller sizes are the quarter-pound rice pot (*cuatroncera*), half-pound (*media libra*), one pound (*arrocera*), and one and one-half pounds (*caldero*).

   The larger sizes are measured according to the radius of the pot at its widest point. The larger sizes are the *catorcera* (14 cm in radius), *quincera* (15 cm in radius), and *veinte* (20 cm in radius), which is the largest that is normally made today. An augmented version of the *veinte* is made from the same mold, but it is manually stretched to 50 cm instead of the normal 40 cm in diameter. Potters also referred to larger sizes, such as the *treinta* (30 cm), *cuarenta* (40 cm), and *cincuenta* (50 cm), but no one makes them.

2. The water bottle, *múcura*. People carry this to the fields when working, and it is valued because it keeps the water cool. (See Figure 7.1 and Photograph 1.2.) Usually the *múcura* is small, no more than 30 cm tall, and holds approximately two liters of liquid. Frequently, it has a finger-loop handle on the neck. It can also be carried in a sack, or a small rope can be strung through the loop handles to suspend it from the shoulder. The stopper for the spout may be made of ceramic or, preferably, wood, since it

can be carved to fit tightly and it also swells when wet, making a tight seal. The *alcarraza* is another small spherical water pot of some 20 cm in diameter; it has two spouts and a hand-sized looped handle for carrying. Although it is now largely decorative, it is known for the ease of pouring. Both the *múcura* and the *alcarraza* are distinctive precolumbian forms made by groups from the central regions of Colombia, and the forms made in La Chamba are plain versions of the precolumbian shapes. The terms *múcura* and *alcarraza* are Arabic in origin, as are almost all ceramic terms in Spanish, showing the Moorish influence on that country. Later, most ceramic forms in Colombia, which are largely precolumbian in origin, were given these Spanish/Moorish names.

3. The water-storage pot, *tinaja*. The distinctive shape of the *tinaja* is an inverted cone; the widest point is at the shoulder, which closes in quickly to form the mouth. (See Figure 7.1 and Photograph 1.3.) *Tinajas* have conical bottoms and were originally designed to be set in holes in the ground, which helped cool the water on hot days. Making the widest point of the *tinaja* near the top means that the water level goes down slowly as water is taken out, a convenient feature for users. The height and diameter of this pot are approximately equal, measuring from 45 to 60 cm in diameter, and the mouth ranges from 15 to 20 cm in diameter. Since a special cover for the mouth is not normally made, an old toasting pan or a small cooking pot may be used as a lid.

Because slip does not completely seal the walls of pots, *tinajas* are porous and absorb water, which sweats through to the outer surface. As the air temperature heats up during the daytime hours, the water on the damp outer surface evaporates, reducing the temperature of that surface. As a result, the water in the pot stays cooler than the air temperature, which guarantees a fresh, cool drink of water during the hot tropical afternoons in La Chamba. After the arrival of piped-in water to the village in the 1970s, people no longer needed water-storage pots, but some of the older people still use them, as do people without piped water who live outside of the village nucleus. Production of the traditional *tinaja* stopped, and today people who want to store water use large cooking pots.

4. Eating bowl, *cazuela*. The form of the eating bowl is adapted from the round base of the traditional cooking pot. (See Figure 7.1 and Photograph 5.2.) It is formed over a hump mold, and in the case of the *cazuela* the mold is made by the ceramist and not by a mold maker. The border is finished when the piece is leatherhard, and knob-like handles are added to each side at the lip. Today, this bowl has become a part of the tableware exported from the region to cities, and it is one of the few pieces used both locally and in the urban areas. It is made in various sizes for the urban buyers. The smallest size is 8 cm in diameter and is made for sauces; the medium-sized bowl is 15 cm; and the large bowl is 18 cm. The *cazuela* is ordered in large numbers by businesses in the neighboring state of Valle, where it is used to pack a popular caramel-like dessert called *manjar blanco*. In Bogotá its most popular use is as an eating bowl in which traditional stews are served.

5. The toasting pan, *tostador*. The *tostador* is a rounded disk, usually 25 cm in diameter and 10 cm deep (see Figure 7.1). It can be used to toast yucca, corn, or other dry foods.

6. The mold, *molde*. Molds are essentially ceramic pots turned upside down and used as molds. Potters frequently make their own molds, but some people are considered good mold makers and make them for others. Although the mold actually looks like a normal pot, it has an unpainted surface that is beige-gray in color. What would be the rim of the cooking pot becomes the base on which the mold stands, and it is made differently. The rim is somewhat thicker, and it is straight, in contrast to the cooking rim which curves slightly outward.

   The mold is heavily tempered so that it is porous, and it absorbs water from the clay, causing the new piece to firm up rapidly and release easily from the mold. Since these are drape molds, the short mold time is critical so that the clay does not dry and crack. Another advantage of the short mold time is that the mold can be quickly used to make the next piece. If the mold becomes so wet that it no longer absorbs water quickly, it is placed outside in the sun to dry.

7. The saggar, *moyón*, or *canasta*. These are the large pots in which smaller pots and bowls are placed for firing (see Photograph 10.4). The saggar is actually an augmented version of the largest

cooking pot made today, the *veinte,* and it is usually 40 to 50 cm in diameter. The mouth is only slightly enclosed, making it easy to load for the firing. It is made with a claybody that has a high percentage of temper, usually sand, to withstand the rapid heating and cooling of the firing process. Both the mold and the saggar are variations on the basic form of the cooking pot.

In La Chamba, people not only use traditional pots to cook and store food and drink, they also use them to store slip and to soak the clay before it is ready to use. They are recycled as planters if they become cracked or slightly broken and are no longer useful for cooking or slip storage. Traditional pottery is still sold throughout the region surrounding La Chamba, and many farm families still use these pots to store foodstuffs as well as water.

Vessel Design Grammar

The design elements for traditional earthenware in La Chamba consist of a small set of alternative forms for the base, body, neck, and handles. These design elements are combined for functional, not esthetic, reasons to produce the recognizable forms of the cooking pot, water bottle, bowl, and others. There is a "grammar," or a set of meaningful guidelines about how to combine design elements to produce pots that are culturally intelligible. Since the grammar of pottery design is a commonly held set of assumptions in a community, it produces a style.

The design of La Chamba pottery starts with a rounded bottom, which is the common shape for most village pottery in Colombia, and it represents a continuity with the precolumbian traditions. The rounded bottom clearly distinguishes the prehispanic-indigenous-mestizo ceramics from the flat-bottomed Spanish ceramics, which are designed to sit on the tile floors of Spanish architecture. The round bottom is a functional shape because it is designed to endure the thermal shock of direct-flame cooking, and also because it can be firmly balanced between three or more rocks, which hold it above the fire to be built underneath. The round shape also adapts to the irregular undulations of the ground. In recent decades flat bottoms have been adopted for tableware forms, such as platters and fish-shaped serving bowls. The bottoms of these forms have been flattened, allowing them to sit on the cabinets and oven shelves of urban customers.

Various forms are used for the main part of the body, including an open shape (bowl), a high, slightly enclosed globular shape (cooking pot), and an enclosed spherical shape (water bottle). The open shape is used for eating bowls and casseroles, and in all cases the wide open mouth is for the ease of serving food. The globular shape of the cooking pot is widest in the middle, or stomach, of the pot to provide an ample volume for the food to be cooked, while it closes in on the bottom to fit the rounded base and on the top to prevent the food from bubbling or spilling out. The enclosed walls of the *olla* are well adapted to the preparation of food, and the broad open mouth permits easy access to work with the food.

Although the base and the body determine much of the profile of a pot, the neck is important in defining its use. The basic function of a neck is to impede water or food from spilling. When there is no neck, such as on serving bowls, it means that there is ease of access to the interior for serving food or drink. An enclosed body wall also helps prevent spillage and lessens the need for an enclosing neck, such as occurs with the *olla*. La Chamba casseroles have no neck, but the mouth is fitted with a seat for the lids, which are used to retain heat while cooking.

The three basic neck shapes are the short neck, the high pouring neck, and the spout. The short neck is used on cooking and storage pots, helping to prevent spillage but still permitting access to stir or dip out the contents. This neck is usually no more than 5 cm high, and it may be 20 cm or more wide. The medium pouring neck, used for pitchers, is 15 cm or more high and the opening may be 6 to 10 cm wide, with a flaring lip that is pulled and smoothed out into a pouring spout on one side. The third neck is a high (15 cm) and narrow (2 cm) spout; it is used for the *múcura* and has the functional advantage of being easily closed with a stopper, making it easy to carry liquids to the fields or other work places.

Handles are important for lifting and carrying ceramics, and all are usually made from coils. Most are stirrup-shaped grasping handles, which are used on pitchers and other pots, such as casseroles and trays. These handles tend to be 15 to 18 cm long and curved to fit the shape of the closed, grasping hand. The second type of handle is a small loop made just large enough to accommodate a finger or rope. One or two of these loop handles are put on small *múcuras* to facilitate carrying them.

The last element of the design grammar is the lid, which was introduced as a part of new tableware designs in recent decades. Lids are made for casseroles, some pitchers, and even teapots, which are occasionally made for urban clients. A small, round, domed lid (10 cm) is made for pitchers and teapots, and larger ones (20 to 25 cm) are made for the casseroles. An oval-shaped, domed lid may be made for the fish casserole.

The grammar of vessel design is the particular way in which the functional elements are combined—the base of a pot with a body form, a neck, lip, and handles or lids. In La Chamba ceramics, each of the elements has a functional purpose, and the pot is made following functional guidelines. However, the elements also have visual qualities that are as much appreciated as the functional ones. The best vessel design combines functional and visual issues in a culturally satisfying manner. During the twentieth century, these design elements were modified and recombined into new forms to create the styles of tableware and "fine" ceramics, and they will probably be recombined and reinterpreted in the future to form yet unknown styles.

Design Styles and Generations

Design in La Chamba ceramics is divided between three major styles: provincial pottery, tableware, and "fine" ceramics, each of which is associated with a different generation. Part of a woman's identity has to do with the ceramic style with which she works, and the generational layering of style can be seen frequently within the same extended family. Grandmothers prefer the cooking-pot style, which has the associations of hearth, nurturing, and the family. Mothers identify with the tableware because it is practical and represents a consistent income. Daughters prefer the one-of-a-kind quality of the fine ceramics with the challenges that it represents in modeling and perfect finishing. The catalogue of forms opens a door to understanding generational changes in esthetics and ceramic styles.

These three styles of La Chamba ceramics have evolved according to the needs of the community and of the larger society. The oldest style, that of provincial pottery (cooking pots and bowls), can be traced to the nineteenth century and earlier; the second style (tableware or *loza)* dates from the 1930s; and the third (fine ceramics) refers to the generation of ceramics developed since the 1960s. The term "fine ceramics" is used locally to refer to pieces that are individually made, that have perfect finishing, and that have some modeling of decorative features.

Although provincial pottery is primarily made by women above the age of sixty, some younger women help their mothers make these pots. Although it would seem that the demand for provincial pottery would be decreasing, the number of households producing it actually increased from twenty in 1972 (Lara 1972, 99) to thirty-five in 1988. This is a 75 percent increase, which is approximately equal to the 70 percent rate of increase for overall production in La Chamba during this time period. This means that the production of traditional pottery is not declining but in fact has increased at a rate comparable to the overall increase of production in the community.

Each craftswoman has a line of ceramics that is identified with her, and although it is generally limited to one style, it may include more than one form or size. This has led to a system of specialization that permits the craftswoman to become highly proficient in the form or forms of her line. Quality control is an important aspect of specialization, and La Chamba women place great emphasis on the quality of the finishing of their pieces. Specialization also permits women potters to establish consistent relationships with wholesale buyers, who know which one to contact for any given form in the repertoire. Specialization also means that women within the extended family can avoid competing directly with each other since each woman specializes in a different form or set of forms.

Ceramics as Iconography

To understand ceramics as a visual medium it is important to consider how ceramics symbolize the values of a society. Each culture has visual values of form, color, texture, and decoration as well as the basic design principles of figuration and abstraction. Of course, there are some visual qualities such as symmetry, perspective, rhythm, balance, proportion, and emphasis that are inherent elements of visual perception deriving from the special characteristics of the human species, but the values of a society include other, nonvisual factors that affect esthetic perception, such as the acquisitive power that a piece represents, the social prestige of the design tradition, and the cultural importance assigned to the medium. These nonvisual factors can augment the perception of the esthetic value of a piece or diminish it. The design elements used in village ceramics are not usually associated with esthetics, but they have an undeniable place in Colombian visual arts.

Village crafts, such as ceramics, are an important part of the culturally authentic experience of popular art and design, and the shapes, colors, and surfaces of traditional pots are key experiences in forming the popular sense of visual expression for most Colombians. Village ceramics provide a link with the precolumbian past and the Spanish colonial heritage, and for the stressed city dweller of today they represent the nostalgia and perceived simplicity of the country lifestyle. Village ceramics symbolize what is authentic in the community, and they are bound to the earth and to the past.

For urban, upper-class Colombians, precolumbian ceramics symbolize their unique cultural identity in the Americas. The presence of precolumbian ceramics in the house permits the owner to project his or her sophistication in appreciating the ancient cultures. For previous generations, the Christian altar and the saint figures were important symbols of the owner's identification with European values, but today the collection of precolumbian figures has replaced the saints as objects of honor within the houses and apartments of the more secular professional elites. In Colombia archaeological artifacts are widely collected by wealthy individuals, who exhibit them in their homes. Although they can be owned privately, it is illegal to export them.

These ceramic pieces do not symbolize European values but rather local autochthonous ones, and the precolumbian figures have become the new secular saints. Although Colombia has incorporated precolumbian art into the national iconography with pride in the achievements of that distant past, ceramics made in the same style by their descendants today are not appreciated in a comparable manner. In fact, they are usually considered poor rural handicrafts or tourist trinkets. Helaine Silverman (1993, 129) describes a similar phenomenon in Peru among people of the same social class. Precolumbian achievements in arts and crafts are more acceptable to the people of the dominant Eurocentric society than is the work of indigenous and mestizo people today, who have a low social status because of their marginalization after the Conquest and Spanish colonial period.

Although the mestizo village ceramics of today have roots in prehispanic tradition, the experience of the Conquest was a crucible in which some elements of the indigenous tradition were destroyed and others reinterpreted or synthesized with European ones. As an element of cultural identity, the village ceramics of today symbolize a set of values quite different from the precolumbian ones. Village ceramics represent the present, the countryside, and the small-town lifestyle that is the basis of Colombian society.

The Culture of Making Pots

Making ceramics is a cultural process of translating the basic sensory experience of the potter into craft pieces, similar to the cultural model of the arts defined by David Bidney (1967, xxxix). The variables that influence craft design and style are synthesized by each craftsperson into a coherent system. In the crafts, it is apparent that individuals have an important role in imagining and creating their visual forms, and individual creativity requires that culture be a fluid system. This concept of the fluidity of culture is inherent in Ralph Holloway's concept of the "arbitrariness" of human behavior (1969, 399), and he suggests even further that "arbitrariness-of-form" is an essential aspect of human behavior (1971, 401ff). Accepting Holloway's point, it can be argued that the central analytical tool for the study of behavior is the process of arbitrary formation of behavior, rather than the final formed product. The forms themselves cannot be the primary unit of analysis because they are no more than interchangeable parts in a procedural continuum that extends from acquisition of behaviors to their being acted out.

The pottery vessel is the manifestation or end product of the process of craft making, and the underlying infrastructure which leads to the making of the pot is drawn from the cultural assumptions and the experiences of the individual craftsperson. The culture of craft is the encoding of human experience into compositions or objects that are culturally recognizable to the viewers. The primary iconic, maybe unconscious, level of coding deals with felt experiences. The organization, classification, and verbalization of visual styles disrupt the continuity between unconscious and conscious levels. However, in art and craft humans give conscious expression to patterns and relationships that are reconstructed from unconscious levels of experience. Thus, art and craft reestablish paralinguistic relationships, an integration between felt experience and forms of culture.

Craft making consists of formalized visual elements that are organized into coherent styles or systems based on the accumulated experience of the craftsperson. Each craft medium and style is an integrated system that is shaped by the visual elements of culture and symbolic systems in the craft making infrastructure of the individual craftsperson. Visual expression in craft is one of the identifiers of human cultural distinctiveness.

Culture and Design Styles

The practitioners of a craft medium form a cultural microcosm in which they manage a similar set of parameters, and the different solutions that they give to their craft expression reflect the dynamic of the culture and result in the style associated with the group. La Chamba ceramics belong to the prehispanic-indigenous design style, which has been consistent for generations. Within a culture there are various internal forces that push toward conformity in design, which results in the recognizable styles associated with ceramics communities. None of these factors alone is sufficient to produce a consistent design style, but together these influences do produce a style. Four factors can be identified in pottery-making communities that work together to produce a consistent style, and they are: intergenerational learning, in-group interaction, market symbolism, and materials and mechanical factors.

The first factor shaping a common style within a community of potters is the transmission of learning from generation to generation. Normally, knowledge is passed from mother to daughter, following the socially established rules for descent and postnuptial residence (Arnold 1993, 188). The intergenerational learning of ceramics occurs especially in conservative communities marked by little social change. Behavior in that cultural context tends toward homogeneity, and the design style in arts and crafts also tends toward uniformity. In this context, the design style tends to remain consistent from generation to generation.

The second factor shaping a common style within a community is frequent in-group interaction (Arnold 1993, 189). Social interaction between potters contributes to their sharing of design information, and leaders within a group influence others to adopt the design styles they have developed. The basic design structure gives coherence and continuity—that is, style—but the specific design elements may be used in more individualistic ways. The effects of in-group interaction can be observed in La Chamba, especially in the social-change process. As Ana María Cabezas began making "fine ceramics," other potters saw the advantages of the new ideas; so many adopted them that they became a new ceramics style.

The third factor is market symbolism. The ceramics of a community with a long history may also have importance in the collective symbolism of the region or the country, and in the market-driven societies of today that becomes market symbolism. In La Chamba, pottery is sold as much for symbolic reasons as functional ones. It symbolizes the authenticity of Colombian food, which is still cooked and served in those pots for special occasions, such as Christmas. This symbolism assumed particular nostalgic power in the social chaos that resulted from the drug trafficking, corruption, high homicide rates, and widespread kidnapping that came to characterize Colombia in the 1980s and 1990s. In the terms of Pierre Bourdieu (1993, 115), La Chamba ceramics have become symbolic goods of large-scale cultural production.

The fourth factor in shaping a style is the common use of materials and mechanical procedures in making the ceramics. The raw materials available to the community will determine the colors and quality of the claybody of the pottery. The special hue of iron red identified with La Chamba pottery comes from the clay itself, combined with the mode of preparing it as slip and the firing process. The shapes and surface textures of La Chamba pots result from the slab-and-coil building technique. These shapes and textures distinguish the work and could not be easily replicated, either on the wheel or with industrial-type plaster molds. So the concepts of shape, line, texture, and color in a given pottery community result from the limits and influences exerted by the materials and mechanics of production on the making process.

The La Chamba Pot

The morphology of La Chamba pottery reflects a generational evolution of design that has responded to market demands. Although La Chamba pottery has been functional historically, the ceramists today are increasingly making special pieces that are primarily decorative. This evolution demonstrates the important role of creativity and design innovation in maintaining tradition. Even with the three distinctive styles that can be identified in La Chamba pottery today, a La Chamba pot has an identity that can be quickly recognized by the urban buyer. The red iron color, the satin-smooth surface, and the impeccable workmanship in the finishing of the piece are qualities that clearly distinguish these pots from those from Ráquira or other ceramics-producing communities in Colombia. There is also a consistency of form in La Chamba pottery, whose bulbous, clean profile lines are undisturbed by added decoration. In addition to this stylistic unity, the other significant feature of La Chamba pottery is its identification with traditional cuisine, which is commonly served in restaurants and urban households in tableware from La Chamba.

8

Contemporary Market Styles: Tableware and Fine Ceramics

During the economic expansion of the twentieth century, La Chamba pottery went through many changes as potters reacted to the new possibilities offered by growing markets. Fundamental changes occurred in the forms of ceramics as the emphasis shifted from functional pottery for use in the local agricultural communities to tableware and decorative ceramics for urban markets. The expansion of the money-based economy stimulated potters to explore new concepts. Instead of making cooking pots designed to withstand the rigors of the open fire, they developed new styles of display ceramics for well-to-do urban customers.

The Styles of the Era of Economic Expansion

The expansion of regional markets into national and international ones in the last century led the potters of La Chamba to develop new styles of work, including tableware in the 1940s and 1950s and "fine" ceramics and figures in the 1970s and 1980s. In contrast to the Provincial style, these pieces are designed for use in urban households on cabinet shelves, on stove tops, and in ovens, all uses foreign to rural households in Tolima. Buyers representing urban merchants and professional designers from official agencies have made important contributions in the development of these new styles. Some have brought actual pots to be copied by the ceramists, others have brought photographs of pots, and others have brought ideas to be developed. So, the innovation in La Chamba pottery during this period resulted in part from outside influences.

Most of the changes have been consistent with the local craft traditions, and the new styles use the same basic forms and working techniques as the Provincial style. This continuity of forms and working patterns results from women always having been the potters. They have consistently maintained the same basic approach to their craft as low-investment handwork adapted to their cycle of domestic responsibilities. Although market demand for La Chamba ceramics has grown, women have not changed their techniques to increase productivity.

The contemporary market-style ceramics are more decorative than the Provincial style because the potters know that most pieces will be displayed as objects in urban households rather than used as functional pottery. Because this style is meant for display, potters burnish the surfaces more highly, and they model figures into the vessel forms to make them visually interesting. The best of these vessel figures become sculptural, and the potters who make them do so with sculptural intentions. These pieces become village art, reflecting the local iconography of domestic animals and tropical fruits. The market economy has given La Chamba potters the freedom to go beyond the relatively fixed system of provincial ceramics to explore and develop the visual possibilities of their medium.

The era of economic expansion has also changed La Chamba potters from being provincial craftswomen to being proletarian workers on contract to merchants from urban Colombia. Although their working techniques and design principles remain the same, they have begun to make new forms of ceramics for urban markets. However, there is no cultural integrity between the makers and the users in these market-based styles because the potters are making ceramics that they do not use, nor do they ever see how their pieces are used.

Contemporary Market Ceramics

The potters of La Chamba distinguish between *loza* and *cerámica,* with *loza* referring to the tableware made by middle-aged women in the community, and *cerámica* referring to the new styles made in recent decades (figures and "fine" ceramics). Both are made with the same local clays, and the fabrication process is essentially the same, but there are differences in the way raw materials are processed and in the finishing of pieces. The differences can be summarized as follows:

1. Claybody. *Loza* is made with a high concentration of the naturally tempered clay from the El Embudo mines, which gives up to 35 or 40 percent of temper in the final claybody. This is required because the pieces may be used as cooking pots. The rapid heating and cooling of pots in cooking can crack them if they do

not have the correct claybody, and the local way to achieve that is increasing the amount of temper. *Cerámica* is made with half as much temper (estimated at 20 percent) because it is not used for cooking. The clays for the claybody of *cerámica* pieces are more carefully cleaned by passing them through a sieve multiple times to remove pebbles and organic material.

2. Slip. In like manner, the slip for *cerámica* is sieved various times whereas slip for *loza* is prepared more rapidly. Only the purest red iron oxide slip is used for *cerámica,* but clay carrying other minerals may be used to mix the slip for *loza.*

3. Technique. The technique of making *loza* is limited to adding coils to a slab base to build the wall of a pot, while the techniques for making *cerámica* include the hand modeling of figurative elements, as well as handles and knobs.

4. Burnishing. *Loza* is *alisada* (smoothed) while *cerámica* is *brillada* (polished). In the former, the surface is stone burnished one time, whereas in the latter, the surface is burnished three or more times with careful attention to each surface detail.

Market ceramics include both tableware and fine ceramics, and most women prefer working with one of these two styles, with tableware being the most popular kind of ceramics made in La Chamba today.

Tableware

Tableware refers to ceramics made to be used on tables, which means that it must be well finished and adapted to serving and eating. The concept of the waist-high table at which people sit to eat was introduced by the Spanish; generally rural, indigenous-mestizo households in Colombia do not use tables for eating. Many of the tableware forms are borrowed from European usage, which represented a new way of using ceramics not based on traditional indigenous-mestizo practices. Only the *cazuela* (eating bowl) is traditional to La Chamba. Since the 1930s, the repertoire of tableware forms has grown from the *cazuela* to include serving platters, plates, water pitchers, cups and saucers, casseroles, and serving ladles. Although tableware forms are derived from European-styled dinnerware, they are made with the thick-walled technique of traditional pottery.

In the Provincial-style pottery, food is served directly from the cooking pot to the eating bowl, which is hand-held as a person sits on a low stool or on the ground to eat. In contrast, the table-style of eating used in urban households requires serving bowls, which are brought from the kitchen to serve food on plates or bowls set on the table. Since serving bowls may be left on the table as people eat, they are expected to be attractive. In La Chamba that is achieved by careful finishing, finely burnished surfaces, and modeled figures.

Since people in La Chamba neither eat at tables nor have ovens to cook with the casseroles, they do not use most of the tableware pieces that they make. Local meals include *sancocho*, which is a stew, and several rice-based meals, all of which are served in the *cazuela*. Since they live in hot country, they normally drink cold drinks, such as juices, rather than the hot drinks for which the cups and saucers are made. When a special meal is prepared for visitors, they prefer to use industrially made tableware, which is perceived to be finer. More prestige is associated with its use. Although urban professionals in Bogotá serve the traditional Christmas dinner of *ajiaco* in La Chamba bowls, the people of La Chamba will serve their Christmas dinner in industrially made creamware.

Although the tableware from La Chamba may be either red or black, approximately two-thirds of the production is black, the color preferred by urban customers. Of all the tableware forms, the item produced in largest quantity is the *cazuela,* which was described under the Provincial style. Today it has been incorporated into the tableware category. The other important forms of tableware that are made today are the casserole, platter, plate, cup and saucer, and pitcher.

1. Casserole (*cazuela cubierta*). A larger version of the regular *cazuela,* it has a lid and two loop handles that project out from both sides (see Figure 7.1). The casserole is made to be used in the oven, but it can also be used over direct flame. It is an adaptation of the traditional cooking pot, being broader and more open. The casserole is a form similar to Spanish village pottery (Llorens and Corredor-Matheos 1979, 93), which was introduced into La Chamba by the requests of urban buyers. Its three sizes are small (20 cm wide by 12 deep), medium (28 cm by 18 cm), and large (35 cm by 25 cm). The loop handles extend out 4 cm on each side.

2. Platter (*bandeja*). It is a flat oval form with raised edges and handles at each end, measuring approximately 30 cm wide (see Figure 7.1). It is used in urban Colombian households both for oven cooking and serving, but its most important use now is decorative.

3. Plate (*plato*). The plate is a Spanish form (Llorens and Corredor-Matheos 1979, 134–35) that marks the cultural divide between urban, Spanish-oriented people, who have traditionally eaten on plates, and the rural mestizo peoples, who have a more indigenous heritage and have traditionally eaten in bowls. It is made in La Chamba but rarely used there. It is approximately thirty centimeters in diameter.

4. Cup and saucer (*taza con platico*). The saucer may be used separately to serve desserts or as part of a cup-and-saucer set. The cup itself is an adaptation of the sauce bowl, with a flattened bottom and the addition of a handle.

5. Covered pitcher (*jarra*). These are water pitchers inspired by the Spanish tradition (Llorens and Corredor-Matheos 1979, 36, 85, 135). They were introduced into the La Chamba repertoire earlier this century (see Figure 7.1). Although the concept is Spanish, the form and texture have the distinctive La Chamba signature. The largest ones, which are basically decorative, can be as tall as 50 cm and 35 cm in diameter. Functional ones are smaller, more in the range of 25 to 35 cm tall.

This is not an exhaustive list of forms because women are constantly experimenting with new shapes. Using established design principles, they developed the new forms of tableware in response to market demand. The synthesis that they achieved in the development of tableware is a balance between the maintenance of tradition and economic vitality. Although the tableware type of production is relatively new, it is made by women who learned traditional pottery techniques.

Fine Ceramics

This style uses new designs introduced since the 1960s, which are identified with careful finishing. Fine ceramics are characteristically red, for two reasons. First, it is a style learned in the classes offered by Artesanías de Colombia, where electric kilns were used, and these kilns do not permit the reduction process, which is needed to obtain black. The other reason is that some of the fine ceramics pieces are too large to fit into the saggars that are used for reduction.

The satin-perfect finish of the surface of fine ceramics is achieved by applying three coats of the finest-quality slip. Afterwards, the surface is burnished to a gleaming coat with a smooth semi-precious stone, which gives smoother texture than would be possible with a softer, grainier stone. Three burnishings are required to achieve the partially sealed, light-reflecting surface identified with fine ceramics. Quality control is important to these pieces, and every border, union, or difficult place to reach is carefully finished. Some potters enhance the satin sheen by polishing the surface with an oil-soaked rag (Méndez 1993, 157) after the pieces are fired.

Although the forms of fine ceramics are new, they use basically the same design elements as *loza*, and, in fact, some pieces are initially shaped on traditional molds. For example, the bottoms of water filters and pitcher-planters are formed on the molds for cooking pots. The most popular forms of fine ceramics are water filters, pitcher-planters, casseroles in the form of a hen, and platters in the form of fish.

The finishing of fine ceramics requires a substantial amount of hand-modeling. The production is occasionally divided in such a way that an older woman will make the base of a piece on the mold, and her daughter will finish it by modeling the upper part. The older women say that modeling is an art requiring special skills that their generation did not learn, and so modeling marks the generational divide between them and their daughters.

The introduction of fine ceramics to La Chamba has been a practical innovation as much as an esthetic one. Since the middle-aged craftswomen dominate the tableware market, the younger women have adopted the new style to gain a niche in the marketplace and to respond to the growing interest in esthetics and design among urban buyers. This style begins to make the transition from pieces that emphasize hand-made quality to pieces that emphasize concept and design.

Two of the aspects of fine ceramics that appeal to the young craftswomen are the selling price and the customized quality of the pieces. A single large pitcher-planter sells for what many dozens of *cazuelas* will fetch. Many younger potters prefer to dedicate more time to the difficult and risky process of making one large individualized piece to sell at a good price than to repeat dozens upon dozens of the simpler forms, which represent almost no technical risk or challenge.

1. Pitcher (*jarrón*). This is a form that crosses between tableware and fine ceramics. Smaller versions of this form (called the *jarra* or *caldera* and discussed under tableware) have a lid and can be utilitarian, but finer and larger versions are exclusively decorative. The largest versions may be used as planters and are 70 cm high and 50 cm in diameter. The base of the larger planter form is

made from the mold for a cooking pot, and the sizes are referred to with the same terms—for example, a *quincera* (15 cm in radius) or a *veinte* (20 cm in radius). Once the base of the pitcher has firmed to the leatherhard stage, the neck and rim are built up using coils. The various stages of making, burnishing, and drying a large piece can take from one to two weeks.

Large pieces are normally made only during the rainy season, when the natural humidity allows each one to dry slowly and evenly. The winds characteristic of the dry period can cause these pieces to dry quickly and unevenly, leading them to crack. Another problem is that the strong winds characteristic of the dry period can blow into the open doors of the kilns during a firing. This is particularly dangerous for large pieces because one side of a hot piece can suddenly cool just at the delicate quartz-inversion stage, causing it to crack. For these reasons most ceramists prefer to make large pieces during the rainy season.

The design of the large sculptural pitcher seems to have originated in La Chamba, having derived from the form of a utilitarian pitcher. The body of the piece is round and approximates a circle in a form dominated by curves. The neck stretches the piece upward and provides a transition to the rim, with the sides flaring up to a softly curved border with a dramatic elegance. The best of these pieces achieve a sculptural quality that goes beyond their cooking-pot origins.

2. Water filter (*filtro*). The traditional water filter in this region of Colombia was made of a porous volcanic stone hollowed out in the shape of a conical vessel and set on a wooden frame. Water was poured into it and filtered as it seeped through the two-inch-thick stone walls, dripping into a pitcher below. By the 1980s potters were making a ceramic version of the water filter, which is more practical than the older stone version. The new design was borrowed from a broken Mexican ceramic filter that someone brought to the community to be copied. It consists of an outer shell, which is actually a tall cylindrical pot approximately 80 cm high and 30 cm in diameter. A conical potlike filter is made with a flange; it is placed inside the shell with the flange resting on the top rim of the shell. Although the outer shell of the filter is slip-painted and burnished, the filter is not. It is left porous so that the

Photo 8.1. *La gallina* (hen casserole). The hen is a popular icon of fertility. The head, wings, and tail of the hen are modeled onto the covered casserole, which is a favorite example of "fine ceramics" tableware made for the urban markets. These casseroles are not traditional pieces, and they are not used in La Chamba. The dimensions are 28 cm high and 25 cm in diameter.

water can seep through it. An opening is cut in the front of the shell, and a pitcher is placed inside beneath the filter to catch the water from the filter. These are quite popular in cities.

3. Hen casserole (*la gallina*). This is basically the same as the regular covered casserole, except that the modeled head and tail of the hen take the place of handles. The basic casserole is formed on a small cooking-pot mold, and the modeled elements are added to complete the shape. Although the idea of a chicken-shaped pot comes from Spanish village pottery (Llorens and Corredor-Matheos 1979, 92 and 119), a similar idea can also be seen in precolumbian Tairona pottery (Labbé 1986, 189). (See Photograph 8.1.)

4. Fish platter-bowl (*el pescado*). The origin of the surging-fish platter design is unknown, but it may have been adapted from Chinese models made during the eighteenth century for the Compañía de Indias (Indies Company), which was a semi-autonomous commercial trading company established by the Crown to coordinate trade with the Spanish colonies in the Americas. The fish platter

Photo 8.2. Surging fish platter. This platter was made by Lidia Inés Sandoval, and she captures the motion of the fish surging through the water. The head, fins, and tail of the fish are well modeled, and the surface is burnished to an impeccable satin sheen. It is 15 cm high, 40 cm long, and 20 cm wide.

in La Chamba is similar in shape to the Chinese versions, an example of which is preserved in the Museo de las Américas (Museum of the Americas) in Madrid (inventory number 15.715). Knowledge of the form could have existed in Bogotá and may have been introduced to local potters. To achieve the fish design, the sides of the basic oval platter are raised higher; the head of the fish is modeled on one end and the tail on the other; and fins are modeled on the sides (see Photograph 8.2). The result is a cross between a platter and an oval serving bowl with the head of a fish, a tail fin, and two side fins. The tail fin is raised into the air and in some examples the head of the bowl-platter is also raised, creating the effect of a surging or jumping fish.

These fine ceramics forms are specialty pieces made only on order, and the best ones are not found in the market. Other forms are made in the fine-ceramics style, including some that are invented as experiments. These experimental forms normally disappear, but the ones that find market acceptance are repeated.

Creativity and Design

Although the ceramics of La Chamba represent a traditional craft, the pieces are individually hand-modeled, which leads to innovation and creativity. The introduction of new designs is one of the most interesting aspects of this tradition. Some of the new designs are based on established La Chamba forms, but others are borrowed from elsewhere. Since each ceramist has a line that she produces, the others recognize the individual elements that distinguish her pieces. Two *cazuelas* that are apparently the same to an outsider can be clearly distinguished by the local potters, and usually there is a "signature" in the pattern of modeling that permits identification of the individual makers. Each ceramist is proud of her pieces.

Major design innovations occurred in the 1930s and again in the 1960s and 1970s. The person who had the most important role in the last period of innovation was Ana María Cabezas, the prime mover behind the creation of the idea of fine ceramics and the designer of many of the specific forms. She acted out her leadership in her role as a teacher, developing new ideas for shapes and textures and teaching them to the younger generation of women potters. In keeping with the domestic responsibilities of women potters, the new style of fine ceramics that she helped introduce was handicraft oriented, and it permitted women to retain the traditional technology and work patterns. The primary characteristic of fine ceramics was a change in the quality of the finished pieces, and it represented greater control and attention to finishing details than is true of the more traditional styles in La Chamba.

Cabezas identifies four sources of ideas for the new designs that she has developed over the years.

1. Precolumbian designs. She has seen prehispanic pieces that have been excavated in the area, and they have given her ideas for new forms. *Guaqueros* (illegal excavators of Indian graves) and farmers have given her ceramics of Pijao design that they have found in surrounding rural areas.

2. Visual material. She also gets ideas from books and magazines that feature ceramics. Although she does not copy the pieces that she sees, she does borrow ideas about developing new designs.

3. Dreams and imagination. Sometimes a new design comes to her in a dream, and with that vision she begins to form the new piece. Once she has developed it, she teaches it to others.

4. Research. She uses an empirical process to try out and prove her new ideas, working on the technical and design problems until

the new shape is acceptable. During the period of this research, she was experimenting with various organic materials to evaluate the quality of black each would produce in local reduction. She was not producing ceramics on a regular commercial basis herself at the time. The role of the innovator is a very specific role associated with being a teacher, and the two processes are integrally related for Ana María Cabezas as she develops the new designs and then teaches them to people who are going to be producers.

In fine ceramics, there is a clear understanding that each form is a special design and that there are informal community patent rights over the design. The person who invents a design has the creator's right to it, and it is considered unethical for other people to copy a design without permission. Another ceramist acquires the right to use a design when the creator teaches it to her, but she should always recognize its origin. In the production of both traditional pottery and tableware the proprietary factor does not exist because the forms are considered the common property of the community. These forms are not individually created designs, but rather the cultural heritage of the entire group. Since most ceramists of La Chamba are not innovators, they freely use traditional La Chamba designs and even borrow designs from other ceramics communities.

The changes in La Chamba ceramics during the twentieth century have responded to larger events that affected the community, such as the opening of roads, which facilitated the transportation of goods and increased demand from urban customers. The local leaders of change were the people who first understood the new opportunities for the craft and led other people to them. This pattern of a small number of individuals introducing innovation in traditional pottery communities has been mentioned by researchers in other communities (Duncan 1998, 40; Hendry 1992, 127; Foster 1967, 294).

One overarching element that identifies La Chamba pottery is its long association with food preparation and storage. Its roots are in an indigenous earthenware tradition that was modified by the Spanish introduction of new foods and eating habits. Since the earthenware vessels were similar for both the Spanish and the indigenous inhabitants of the Americas, the synthesis between them was easy, leading to regional versions of mestizo domestic pottery in Colombia today, including La Chamba. It is this cultural history of La Chamba along with its contemporary cultural context that establishes the parameters within which the local potters make decisions about their craft. The cultural continuity with the past in La Chamba has permitted potters to maintain the integrity of the principles of ceramic design inherited from the indigenous traditions of the region.

Authenticity and Income

Crafts were historically made in La Chamba for domestic use and for local trade. However, as crafts have become commodities in recent decades, the economic context in which they are produced has changed to include large-scale contracts, proletarian workstyles, and middlemen. According to Néstor García Canclini (1990, 228), the pressure to meet market demand leaves little time for symbolism and concerns about authenticity in ceramic design for most Latin American potters.

Authenticity of form and technique is a concern for cultural researchers and bourgeois urban buyers, but the subsistence potter is frequently concerned only with what will produce more income. When the economic development specialist tells the potter that "authentic" pots sell better, the potter may adopt that form or procedure in order to increase sales. Income provides the potter's household with food, clothing, and other necessities, a consideration that takes priority over cultural history or accuracy.

Traditional village and indigenous crafts are not disappearing, but they are in the process of transformation into new and more contemporary shapes. In some cases, workers have been recruited to make crafts with mass-production techniques in factories, and professional designers working with development agencies have been contracted to design new, more marketable forms that have the look of traditional crafts. Although many craftspeople, especially women, continue making domestic styles of crafts, increasing numbers of young people look at crafts for their employment and income potential, which frequently means innovations and new styles.

Innovation and Change in La Chamba Ceramics

Although innovation and creativity do occur in village craft ceramics, in La Chamba only a few isolated individuals, such as Ana María Cabezas, are known as innovators. She introduced new forms and new finishing techniques and taught them to many potters. In her research among Mexican village potters (1992, 172), Clare Hendry also found only isolated examples of innovative potters. In Latin American villages people who differentiate themselves from the group can be socially discouraged from their eccentricities. June Nash (1985, 48) and Ruben Reina (1963, 18ff) both reported cases of Mayan potters who were sanctioned socially for making innovations in their ceramics designs. George Foster, working in the rural Mexican community of Tzintzuntzán (1967, 296), found that the potters were less likely to be innovators than people in the general population of the town. He concluded that the lack of technical control over the outcome of firings, such as concerns about cracking, leads potters to be conservative (ibid., 300–301). The habit of conservatism in turn stifles innovation.

Among Pueblo potters Ruth Bunzel (1929, 86–88) noted that only two individuals had introduced significant style changes in the years before her research. It must be mentioned that innovation in Pueblo pottery has increased dramatically since Bunzel's study, and Lydia Wyckoff's (1985, 86ff) study of Hopi potters on the third mesa found that they were equally divided between the traditionalists and the innovators.

La Chamba potters tend to be conservative in retaining both traditional forms and techniques of working, and most are more interested in the technical qualities of their pieces and the efficiency of the production process than in the formal characteristics of their pots. Most village potters mechanically repeat the forms they have learned to make, so that craft becomes a system of hand production without the intention of inventing new forms, altering the techniques, or experimenting. Since any error or change in the composition of a claybody, drying process, or firing procedure can lead to increased losses in the firing, that also means greater economic losses. As Foster suggested (1967, 296), there are functional advantages for village potters to be noninnovative or nonexperimental as they try to avoid losses in their work.

The provincial domestic pottery of La Chamba represents a continuity of design with the indigenous past, while the newer styles identified with the era of capitalist expansion (tableware, fine ceramics, and figures) show European influences. Although the people of the La Chamba area resisted the Spanish presence and influences during the colonial period, the market forces of the twentieth century have brought a more extensive borrowing of European ceramics forms than at any previous time.

Conclusions

While many older artisans in Colombian pottery-making towns, such as La Chamba, continue making provincial country earthenwares, the younger

generations are diversifying into art and industry, as well as fine-craft ap-
proaches to the medium. Young ceramists from village pottery backgrounds
are art potters who have discovered that for carefully executed one-of-a-
kind pieces they receive significantly higher prices, such as for the upscale
version of the common tableware, which is called "fine" ceramics. It sells for
higher prices and is an attractive stylistic change for the younger generation.
Today ceramics represent a diversified and dynamic craft that potters value
for its income potential and that urban customers value as an expression of
cultural memory and national identity.

9

Figurative Ceramics

Art or Commerce

The figurative ceramics made in La Chamba today date from the last few decades, a period during which the urban market for village crafts has expanded. Figures represent an abrupt change from the idea of ceramics as functional vessels to ceramics as an expressive medium. La Chamba figurative ceramics celebrate the concern that is most important to agricultural communities: fertility. La Chamba figures celebrate the abundance of nature by such means as a canoe full of plantains, a bowl filled with fruit, a surging fish, and—the epitome of fertility—the hen. These articles reflect the fertility of the tropical surroundings of La Chamba in the Magdalena River Valley. The new generation of La Chamba potters are the figure makers, and they are known for their skill in modeling. Eduardo Sandoval has emerged out of the generation as the only man to make figures.

Social Change and Figuration

Colombian potters abandoned the prehispanic figurative traditions after the Spanish Conquest because of their iconographic references to belief systems that were prohibited. The art of the feudal elite during the subsequent centuries was largely Christian and was drawn from European art and craft traditions. Polychromed wood was the most popular medium, and indigenous craftsmen in Ecuador and elsewhere learned to make these figures. Ceramic figures were not important during the colonial and Republican periods of Colombian history, and most village potters made functional vessels, not figures. There was no demand for ceramic figures in either regional or national markets, and La Chamba potters apparently did not make them.

The economic expansion since the 1950s has created a market for La Chamba figures. This expansion and the urban demand for decorative ceramics have allowed La Chamba potters to explore figuration as an expressive style for the first time since the Spanish Conquest. They have responded by developing a line of vessel-based figures, especially the hen and the fish, and some stand-alone figures of humans and animals. However, it is interesting that the women potters of La Chamba have made their best figures when they are incorporated into vessels. Few have developed a sculptural style, as has occurred in other Colombian ceramics centers, such as Ráquira (Duncan 1998, 91–107) or Pitalito (Villegas and Villegas 1992, 78–79).

The growth in urban markets for decorative ceramics in recent decades has made it possible for La Chamba potters to begin making figurative pieces, but their work is generally limited to a narrow range of forms that are commercially successful. Urban collectors of art consider La Chamba figure makers to be artisans making craft objects, rather than artists creating sculpture. So the subordinate status of the La Chamba potters within the larger society reemerges in the definition of their figures as craft rather than art.

Ceramics as Art or Craft

In Latin America the distinction between art and craft is frequently based on ethnicity and residence, with art understood to be primarily urban and Eurocentric while crafts are seen as being primarily indigenous or mestizo and rural (García 1990, 224–25). This view contrasts the urbane and cultured artist, who creates one-of-a-kind works in thoughtful isolation, with the craftsperson, whose expression is collective, anonymous, repetitive, and uncreative. In this hierarchy, art has a high social status, and crafts are relegated to the lower social status associated with indigenous and mestizo peoples. If potters make figures with the intention of being expressive and decorative, should theirs be considered a village art or a provincial craft?

Clare Hendry (1992, 2) says that we should not make a sharp distinction between art and craft because both require visual skill in the use of materials and the techniques of a medium. However, she suggests that we can distinguish between the artist's emphasis on the abstract qualities of a piece (that is, history or idea of the form, texture, color, and so forth) and the artisan's emphasis on the concrete, technical qualities of those same aspects. The artisan may work to repeat a form quickly and produce a high volume of pieces, or she may work to control the quality of the craftsmanship in a lower volume of pieces. The craftsperson creates art when he or she uses visual elements, such as shape, texture, or color, to make a piece that challenges the observer esthetically. Art ceramists transform the inert material of clay into a symbol of being and creativity, converting technology and utility into an expression of nonverbal, conceptual values.

Ceramics is an art that is accessible to all members of a society because it has its roots in everyday life and function. Furthermore, its close relationship with daily life has largely determined the visual qualities of ceramics. Philip Rawson (1971, 9) suggests that this connection with ordinary experience gives ceramics its special esthetic interest. Not only is pottery one of the oldest media of visual expression, but the various stages of its evolution have reflected important social, economic, technological, and esthetic aspects of society (Cooper 1981, 7). The making of figures may be an esthetic use of ceramics; however, village potters frequently make figurative ceramics that emphasize narrative intentions more than esthetic ones.

Figurative Ceramics in the Upper Magdalena Region

Figurative pieces were a part of the precolumbian ceramics tradition of the Upper Magdalena region, but until recently the ceramics of the historical era have not included the figure. A dramatic renewal of figurative ceramics occurred in the town of Pitalito in Huila, where the Vargas family developed a distinctive style. This Pitalito (Vargas) style of figure making became important to La Chamba potters because it showed that ceramic figures can be economically successful, and this has stimulated potters of the younger generation to make figurative pieces.

The precedent for the Vargas tradition of making ceramic figures began with Doña Aura Muñoz de Vargas in the 1940s and 1950s. She made figures and nativity scenes in ceramics as a sideline activity, like many other women, but not with the idea of producing them commercially. As a child, her daughter Cecilia learned to make dolls, houses, and other playthings from clay, but she considered them simply as children's toys. However, by the 1960s, when Cecilia Vargas was a young adult, she began making pieces for sale, realizing that there was commercial potential in these childhood objects. By the 1980s she was recognized not only as a successful craftswoman but also as an important artist representing autochthonous small-town and rural values. The demand for her pieces was so strong that she sold her work at prices considerably higher than traditional village ceramics. Her children learned the style and in turn became successful artisans on their own.

The Vargas family is internationally known for making ceramic buses, called *chivas*, and rural house scenes, which narrate life in the region. The national and international success of the Pitalito figures led to a gradual expansion of the Vargas family business to include several workshops now run by the family. Potters in other parts of Colombia and in Ecuador eventually began copying the successful figures, and this has now become an international craft style. These spinoff copies of the Pitalito style have usually been of a lower quality, but they are also less expensive, which has made this popular art form more accessible to a wider range of people.

The Vargas family in Pitalito has played an important role in reviving figurative ceramics in the pottery-making villages of the intermontane valleys of southern Colombia, where the indigenous-mestizo heritage is the strongest. The potters of La Chamba have reacted to the Pitalito success by undertaking their own experiments with figure making. Since they did not have a preexisting style for figures, they borrowed extensively from other ceramics communities in Colombia and elsewhere.

La Chamba Figures

In addition to seeing the success of the Vargas family, La Chamba potters have been stimulated to make figures by competitions organized by various state and national institutions. Potters have responded by portraying elements of their surroundings in ceramics, including domestic animals and fruits, among other figures. One institution that has organized figure-making competitions has been the Museo de Artes y Tradiciones Populares (Museum of Popular Arts and Traditions) in Bogotá. For many years, this museum had an annual competition for nativity scenes, and the museum staff has also encouraged other figurative themes. These competitions, coupled with the existing market for figures, have encouraged a few La Chamba potters to produce figurative ceramics.

Historically, in the mestizo-indigenous villages of Colombia, women have made the domestic pottery for cooking and serving, and men have made figurative ceramics, especially the human figure (Duncan 1998, 92). This holds true in La Chamba, where a man, Eduardo Sandoval, has been a leader in figurative ceramics. He makes nativity sets, scenes of people working, and sculptures of the human figure adapted from well-known Colombian artists. On the other hand, his sister, Lidia Inés Sandoval, is characteristic of women figure makers, modeling figures onto vessels used for food, such as the fish platter. Like some other women potters of her generation, she also makes figures of domestic animals, especially the burro or donkey.

Pitalito *Chivas* and Houses

The buses or *chivas* of the Vargas Pitalito style are painted with
bright enamel colors, and the elaborate designs are similar to those
used on local buses in this part of rural Colombia. Miniature people
are placed on the benches of the bus, and their stalks of bananas,
sacks of oranges, and other goods are piled on top. These *chivas* are
palm-sized pieces, ranging from ten to twenty centimeters long. They
are popular with city dwellers in Colombia and with foreign tourists
and have become a popular export. They can be found in museums
and craft boutiques from Bogotá to New York and Paris. The *chiva* is
used for display in the urban households of Colombia and elswhere,
and its bright colors and display of tropical plenty suggest well-being,
rural tranquility, and occasionally humor.

The real *chivas* are the common form of transportation for
country people in many regions of Colombia. These buses are made
locally, using the motor and chassis of older two-ton trucks, which
have been converted from their earlier uses as farm trucks carrying
cattle, corn, or potatoes to market. Fords from the late 1940s and
1950s are popular, and the ceramic replicas accurately reflect the
make and style of the truck. Usually only the hood and front fenders
of the original truck are intact; the body of the bus is built in wood.
For seats it has a series of rustic wooden benches, and one side of
the bus is left open so people can enter and leave. The roof is a
platform for loading agricultural products and supplies for passengers, and men frequently ride on the top when the regular seats are
filled. These buses are given suggestive, frequently *machista* names,
such as "Yo también fui último modelo" (Once I was the latest
model), "Viejito pero con ganas" (Old but with desires), "Llegó mi
querer" (My loved one arrived) (Calderón 1993, 157), "La Infiel"
(The unfaithful woman), and "La Cansona" (The tiresome woman).
These names are painted on the front bumper of the bus.

Ceramic scenes of households are also made in Pitalito, usually
showing the small, one-room country house with white-washed
walls and thatched roofs typical of the indigenous architecture of
this region. The members of the household are shown in their daily
activities, while chickens peck for food and the pig rests in the shade.
These pieces show the richness of the tropical landscape in the

vegetation and fruits, each of which is individually made in miniature sprig molds. Another popular theme is the canoe filled with fish, tropical fruits, and flowers on the way to market. In visits in 1995 and 1998, we saw new themes in the Pitalito style. One is Noah's Ark with African animals (elephant, giraffe, zebra) intermingled with Colombian animals (parrots, toucan, butterflies). Another is a jetliner with chickens, potatoes, and other goods loaded on top of the wings and fuselage, with passengers waving good-bye out the windows of the plane.

Human Figures

La Chamba potters portray human figures in nativity scenes and in scenes of work in the local village. In recent decades, the nativity scene has become a standard subject in the village-ceramics tradition throughout Colombia. The nativity has not been historically important in village Colombia, and its popularity today among potters responds to its commercial possibilities more than to religious values. For example, a figurative ceramist like Eduardo Sandoval can make eighty to a hundred nativity sets per year to sell during the pre-Christmas season. Figurative ceramists do not produce in high volumes like functional potters, but they sell their pieces for higher per unit prices.

The nativity scenes include the standard set of figures: Joseph, Mary, the Christ child, the three kings, a cow, and a donkey or other domestic animal. The figures are shown regarding the Christ child in worshipful poses; the three kings wear crowns and hold the gifts they have brought to the child. (See Photograph 9.1.) Since these figures are hand-modeled rather than cast, they include details of hair and clothing texture that are not found in the mass-produced nativity figures from other communities, such as Ráquira (Duncan 1998, 102).

La Chamba potters also portray local work scenes, and they draw heavily from the Pitalito style for these figures. This was a genre pioneered by Eduardo Sandoval, and his ceramic figures reflect the river life that he observed daily from his house, located on the river near the Chapetón landing. His father worked the river with rafts and canoes, transporting farm produce from field to market. As a potter, the younger Sandoval narrates that lifestyle in his portrayals of men in canoes transporting loads of plantains or other fruits. (See Photograph 9.2.) He does not give much detail to the face or anatomy of the

Photo 9.1. Nativity scene. The nativity scene is a recent theme in La Chamba ceramics, developed in response to requests from urban buyers. The figures in this nine-piece set are 15 cm tall. All are facing the diminutive Christ child in the center. This is an early example of Eduardo Sandoval's work.

figure, and that has the effect of emphasizing the load of food, which he does represent with careful detail similar to the sprig-molded fruits on the Pitalito buses. His figures are usually small, ranging from 10 to 20 cm tall, and he finishes surfaces with the immaculate detailing that is a signature of his work. He uses only the finest quality of slip, and he burnishes it to a satin sheen.

A few potters have made the figure of the *mohán,* which is the shaman from the Pijao tradition discussed in chapter 2. They portray the *mohán* as a figure in a squatting position smoking a cigar. The static squatting position emphasizes that the shaman uses his or her spiritual powers rather than physical ones, and the smoking of a cigar is associated with the power of nature represented in tobacco. According to the legend, if someone is in a canoe on the river and sees the *mohán* sitting on the river bank, they should not try to approach because they will be caught in a whirlpool, sucked down, and drowned. The story teaches that the spiritual powers of the shaman are great and should be respected by normal humans. The *mohán* became a

Photo 9.2. Canoe with plantains. One of the most common scenes at Chapetón, the river landing in La Chamba, is the arrival of canoes filled with the agricultural produce of the region, ranging from plantains to watermelons. This is an early piece by Eduardo Sandoval, and it shows an interest in fruit that continues in his current work.

subject for figurative ceramics in the 1980s as people explored the precolumbian roots of their culture.

Animal Figures

Women primarily make animal figures, especially the domestic animals that they usually tend, including donkeys, cows, pigs, and chickens among others. These figures represent what people observe around them, but they are also successful in the urban markets. Like the human figures, they are usually small, being under 20 cm in height and length.

Lidia Inés Sandoval and other potters make small donkeys carrying loads, much as they actually do in the community. Sometimes the animals are shown carrying pots, a form that is similar to the Ráquira pony from Boyacá (Duncan 1998, 99–101), suggesting that La Chamba potters may have borrowed the idea from there. The donkey was a Spanish introduction to the Americas, and potters portray it with the Spanish- or Moroccan-style side-carriers, which emphasize its Iberian origin. These carriers are made of wood in an L-shape; the foot of the L is a shelf that supports the load. One is slung on each side of the donkey, and they are tied together with ropes across the animal's back. Pots of water, bunches of plantains, and other heavy loads can be carried that way.

Chickens, more specifically hens, are another popular subject for the ceramic figures made by women, and they may be made as stand-alone figures or as casseroles, which will be discussed below. In fact, many families keep chickens, which are usually left to range freely around the house, so they are common figures in the domestic world of women and children. A popular version of the ceramic hen is a container with miniature pots and baby chicks inside. The top half, which contains the modeling for the head, wings, and tail feathers, can be lifted off, although it is tied to the bottom half with a dried plant fiber. Children love the small pots and baby chicks that they discover hidden inside the hen, so relatives and friends frequently buy these hens as gifts for them. They are in the blackware style and measure approximately 10 cm high.

The pig is another ceramic figure that women potters make, and they may make it purely as a decorative figure or as a piggy bank. In households that have a pig, the women usually feed and care for it, so they also closely observe it. They usually represent the pig as voluminous and round, empha-sizing the idea of fullness, which is an attractive idea in a community where many people live close to the edge economically. One representation of the pig is a sow nursing piglets, a good image because it means prosperity. A woman who has a sow can sell the piglets, and that represents an additional source of income for her household.

Potters also portray some common wild animals in La Chamba figures, including birds and turtles. Some figurative potters have made ceramic doves that are similar to Mexican versions. Water animals are also important since La Chamba is located at the confluence of small waterways and the Magda-lena River. The water animals include fish, turtles, and serpents, with the first being the most popular and the latter two being made only occasionally. Since they are typically made as vessels, the fish will be discussed as vessel-based figures.

Vessel-Based Figures

The best figures esthetically are animal shapes incorporated into vessels, and these are usually hens, fish, or piggy banks. The reason these forms are most common is probably that women deal with these animals daily. They are the family food, and women observe them closely. These figures are based on European, or even Chinese, models, as described in chapter 8.

Potters make the hen casserole by adding a head, wings, and tail feathers to the undecorated round casserole. Skilled modelers incorporate the figurative elements of the hen very well into the casserole, making it one of the best figures produced in La Chamba. (See Photograph 8.1.) Although details like the comb, beak, and eyes are apparent, all of the features are highly stylized. Potters represent the wings as raised feather-like parallel patterns and the tail as a fan with lines representing clumps of feathers. The hen bulges out into the full body of the casserole, which is intended to hold a good volume of food. The back is a lid, and the knob on the lid is commonly represented as a baby chick. The potter makes the bottom half of the casserole from a slab on a hump mold, and the lid is from another slab.

Lidia Inés Sandoval and her mother, María Isabel Valdés, collaborate in making the fish shape from an oblong platter complete with a head, tail, and fins (see Photograph 8.2). After the mother makes the slab and builds up the walls, her daughter models the features of the fish. A wide range of fish forms exists, and the most dynamic are in the form of a surging or jumping fish with its head and tail raised high in a curve. These forms seem to have been made by observers who have watched fish and understand their movements. In contrast, others emphasize the horizontal line with the head and tail on the same plane as the rest of the body, suggesting stillness and inactivity. While some potters make open fish platters, others make enclosed ones with lids. In the latter case, the dorsal fin becomes the knob for the lid.

The piggy bank has become a popular form in recent decades (see frontispiece), not just in La Chamba but also in many other pottery-making communities in Colombia (Duncan 1998, 102). La Chamba piggy banks may be produced in large quantities. First the potter makes the bottom of the body as a pot on a small hump mold like regular pots. When the bottom has firmed up to the leatherhard stage, the potter turns it upside down and places it in a bowl to simplify turning it while she completes the top part with coils. She adds the coils gradually, until the body becomes a closed sphere. After it firms up, she models the ears and snout onto one end and the tail onto the other, and cuts a coin slot into the back of the animal. This process was well documented by Gertrude Litto (1976, 149).

There have been other experiments with vessel-based figures, such as the Indian-motif planters that some people borrowed from Ráquira in the 1970s. This planter was made from the base of a traditional pot and had a small face modeled into the neck area. A featherlike headdress band was modeled around the mouth of the pot, and on the sides were ears decorated with ceramic earrings. This form was popular at that time in the Bogotá market, and a few women tried making it, but they did not have much success. Their planters were more carefully modeled than the mass-produced plaster-mold planters from Ráquira, but since the La Chamba potters hand-built each planter, they could not compete with the Ráquira potters in price. Eventually, they stopped making the Indian-motif planter.

La Chamba potters have borrowed extensively from other ceramics traditions to enrich their figure making. However, that has not been sufficient for them to become as successful with figures as they traditionally have been with vessels. A few people have learned the modeling and conceptual skills to become good figure makers. As creative people frequently do, they have borrowed extensively from other art and craft traditions in Colombia, Mexico, and Europe for their figurative pieces.

Eduardo Sandoval: Craft Meets Art

Eduardo Sandoval is one of the potters responsible for introducing figurative ceramics into La Chamba. He learned to make ceramics with his mother, and as an adolescent he dedicated himself to making figurative shapes. In 1981, after completing high school in El Guamo, he went to the Escuela de Artes de Bogotá (School of Art of Bogotá) to study art and design. After his studies were finished, he remained in Bogotá, which afforded him greater contact with the urban-based markets where he sells his work. His wife is also from a family of ceramists, the Paéz family from Ráquira, the other important traditional ceramics center in Colombia. Sandoval's work has been widely recognized in Colombia, and he has received a number of prizes, including the Medal for Craft Mastery awarded by Artesanías de Colombia in 1990.

Throughout his two decades in Bogotá, he has returned home to obtain the local clay and slip and to bring pieces to fire in his mother's kiln. He explained that he cannot obtain the same results with the materials and kilns available in Bogotá. He packs the dried ceramic pieces very carefully and personally carries them on the 150-kilometer-mile trip to La Chamba for the firing. During the 1980s he also traveled to Italy to observe the ceramics traditions of that country. His art study in Bogotá and travel to Italy are unheard-of experiences in Colombian village craft traditions.

Eduardo Sandoval's early figures were based on village scenes from La Chamba; however, by the 1990s he had begun making compositions based on traditional European still-life forms. In these he uses European images of bowls of fruit, but his compositions overflow with fruits in the baroque style of colonial churches in Colombia. (See Photograph 9.3.) He mixes European and American fruits in a visual metaphor of the tropical richness of the Americas and perhaps more specifically the richness of the Magdalena Valley. These pieces are used as sculptural centerpieces for tables in upscale Bogotá houses.

Sandoval has also been making figurative sculptures that refer to the well-known figures of Colombian painters, including Fernando Botero (nudes and horse-mounted figures) and Ana Mercedes Hoyos (fruit sellers from Cartagena). These figures have been a commercial success, but they also represent the tension between art and craft in his work. His control of the ceramic medium competes with the best of three-dimensional art in Colombia, but he is coming from a craft tradition that makes it difficult for him to enter the world of gallery art. His centerpieces and artist-based figures allow him to combine his interest in sculpture with his craft skills to attain a recognition that goes beyond the usual levels for ceramics in Colombia, and his pieces are sold today in New York and London, among other places.

Sandoval's human figures from the 1980s were relatively small, only 15 cm high, but his sculptural pieces from the 1990s are larger (60 to 70 cm). The still-life centerpieces are 35 to 40 cm high and only slightly smaller in diameter. Sandoval's work is about the esthetics of surface, and his pieces are known for their impeccable finishing, which is a characteristic of La Chamba ceramics. He makes some of these centerpieces as blackware, and is the first potter to make fine ceramics in this color. In the late 1990s he began experimenting with areas of rough unburnished surface on some pieces, creating a contrast with his otherwise highly burnished surfaces.

Eduardo Sandoval's sculptural compositions sell for hundreds of U.S. dollars, prices far removed from the pennies-a-pot pricing of traditional village pottery. Although he continues using La Chamba technical processes, the composition and content of his work is now oriented toward international ideas. He and Cecilia Vargas of Pitalito are rare examples of Colombian craftspeople who have transcended their village craft origins to receive recognition at the national and international levels. Louana Lackey (1982, 147) also describes the international recognition gained by "aberrant innovators" among village potters in Mexico. These examples from Colombia and Mexico show how international crafts markets influence local, domestic

Photo 9.3. Eduardo Sandoval centerpiece. This is a European-style still-life with a mixture of fruits from Europe (apples, pears, and grapes) and Colombia (granadillas and bananas). Although this is a European form, it celebrates the abundance of fruits and vegetation that is characteristic of La Chamba. This piece is 35 cm high and 30 cm in diameter.

craft traditions like La Chamba's. Eduardo Sandoval represents a generation of innovators among whom esthetics dominate crafts concerns, and they give more attention to the visual qualities of their pieces than to production goals.

The Visual Qualities of Figures

Figurative pieces are hand modeled so that each is a one-off piece, meaning that it has individual modeling though it is one of a series of similar pieces. Occasionally a ceramist even makes one-of-a-kind pieces, which are unique in their composition. Since figurative pieces are individually modeled, they sell at higher prices than Provincial-style cooking ware, and they sell quickly, often before they are made. The modeling style in most pieces is rustic, with stylized features and only minimal details. Potters model in eyes, ears, noses, and mouths, but they do not portray them realistically. The overall figure is important but the individual detailing is not, so hands, feet, and even facial features are stylized.

La Chamba figure makers use two surface treatments: the natural clay finish and the burnished surface. Women potters use the natural clay surface when they make stand-alone animal figures, such as pigs, donkeys, and turtles. The naturally occurring temper in the claybody contributes to a gritty surface that expresses the tactile quality of these animals. This surface may even be scraped to emphasize its grittiness. These are among the rare pieces made in La Chamba that are not painted with slip.

The burnished surface is used for all of the vessel-based figures, including hens, fish, and piggy banks, and also for human figures and birds. These pieces are painted with the slip used on fine ceramics, and they are carefully burnished. Since the vessel-based figures in fine ceramics are functional (such as the covered hen casseroles or fish-shaped platters) and may be used as fine tableware in the houses of urban customers, they are given the best finishing possible. This satin luster is characteristic of La Chamba ceramics and identifies them wherever they are sold.

The potters of La Chamba have been successful in modeling figures onto vessel forms, but their attempts to make stand-alone figures are more rustic and generally lack the craft professionalism found in their pots and bowls. Potters have borrowed most of the ideas for stand-alone human and animal figures from other pottery-making communities. That foreignness is reflected in the hesitant and tentative nature of these borrowed figures, and this is particularly true of those made by the older generation. Figures seem to be an alien concept that they have not been able to appropriate. The younger generation of potters has more manual skill in modeling, and they make vessel-based figures with more confidence, giving them a creative integrity appropriate to their cultural imagination.

Art or Commerce

La Chamba potters began making figures during the economic expansion following the 1950s because of the demand for them in urban markets. The vessel-based figures of fine ceramics (especially hens and fish) are consistently compelling in their composition and finishing, and in these pieces La Chamba potters have achieved the union of art and commerce.

Although the artistry of some stand-alone figures is strong enough to receive good reviews internationally, such as the work of Eduardo Sandoval, most figures are not. However, the commercial success of the figure makers has encouraged younger potters in La Chamba to experiment with figurative pieces, leading to another style in La Chamba ceramics.

10

Clay and Beehive Kilns

Indigenous Technologies

Clay, tools, and the kiln constitute the technology of La Chamba ceramic production, and it is almost exclusively of prehispanic origin. It is an inexpensive, nonintrusive technology that has little effect on the normal operation of the household. No machinery is involved, and the work can be done in conjunction with domestic tasks. The work produces little dust, and the cleanup afterwards is easy. One morning the potter mines the clay, then cleans and mixes it by hand, and by the next day she can use it. She does not employ any complex tools or machinery, and there is no long-term storage of raw material or finished products. No significant capital investment is needed, and the basic production processes can be learned by any twelve-or thirteen-year-old.

Raw Materials

Three kinds of clay used in ceramics production are deposited in the soils around La Chamba. One is heavily saturated with red iron oxide and is used as slip (*barniz*) to paint the surface of pots. Another is a highly plastic clay particularly well suited for the coiling process. It is dark gray or black when mined but fires to a beige color. The third type is heavily mixed with sand as a natural temper, and it is an important ingredient to prevent pots from cracking in the fast, direct-flame firings used in La Chamba. The claybody that is normally used for traditional cooking pots is a mixture of one-third plastic clay and two-thirds of the sandy clay. The first clay gives the plasticity and cohesion needed for coiling pots, and the sandy one creates a porous, open body required for pots to survive the thermal shock of the direct-flame cooking process. The body is strong in the green state and will withstand the pressure of the burnishing process with almost no breakage. The claybody used in the fine ceramics of recent years is composed of up to 75 percent plastic clay with the remainder being sandy clay. This mixture gives a more finely textured surface, which facilitates the intense burnishing of the finer pieces.

The sandy clay is taken from the communal, public mine called El Embudo (The Funnel), located in a field at the intersection of the roads leading to El Espinal and El Guamo, with the road to El Espinal running along the eastern edge of it. The surface of the field is pockmarked with holes where potters have been mining clay. The clay deposits are located under 20 or 30 cm of topsoil, and the vein of clay is usually no deeper than one meter. A maze of paths has been worn through the grass to the areas where the clay deposits are the most promising. A potter brings a donkey to carry the clay back home, and she is usually accompanied by a friend or family member. (See Photograph 10.1.)

Plastic clay comes from El Olvido (Forgetfulness), an area of eighteen hectares that is located between Agua Dulce (Sweetwater) Creek and the Magdalena River. The clay from El Olvido has little natural temper and cannot be used alone in functional kitchen ware, but it is used for decorative pieces. The best plastic clay comes from the Rodríguez farm, and the clay

Photo 10.1. Loading clay on a donkey. This potter, assisted by a friend, is loading clay onto a donkey for the trip home. She mined the clay from the hole to the left with the indigenous Andean-style digging stick that can be seen in the hole. She breaks out clumps from the vein of clay and puts them into burlap bags of forty to forty-five kilos each for transport home.

Mining Clay

Two or three times a week, Anatilde Prada de Silva goes to the mine early to dig the clay that she will need for the next few days' work. She normally takes one of her children with her and the donkey to carry the clay back to the house. It takes her twenty minutes to walk to the mine, which is located where the road divides for El Espinal and El Guamo. She begins by removing the shallow topsoil layer with a steel-tipped version of the Andean digging stick (*barretón*) to get to the clay deposits. The *barretón* is the prehispanic digging tool still used by indigenous and mestizo farmers in this region of Colombia. Although mining the clay is a job performed primarily by women, in 35 percent of the households men occasionally help the women by doing the mining.

Anatilde Prada usually goes back to holes where she has found clay recently. During the dry season, the previously dug holes are dry, which make it possible for her to dig in the same place, following a vein of clay. Mining in the rainy season is harder because the existing holes fill with water, the earth becomes heavy, and the clay is slippery and difficult to dig. She places hand-sized chunks of clay into one of the burlap bags brought for that purpose, until two bags are filled with thirty to forty kilos each. While the child controls the donkey, she lifts the sacks onto each side of the animal. By shortly after 8:00 A.M. she is back at the house and ready to begin making bowls.

---

deposits there cover fourteen hectares located on the east and north sides of a curve in the Inga Creek. At one time, three members of the Rodríguez family owned sections of this mining area, and would not give potters permission to mine there. Since the plastic clay is necessary for the claybody, people would go at night to mine the clay without the permission of the owners, giving rise to a continuing conflict. Dean Arnold (1993, 64) described a parallel situation in Quinua, Peru, where stratagems for getting clay from an uncooperative landowner included getting him drunk and then taking the clay while he was not being vigilant. In the mid-1990s, Artesanías de Colombia negotiated the purchase of the Rodríguez land, solving a major problem for the community.

The mined clay contains contaminants such as small stones and roots, and when it is brought home it is spread out to dry, after which the boys of the household pound it with a club on the cement floor of the porch, breaking up the clumps. In the next step, an older son or the mother will pulverize it in a large wooden mortar (*pilón*) until it is reduced to a fine powder. This is the same type of *pilón* used in this region for pounding rice or corn to prepare it for cooking. Once the clay is pulverized, it is passed through a sieve to eliminate stones and other foreign objects, and then it is soaked in an old cooking pot until ready for use.

Slip Clay

Two kinds of slip are used for painting pots, and they are graded according to the intensity of the iron red color they produce. The slip that is considered inferior comes from El Olvido, and it is used only on the less expensive traditional cooking pots. It fires to a pale, opaque iron red, and yellowish stains bleed through it at unexpected places. Since this color irregularity is undesirable, the slip is not prepared carefully, which probably leads to a further decline in its quality.

The fine slip is made from clay that comes from the opposite side of the Magdalena River, in the foothills of the eastern range of the Andes. The people prefer this slip because it fires to a well-saturated, high-value iron red, and the fine particles of the clay permit the perfectly burnished finish required for fine ceramics. This clay is obtained by crossing the Magdalena by canoe and walking a few kilometers to the ridges where the deposits are located, an area that is pock-marked with holes ceramists have made digging out clay. A set fee is paid to the owner of the land for each five-gallon can of clay excavated. Slip clay is pulverized and then soaked in an old cooking pot until it reaches the consistency of cream, and then it is strained to eliminate pebbles, roots, and other foreign matter. La Chamba ceramics are identified by the porous quality of the claybody and the satin quality of the slip-painted surface, so the qualities of the clay itself create much of the identity of this ceramics tradition.

Before the dry clay can be used, it is soaked in old cooking pots for a couple of days, and it is well mixed to make sure that it has an even consistency. One cooking pot of clay can provide enough clay for a day of work for a maker of *cazuelas*. When the clay is ready, the potter takes it from the pot to dry and then wedges, or kneads, it on the ground with dry powdered clay until it reaches the consistency of dry bread dough. After wedging, the clay is ready for use. Since bowls and the bases of pots are made with slabs, the clay does not require much plasticity, and the clay is sufficiently plastic for the coiling process used in La Chamba.

Tools

In addition to the hump mold, which is usually a pot or bowl turned upside down, the tools of ceramics making in La Chamba include a polishing stone, a gourd scraper, a trimming (that is, fettling) knife, saggars (pots that contain smaller pieces for the firing), and the kiln, each of which is made locally. Traditionally, polishing stones were well-rounded river stones, but today many people use tumbled semiprecious stones bought at fairs. These highly valued stones are kept in a special box so that they are not misplaced or lost, and disputes may arise over a favorite stone that cannot be found. The polishing side of these stones may be concave or convex according to the surfaces on which they will be used. A normal table knife is used as a fettling knife, and gourd (*calabazo* or *totuma*) scrapers are used to smooth the surface of a pot. Ten of these scrapers can be made from a medium-sized gourd, and a boy will make them for the equivalent of fifty U.S. cents. Scrapers are also made from pieces of plastic found around the house, and dried corncobs may also be used to smooth out rough places on the wet or leather-hard surface of a pot. Ninety-nine percent of the potters in the Department of Tolima report working with the same manual techniques used in La Chamba (Artesanías de Colombia 1998, 92–93).

The History of the La Chamba Kiln

The kiln used in La Chamba at first appears to be unique because it does not have a separate firebox. This is explained by its derivation from the traditional beehive-shaped bread-baking oven found in this area of Colombia. That oven was originally introduced into Colombia by the Spanish, who in turn borrowed it from the Muslims. Baking-shell ovens were used in the Middle East at least in the first millennium B.C. A fire at the bottom was the source of heat, and there was an open draft hole in the top of the shell. These shell ovens are still used today to bake flatbread in various parts of the Muslim world. A downdraft version was made in the countries of northern Africa, in which the top hole was enclosed and bread was introduced through an opening at floor level. It was this version, called the *horno arabe* in Spain (Lister and Lister 1987, 54), that was brought to Colombia. It is used for baking bread throughout the Americas, from the Pueblo Indians in the U.S. Southwest to the Andean countries of South America. In La Chamba it was adapted for firing ceramics.

For making ceramics, Spanish potters adapted the beehive shape to the Mediterranean kiln, with the firebox located directly under the ware chamber. That kiln was adopted by potters in the Department of Boyacá, where the Spanish presence was more influential during the colonial period (Duncan 1998, 176–77). In contrast, the potters of La Chamba borrowed only the idea of the shell of the kiln without the firebox. So the potters of La Chamba essentially use the bread-oven version to fire ceramics, a process that is more closely related to the indigenous open-air firing.

Similar beehive kilns are used throughout this region (Litto 1976, 146 and 155), but in La Chamba the shape of the bread kiln was enlarged for the firing of ceramics. Some households have a second, smaller kiln for baking bread that resembles the ceramics kiln, and both may even be placed side by side.

The Architecture of the La Chamba Kiln

The La Chamba kiln appears to be a giant cooking pot turned upside down (see Figure 10.1). By European and Asian standards, it is technically not a ceramics kiln because it does not have a firebox or chimney and the door is not closed. It is a downdraft kiln, in which heat rises to the dome and flows back down to escape out the crawl door and the two exhaust holes placed on each side of the kiln. This firing process uses relatively little fuel, is quite rapid (needing as little as two hours), and is well adjusted to the high-thermal-shock claybody and the absence of glazes characteristic of La Chamba ceramics. It is inexpensive and efficient, and as such is a good example of low-tech, appropriate technology.

This kiln permits the people of La Chamba to continue a precolumbian style of firing that is well adapted to their needs. In that style, firing was done by forming a mound of pottery and wood, which was loosely covered with large pottery shards to enclose the heat. The bread-oven-type shell kiln of today replaces the pottery shards of the precolumbian firing. In fact, it is more of a heat-containing shell than a true ceramics kiln. The interior diameter of the kiln is usually about two meters, and the height at the center of the peaked dome is just under two meters, which gives a large kiln of almost six cubic meters. However, the practice of loading with saggars does not permit all of the space to be used because pieces cannot easily be stacked in the upper part of the kiln, so the effective loading space is closer to five cubic meters.

The kiln described by Louana Lackey (1982, 114) for Acatlán, Mexico, seems to be another adaptation that follows the same principles as the La Chamba kiln, except that it is not enclosed at the top. It is a circular wall,

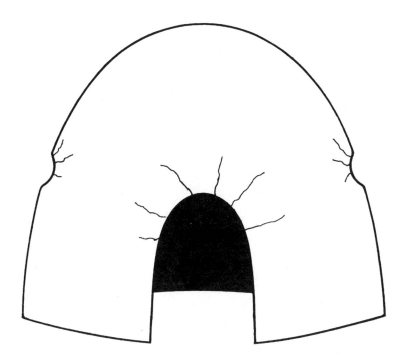

Figure 10.1. La Chamba kiln. This sketch depicts a shell kiln without a firebox. A normal-sized one is 2.25 meters in diameter and 1.75 meters high. The crawl door is 60 to 70 cm wide and 85 cm high. Exhaust holes of 15 cm are placed on each side of the kiln at about the height of the door.

about waist high, that contains the pottery to be fired. Wood for the firing is placed on the ground in the bottom of this "ring kiln" and covered by a layer of shards of broken pots; then the pieces to be fired are placed on top until the stack of pieces is 50 to 70 cm higher than the kiln wall. The top of the pile is covered with two layers of broken pot shards to enclose it and retain the heat. Like the La Chamba kiln, this forms a shell that retains heat in a firing procedure similar to the prehispanic-indigenous open-air firings.

In contrast, the Mediterranean-style Spanish kiln, which is used in Boyacá, the Southern Highlands, and the Cauca Valley of Colombia, requires two days for each firing and an estimated 200 to 300 percent increase in fuel, and it only gives a 25 percent increase in temperature. Although the Mediterranean-style kiln does improve the retention of heat and temperature control, this is of no advantage for the unglazed, heavily tempered ceramics from La Chamba.

Building the Kiln

Although many people know how to build kilns, some are recognized as more skillful than others. Kiln makers are men, primarily because they carry out all major construction projects, and the kiln is built with an adobe technique similar to that used in making bread ovens and houses. Ernesto Habiles built many of the kilns in use in recent years. They are usually built on a slightly higher point in the ground to insure that water drains away, keeping the kiln floor dry.

First a bamboo frame is built in the shape of the kiln, and adobe walls 25 to 30 cm thick are laid in over it. The adobe walls are heavily tempered with sand, and organic fillers like straw are also intermixed. A crawl door, approximately 70 cm wide and 1 meter high, is left in the front wall, and draft holes, which are 15 cm in diameter, are made on opposite sides of the kiln halfway up the wall. Once the wall is complete, the surface is smoothed over with soft clay to produce a seal. Cracks that develop in the walls over the years are resealed with a similar adobe-clay mixture. After the walls have dried sufficiently, a fire is built inside the kiln to burn away the bamboo frame and harden the walls. Subsequent firings complete the curing and hardening of the kiln, which has a life expectancy of ten to fifteen years and may last longer. The materials to build this kiln can all be obtained locally and cost approximately sixty U.S. dollars.

Kiln Demographics

There are sixty-two kilns in the village, and each is the focal point of a family or neighborhood network of potters. There is approximately one kiln for every two houses, and an average of three ceramists share each kiln. However, in reality there tend to be three distinct patterns of kiln use in the community. One is the nuclear-family kiln, primarily used to fire the production of one woman and perhaps that of her daughter. The second pattern is the extended-family kiln, shared by the women of the matrilocal family network and maybe used by four or five women. Before running water was introduced into the community, open wells were the focal point around which the extended family network was organized, but now kiln sharing seems to be the most important focal point for the extended family. Eighty-four (74 percent) of the potters fire their work in their own personal kiln or the kiln of an extended-family member or neighbor.

A small third group (9 percent) does not have a kiln nor access to a kiln belonging to the extended family. These tend to be young women who have not yet established working relationships, and they have to rent or borrow a kiln from a neighbor or take their ware to Artesanías de Colombia to fire. Another group (15 percent) of mostly older women sell their work unfired to a local middleman, usually because they are unable to fire the work themselves.

Firing the Kiln

Firings are normally done on Saturdays because the middlemen arrive on Sunday to pick up orders. In preparation for a firing the potter brings her pieces from her house to the kiln, and children help carry them. (See Photograph 10.2.) *Cazuelas* and other small pieces are placed inside of saggars for the firing, and they are lined up by kiln loads. (See Photograph 10.3.) The saggars (*canastas* or *moyones*) look like large cooking pots.

The first ten saggars are placed on the floor of the kiln in four rows, making a 2–3–3–2 pattern that conforms to the round shape of the kiln. A second level of saggars is placed on top of the first level, and the loader tries to place them in such a way as to receive the flame rising from the floor of the kiln. In some

Photo 10.2. Carrying *cazuelas* to be fired. A firing is in progress in the Prada family compound. In the center a nephew carries *cazuelas* to be fired. On the left, local reduction is being done in the smoking saggars from the last firing.

Photo 10.3. Loading *cazuelas* in saggars. The *cazuelas* and other small pieces are placed in saggars for firing. Firewood for the kiln leans against the wooden building behind the potter, and a daughter is bringing more pieces. Wire handles are inserted through holes in the saggar walls to facilitate pulling the hot saggars out of the kiln at the end of the firing.

Photo 10.4. Loading the kiln. For the first firing of the day, one person loads the kiln from the inside as a helper brings pieces to the entrance. All the pieces on the ground level next to the fire are placed in saggars for protection, including cooking pots and *cazuelas*. Large pieces are placed without saggars on the second level. Firewood lies on the ground to the left of the kiln.

Photo 10.5. The firing. Saggars or cooking pots, depending on the kind of ware made by the potter, are stacked on top of each other in the kiln, with the heavier saggars on the bottom. Spaces for the firewood are left between the saggars or pots. The door stays open during the firing.

cases the kiln load may include up to eighteen or twenty saggars. Larger saggars (50 cm in diameter) are used if a man is loading the kiln. However, if a woman has to load the kiln herself, she uses smaller ones (40 cm in diameter). While the larger saggar holds twenty-four *cazuelas,* the smaller size holds eighteen. In some cases a mother and daughter may combine their work in one firing, so that a load of tableware in saggars may be placed on the first level, and cooking pots are stacked on top of them to form the second level.

The firing requires the collaboration of at least two or three people, preferably two who load and unload the kiln, and one who organizes the pots into groups for cooling. The strongest, usually a man, places the pots or the saggars in the kiln and takes them out at the end of the firing. (See Photograph 10.4.) The second person may assist the first one in lifting the heavy saggars into the desired position in the kiln and later in removing them.

Traditional cooking pots are too large to be placed in saggars, so when they are fired the first layer is placed directly on the floor of the kiln, and other layers are stacked on top. Since these pieces lie directly in the fire, they heat up quickly, creating a danger of cracking. (See Photograph 10.5.) Gusts of wind can also blow in the open door of the kiln, suddenly cooling one side of the hot pots near the door, another cause of cracking, but the heavily tempered claybody helps to control this problem.

Photo 10.6. Unloading hot saggars. Once the kiln is hot, loading and unloading are done outside the kiln by men using long poles.

The first firing of the day lasts about three hours and normally starts early in the morning, after the chill of dawn has passed. People prefer to do two or three firings in one day, ending by mid-afternoon, but during rush periods they may do additional firings, completing the last one after dark. Once the kiln is hot, the subsequent firings can be completed in two hours. A potter who has to borrow a kiln might have to fire on Friday if it will be used by the owner on Saturday.

Once the kiln is hot, all movement of the saggars in and out of it is done with wooden poles called *palancas,* which are 3 or 4 meters long and 5 to 7 cm in diameter. (See Photograph 10.6.) A steel-tipped pole, called a *garabato,* has a hook to catch the edge of the saggars, and it facilitates pulling them out of the hot kiln. Sometimes loop handles, which are perfect for the *garabato,* are made by drilling two sets of holes in the neck of the saggar and running a heavy wire between them. Cracks in saggars are also repaired by drilling holes along each side of the crack and wiring it together. A bucket of water is kept near the door of the kiln to moisten the poles so they will not burn while the hot saggars are being removed. If a pole begins to smoke, it is immediately plunged into the bucket of water.

When the slip-painted pots and bowls reach a deep plum-red color, called

Firing the Kiln

On Saturday morning Don Roberto fires Doña Julia's pots in their kiln, located on the edge of a hill overlooking the Magdalena River. Scattered around are shards from earlier firings, testifying to the fact that pieces do not always survive. He has to do two or three firings during the day to fire the production of the week. Doña Julia helps him, but as the man he is responsible for the heavy lifting and for managing the fire itself. He uses a long pole to place the pots in rows inside the kiln. Doña Julia brings the pots and places them around the mouth of the kiln as he continues the loading. Later, wood is placed between each row of pots for the firing. A second layer of pots is placed on top of the first layer, and finally a third layer completes the loading. The pots are stacked as far up as he can reach inside the kiln.

Long poles of wood the length of the diameter of the kiln are placed between the rows of pots, and the fire is started. Don Roberto will add wood little by little to build up the flame over the next two hours. During this time he never leaves the kiln for more than a few minutes, and during the later stages of the firing he cannot leave at all. Doña Julia spends most of the time in the nearby kitchen, but she comes over periodically to check on the progress. He watches and controls the fire through the door of the kiln, which is never closed. After about two hours, when the pots have acquired the right dull red color, Don Roberto lets the fire burn down. As the open flame dies out, he begins to remove the pots, dragging them to a cooling area. As soon as the kiln is empty, he will fill it with the next load of pots and repeat the process.

After the firing is complete, the pots will be stacked along the back of the house, waiting to be picked up by the intermediary who ordered them. During a productive period, the wall of pots next to the house can be head high and ten meters long. The bright red of the new earthenware contrasts with the whitewash of the wall to make a scene of color fields that would make an abstract expressionist painter happy. The newly fired pots have a deep red iron color and satin-smooth texture, but in more practical terms the pots are important to the potters because they represent the income that the family will have until the next production cycle is completed.

rojo transparente, it is time to take out the pieces. As the strongest person lifts and drags the hot saggars out of the kiln, the second person picks them up with a shorter, 2 meter pole and carries them a few feet away to cool. This pole is also sheathed in metal. This is a hot and uncomfortable job, especially for the two people working at the mouth of the kiln, where the temperature can rise to fifty degrees centigrade and more. Some people wear hats, long-sleeved shirts, and towels or scarves around the neck to protect themselves from the heat, but others use no such protection. When the person working in the mouth of the kiln gets too hot, they move away and cool down before continuing.

Medium density wood is used to fire the ceramics, and it is placed on the floor of the kiln in the open areas between the saggars. These areas are called the *calles* or streets, as if the saggars were buildings. In the past, men in the family gathered and prepared the wood for firing, but increasingly women buy it ready to use from specialized wood suppliers. Wood is bought in bundles of ten to twelve poles, each approximately 3 meters long and 5 to 7 cm in diameter. The small diameter of the poles permits them to burn quickly, which heats the kiln faster. Four bundles are used in a normal two-hour firing, and the fire has to be stoked by the addition of wood throughout the firing. Temperatures at the height of the firing range between 700 and 800 degrees centigrade, according to tests made with Orton cones during our research. However, Lawrence Kruckman and Michael Milligan (1978, 58) measured firings over 800 degrees centigrade in their research in La Chamba.

People determine when the firing is complete by the color of the pots in the kiln, the amount of wood used, and the time elapsed. Since the La Chamba kiln is not an enclosed, sealed kiln, the color of the fire cannot be read the same way that it is in European or Asian-style kilns. When the people decide that the pots have reached their proper temperature, they let the fire die down to coals before unloading the kiln.

Oxidation or Reduction

Oxidation and reduction refer to the amount of oxygen present in the firing and cooling of ceramics. Oxidation means that there is a free flow of oxygen in both stages, and reduction refers to oxygen deprivation in one of the stages. La Chamba ceramics are fired in oxidation. In fact, neither the kiln door nor the draft (flue) holes are closed during the firing, which allows a free flow of oxygen for the fire. However, post-firing reduction is used in La Chamba, and this is done by pouring flammable organic material (dried pulverized donkey dung) over the hot pots inside a saggar after it is pulled from the kiln. The dried dung bursts into flame, and the saggar is quickly covered to starve the fire of oxygen. To complete combustion the fire is forced to suck oxygen from the slip surface of the ceramics, altering that layer and turning it ebony black. When the firing is finished and the saggars are pulled from the kiln, those intended for oxidation are grouped together on one side of the kiln and left to cool freely in the open air, and they will be the typical La Chamba iron-red color. Saggars that have pieces intended for reduction are taken to another side of the kiln. A couple of gallons of donkey dung are dumped inside the saggar and quickly spread around the pots with a stick, and the saggar is immediately covered with a piece of sheet metal to seal the fire inside. Smoke billows out of the saggar under the metal lid, and by the time the kiln is empty the fifteen or so smoking saggars make it impossible to approach the reduction area.

A flame licking out under the cover of the saggar means that oxygen is leaking in, and it must be put out immediately or the reduction will not be complete. That would produce pieces with a crazy-quilt pattern of reddish and blackish spots with no clear color definition. The person in charge of this part must watch each saggar, and if a flame appears it is quickly smothered with more dung or with leaves. Each saggar is left covered twenty minutes or longer to complete the reduction process.

Humoral Theory, Clay, and Firings

Health for both men and women in La Chamba is understood in terms of a balance in the humoral (or hot and cold) elements of life. It is important not to have sharp contrasts of "hot" and "cold" elements, which can lead to health problems. The humoral theory of illness and health was developed by Hippocrates, who suggested that matter itself was composed of four essences: heat, cold, wetness, and dryness. This system has been adapted to many different cultural contexts, and the definition of "hotness" and "coldness" depends on the particular cultural classification used (Mathews 1983, 841). In his explanation of humoral theory, George Foster (1988, 121) indicates that health is equated with body temperature balance, and illness results from imbalances caused by "hot" or "cold" experiences. Although humoral theory was originally a Mediterranean concept, it meshes well with indigenous concepts in the Americas of "humors" that affect health and well-being. It is common in rural Colombia (Duncan 1998, 64).

Humoral theory also has gender connotations in La Chamba, with women being "cold" and men being "hot." Women mix the moist clay and work with it to make pots, both of which are considered "cold" experiences because they involve contact with the damp, cool clay. I suggest that one of the reasons men rarely make pots is the belief that this "cold" activity may drain their heat, or maleness. Small boys do work with clay in some instances, but after they become sexually mature at adolescence almost no males do.

In contrast, men are expected to fire the kilns, which is the "hot" experience in ceramics making. Even if men and women are doing the firing together, men will do the hot work in the mouth of the kiln, loading and unloading saggars. Although it is more logical for men to handle the heavy saggars because of their strength, it is also thought that the heat affects them less because of their "hot" nature. Excessive heat is thought to be more dangerous for women, especially during their menstruation, and some people believe that the heat of the kiln can make young women infertile, so many younger women avoid it as a health precaution. Although men are usually the ones exposed to the most intense heat, it is usually women who do reduction, a task that involves substantial smoke inhalation and can be equally unpleasant.

Individuals of both genders must avoid cold or cool experiences on the firing day. They cannot bathe, or get caught in the rain, or stand in the wind. After experiencing the intense heat of the kiln, the body and the spirit must cool down slowly and naturally because sudden exposure to a cold experience could make a person sick. After the firing people will stay close to the house and give their body time to recover from the extreme heat.

The heat of the kiln and the smoke from the reduction process are intensely physical experiences, and both make the firing an unpleasant and potentially unhealthy task. Usually, the arduous work is ameliorated by the company of friends or family members, who come to watch and talk while the firing is going on. The firing is one of the most important moments of male-female collaboration in the community, and the men relieve the difficult work of the heat and the lifting by making gibes that have sexual overtones, comparing the poles to their own sexual organs and the pots to the women. The women counter by disparaging the men's strength and virility, turning their collaboration into a theater of social relations and gender commentary.

Gender and the Kiln

La Chamba women repeatedly asserted that the firing is a man's job, and most women explain the need for a man to assist with the firing in terms of the greater strength needed to load and unload the heavy saggars from the kiln. However, the census made for this study revealed that husbands do the firing in only 46 percent of the households. Observation in the community suggests that teenage sons, most of whom are no stronger than their mothers, are frequently the "men" who help with the firing. If there is no male in the household who can or will help, the woman may hire a man to do the firing for her.

Who fires the kiln is an indication of the gender roles within a household. In nuclear-family households where there is a strong male presence, the husband tends to take responsibility for firing the kiln. However, in matrifocal house complexes where men have more marginal roles, women are more involved in the firing. In matrifocal households, especially those without a male head of household, a brother or older son usually performs the man's role in firing.

The Prehispanic Origin of La Chamba Technology

The prehispanic-indigenous technology used by the women of La Chamba is similar to that used throughout the Americas in indigenous pottery communities. Hand modeling and coiling are the primary production techniques, and they are well adapted to the requirements of household production, entailing minimal investment and space requirements, and flexibility in the number of forms made. With these techniques a potter can make cooking pots, water storage jars, water bottles, serving bowls, and many other shapes, although most women working in a traditional workshop limit themselves to just two or three forms. The flexibility of the modeling and coiling system is important in allowing potters to keep up with the shifting demands of the buyers. The part-time potter can adapt her production to the specific forms needed in the market at any given moment, and she can easily fire these traditional pots in inexpensive open-air firings. The major limitation of this system is its low productivity, which means low returns for the potter.

The prehispanic-indigenous techniques used by the women in La Chamba include the following:

1. The turntable plate. Placing the pottery on a bowl or broken pot shard to turn it while coils are being added is common in indigenous communities in the Americas, from Mexico (Lackey 1982, 65) to Peru (Litto 1976, 29). This "turntable" is rotated by hand or foot while the potter is adding coils or finishing the surface. Since La Chamba women work sitting on the floor, some are quite dexterous, using their toes to turn the pot while they work on it.

2. Coiling. Making pots by hand coiling is the most important technique in La Chamba, and it is a common prehispanic-indigenous practice.

3. The slab and coil technique of pot construction. The base of pots, especially larger ones, is made from a slab, and the top section is completed by coiling. This combination of techniques is also described for Acatlán, Mexico, by Lackey (1982, 78) and for Atzompa, Mexico, by Clare Hendry (1992, 66), both mestizo-indigenous communities like La Chamba that use techniques of indigenous origin.

4. Use of ceramic molds. At least parts of most La Chamba vessels are made on ceramic hump molds following precolumbian practices, but European-style plaster molds made in vertical halves are not used. Lackey (1982, 66–68) described the use of similar ceramic molds in Acatlán.

5. Slip decoration. Decoration with slip is a prehispanic technique that was used in the region of La Chamba by the Pijaos (Rojas de Perdomo 1985, 214).

6. Open-air firing. Prehispanic and indigenous potters have traditionally done open-air firings, and the La Chamba style of firing is an adaptation of this process. The La Chamba kiln is more of a shell in which to fire the works than a true kiln. Wood is laid directly around the pieces to be fired, as it is done in open-air firings. But instead of covering the mound of pots to be fired with broken pot shards, in the indigenous manner, La Chamba potters have adapted the Spanish bread oven to enclose the heat of their open-air-style firing.

7. Use of the *barretón*. An indigenous Andean-style digging stick is

used to excavate the clay. The *barretón* today has a metal tip which facilitates its use.

8. Working on the ground. In the indigenous style, the potter works seated on the ground, in contrast to the Spanish practice of working at a table. No La Chamba potter was observed seated at a European-style table; however, some potters did work while sitting on indigenous-style, ground-level stools (approximately 15 cm high) with work platforms or tables at the same height. These ground-level wooden platforms are essentially smooth surfaces on which the work can be contained and organized. That La Chamba potters work exclusively with techniques of indigenous origin indicates the prehispanic roots of this tradition.

La Chamba Ceramics and Its Future

The ceramics of La Chamba represent a body of work that is unified in terms of technique, form, and social organization. The technical aspects of ceramics production conform to the prehispanic-indigenous style, and it is a simple household production system that relies on the collaboration of the extended family. The use of the slab and mold technique, coils, modeling, and slip decoration, and the style of firing all indicate the precolumbian origins of this ceramics tradition. The women potters of La Chamba have maintained a system that is well integrated with their esthetic values and household lifestyle. They use traditional craft procedures and technology, which makes them purists and traditionalists in method. Even as they expanded production to meet market demands during the last half of the twentieth century, they retained the indigenous working techniques that characterize Tolima ceramics.

I I

La Chamba Women and Craft Capitalism

La Chamba ceramics are commodity goods within the market system of today's global capitalism. Global markets for traditional crafts feed the tourism industries, both national and international, and the boutiques of exotic objects that may be found throughout the world's urban centers. International networks of craft capitalism contract the work to be done by craftspeople in remote villages, and then resell it to urban customers and tourists looking for cultural traditions or exotica. The unregulated nature of this market system has favored the merchants and middlemen and has led to the economic exploitation of vulnerable women and children.

In Latin America women are frequently the people who make the crafts, and their position is at the bottom of the subcontracting chains that characterize this branch of capitalism. In La Chamba gender ideology limits women to home-based work and constrains them from competing freely in craft capitalism. These constraints inhibit them from traveling to better-paying markets, from investing in technology that would increase their productivity, and from becoming full-time capitalist entrepreneurs. The only economic option for most women is to work as poorly paid craft potters and to augment their production through the unpaid work of their children and older relatives. Their culturally driven definition of themselves as mothers and wives is contrary to the demands of the unregulated free-market system, and their low, castelike status reinforces their gender vulnerability within that system.

Ceramics as Domestic Economy

The primary value of craft work for the women potters of La Chamba is not to make a profit but to provide for the needs of household members. Women work toward strengthening the family and contributing to its status within the community. That economic logic leads home-based women workers to work for less than the legally established minimum wage in order to provide for household needs. Since a woman's income from ceramics usually supplements her husband's income as a day laborer in agriculture, women do not have to maximize their earnings. Their marginal earnings lead to negligible capital formation and little surplus income with which to invest in technology and increase productivity. As a result, there is little economic differentiation between one household and another in the community.

The women of La Chamba regard making pottery as another nurturing role, like preparing meals and washing clothes. Nola Reinhardt (1988, 19) described this orientation as "subsistence household production" in her study of small farmers in Colombia. In our household survey, the young potters expressed their objections to the hard work and the poverty associated with ceramics, but if they do not make ceramics, they have to move away from home to find work. Since that leads to social displacement and separation from the family, it is not an acceptable option to many, so they remain in the community and endure the hard work and low pay associated with their craft.

Studies of home-based industries in Colombia (Gladden 1992 and 1993), the Americas (Benería and Roldán 1987), and other parts of the world (Standing 1989) have focused on the economic exploitation that frequently accompanies this type of work. The piecework produced by women working at home usually earns less than the already low minimum wages of these countries. In craft capitalism, the added value on the final sale goes primarily to the professional people in marketing and distribution, producing inequities in the profits between the craftspeople and the final sellers.

The markup on a pot sold in Bogotá can be two to four times the price paid to the potter. For example, a ceramist in La Chamba may receive $1.00 U.S. for a pot that will be resold in Bogotá for $3.00 to $4.00 U.S. And when the same pot goes out of Colombia to a northern-hemisphere country, the disparities are even more pronounced. In the 1990s, prices of La Chamba ceramics sold in New York City ranged from twenty-five to fifty times the price of the same piece in the community. By the late 1990s La Chamba ceramics could be ordered over the Internet from suppliers in the United States at twenty times the average amount received by potters for making similar pieces. The low compensation of potters is complicated by the fact that they are also required to absorb all of the capital costs of production.

In a worker-friendly economy, workers can expect their income to cover the cost of their labor (at least a minimum wage) as well as the costs of production. However, the home-based potters of La Chamba provide the complete infrastructure of production (the workshop, molds, tools, and kilns) and the raw materials in addition to their labor, and they still earn less than the minimum wage. They work in their houses, which they do not consider a capital expense, and the costs of their tools and kilns are low enough that they are not calculated either. So in this home-based economic system, women absorb all of the costs of production, which passes that expense from the owners of capital to the workers without compensation.

Colombia has its own system of subcontracting craft work at unreasonably low prices, which follows the global restructuring of the international economic system. Women in La Chamba are affected by this process because the subcontracting chains—specifically, the middlemen and urban retailers—pay them the lowest prices possible in order to improve their own earnings. The resellers of La Chamba ceramics can protect themselves from the low prices of pottery by increasing the volume that they buy and resell. However, as the producers of ceramics, women cannot so easily expand the volume of their production because of the limits of their technology, their lack of capital, and their dual status as potters and homemakers. The household obligations implicit in their gender role also constrict their ability to work with the dedication and profitability comparable to that of men. Gender roles combined with the economics of home-based contracting relegate these women potters to the lowest levels of income in Colombia.

Family and Household Economic Theory

Stephen Gudeman (1978, 1986, 1992b, 1998), Gudeman and Alberto Rivera (1990), and Alexander Chayanov (1966) have described the rural household as an economic unit in which people make decisions that are not necessarily market oriented. Gudeman and Rivera (1990, 2) suggest that people working in the rural family economy of Colombia understand that their livelihood comes from the earth, given by Providence. The house is the center of the material culture and a metaphor of the household economy. The successful household economy is one that has something left over after the required expenditures. The household as an economic unit is not intended to create profit but rather to create savings, in contrast to corporate production, which is intended to generate surplus income. In the household economy people save the excess income over expenditure, while in the corporate economy people invest it (Gudeman 1992b, 144–45).

In a related line of analysis based on studies with Russian peasant farmers, Chayanov argues that economic decisions are directed to produce a livelihood for the household rather than to generate profit or capital. According to his analysis, traditional rural economic behavior is oriented toward subsistence on a self-replicating family farm. He suggests that people in the peasant household economy will exploit themselves to maintain a subsistence living, working for less than minimum wage. During times of shortage, the people of a household increase their workloads to achieve subsistence (1966, 113–15), but in times of plenty they do not maintain the increased workloads in order to create profits or capitalization.

Women potters have a critical role in the household economies of La Chamba, and their economic decisions tend to follow the theories of Gudeman and Chayanov. Their economic strategy is to make minimal investments in their production and save their earnings for household needs. They do not make expenditures in infrastructure or equipment, which they see as taking resources away from the family. Through household-based production, they add to the family income by using the interludes of time that they have between domestic tasks and by using the labor of their children. They also see the education of their children as ultimately the only way to produce economic progress and improve the status of the family.

In a study of women weavers in Guatemala, Tracy Ehlers (1990, 161) documented a similar pattern of economic decision making. However, when women did attempt to achieve economic growth by commercializing their craft, they were limited by two factors. First, women were undercapitalized, and to expand their production, they had to rely on the unpaid labor of family members, especially daughters and daughters-in-law. In contrast to men, they did not have access to capital-intensive technology to expand production. Secondly, women worked in internal markets and had little access to external markets, which men controlled through investing in transportation. As a result, the Guatemalan weavers were forced to rely on the household economic model, based on the efficiencies of the domestic economy. Having little opportunity to expand the economic scope of their production is a problem that commonly limits the work of Latin American craftswomen.

The Logic of Income Calculation

The economic logic of the women of La Chamba is to develop social capital by supporting the family; it does not include accumulating capital in the form of money. Since the household is tied together in work and poverty, each person is critically needed for what they can contribute to the family subsistence. Annis (1987, 60–61) describes this approach to household economics among Guatemalan small farmers and weavers as the binding together of the family in its poverty. There is rarely an opportunity to accumulate a surplus for a "rainy day." La Chamba women increase their income-producing work as the number of dependents in the family (children or older relatives) increases or as the level of the husband's income decreases. Inversely, if a woman lives in a small household or has a husband with a good income, she engages in less income-producing work.

Karin Tice (1995, 172) also found among Kuna women *mola* makers that their incomes negatively correlated with the incomes of their male partners. Among the Kuna the "household maintenance strategies" of women depended on whether they had to produce cash income for food purchases. If their husbands provided the food, the women made fewer *molas* (cloth panels made with complexly sewn patterns), but if the husbands did not provide food, the women increased their production to generate additional income. In La Chamba, women follow similar strategies for maintaining the household, increasing or decreasing their ceramics production according to how much income is required for household needs.

June Nash (1985, 57) and Sheldon Annis (1987, 128) also found with Mayan craftswomen that their motivation to work was based on the income needs of the household, not on a desire for money as capital. Scott Cook (1990, 114) found among Mexican home-based craftswomen that they understood their work as an extension of household activities. Rather than "working" (*trabajando*), they were "helping out" (*ayudando*) the household. They saw their work as bringing in cash for the family, but they did not think in terms of profits.

Women potters making ceramics within their domestic cycle do not calculate their hours of work as a specific cost of production, which suggests that they do not consider time to be economically significant. We did not record instances of women calculating how many hours they had worked on an order, either in our interviews or in our observations, and Dean Arnold (1985, 220) observed the same phenomenon in Peru. However, potters do calculate the schedule and the size of the order to be filled, and if they see that they cannot fill it, they will ask a relative for help. This indicates that they are very much aware of the time required to fill an order, even though they are not calculating the hours worked as a specific expense. La Chamba potters combine home-maintenance work with making ceramics in their daily work cycle, which is commonly twelve hours or more. Although the organization of work fluctuates from day to day, we observed women working from six to eight hours per day on ceramics and another six to eight on household tasks. This varies from household to household according to the size of the family.

As suggested by Gudeman (1992b, 142), the home-based craftswomen in Latin America tend to work according to the economic needs of their households (cultural capital), rather than maximizing their earnings (predatory capital). Studies in other countries done with workers in various craft media demonstrate this same pattern of work, ranging from textiles in Panama (Tice 1995, 172) and potters in Mexico (Nash 1985, 57) to weavers in Guatemala (Annis 1987, 128). The potters of La Chamba calculate the economic return they need from their work based on the consumption level of their household.

Gender and Income

Like rural households in other areas of the Andes (McKee 1997, 19–23), most households in La Chamba need multiple sources of income to have more than a subsistence level of existence; agriculture and ceramics are the most common ones. In the early 1970s, 129 (72 percent) of the households earned some income from ceramics (Lara 1972, 84–85). Agriculture was second in importance with 88 (49 percent) of the households having income from this source. Income from any one activity was frequently insufficient to support the household, and the common pattern has been to combine a man's agricultural income with a woman's income from ceramics. When the household survey for this study was done in the late 1980s, 170 (92 percent) of the households earned income from ceramics, an increase of 20 percent when compared to Carmen Lara's study fifteen years earlier and evidence of the growing commercial importance of the craft.

The economics of ceramics in La Chamba depend on whether a woman or man is a household's primary income earner. In 135, or 73 percent, of the households, a man is the head of the family, and in most he also has the largest income. In those cases the woman's income from pottery provides an economic cushion that protects the household from the irregularity of the husband's wages from day labor. It also provides additional funds for special expenses. However, in 49 (27 percent) of the 184 households in La Chamba, women are the primary income earners and the heads of the household. Unless there is an older child living at home, households headed by women usually have only one income, which means that they are poorer than the normal two-income family. Although the income of women household heads completely determines the economic status of the family, all continue to follow the "household economics" model of making pottery as a domestic task rather than adopting mass-production techniques that would increase their income.

Household Income: Agriculture and Ceramics

Although most households in La Chamba depend on the combined earnings of the men in agriculture and women in ceramics, it is difficult to calculate household income accurately because it is not stable from month to month. During this study the legal minimum monthly wage on the commercial farms surrounding La Chamba increased from 13,557.60 pesos ($96.34 U.S.) in 1985 to 236,460 pesos ($139.78 U.S.) in 1999 (see Table 11.1). These figures are limited by the fact that agricultural work tends to be limited to the planting and harvesting seasons, and there are months when La Chamba men may have little or no income.

On the other hand, calculating the income from ceramics is complicated by the fact that there is a variable price structure for La Chamba ceramics. A potter may accept a low unit price on high-volume orders from middlemen, while she expects a middle-range price on retail sales to people from the region and even higher prices for retail sales to visitors from Bogotá. However, most ceramics are sold at low unit prices in high-volume wholesale orders, but even the prices of these orders may vary according to the size of the order, the prestige of the potter, and the profit targets of the middleman.

The highest prices are paid to established potters by organizations devoted to promoting the arts, and the lowest prices are paid by middlemen representing the lowest-cost craft stores. The base wholesale price in La Chamba for a dozen *cazuelas* in 1985 was 225 pesos, but that could range up to 400 pesos. Over the next fifteen years the highs and lows ranged from 800 to 1,600 pesos in 1990, 2,500 to 3,500 pesos in 1995, and 5,000 to 7,000 pesos in 1999. Potters also make some retail sales to tourists from Bogotá, and over the period of this research, this local retail price increased from 1,000 pesos in 1985 to 4,000 pesos in 1990, 7,500 pesos in 1995, and 15,000 pesos in 1999. In 1999 a potter might sell one dozen *cazuelas* at 5,000 pesos as part of a large order from a middleman or at 15,000 pesos in a retail sale to a tourist. However, the majority of the sales are to middlemen at the lower price.

Table 11.1. Colombia's Minimum Monthly Wage and Consumer Price Index
Increases, 1985–1999

Year	C.P.I.[a] (%)	Minimum wage (pesos)[b] Amount	%	Exchange rate[c]	Minimum wage (U.S. dollars)
1985	24.0	13,557.60	20.0	140.73	96.34
1986	19.0	16,811.40	24.0	192.35	87.40
1987	23.3	20,509.80	22.0	241.39	84.97
1988	28.1	25,637.40	25.0	296.36	86.51
1989	25.9	32,559.60	27.0	377.92	86.15
1990	29.1	41,025.00	26.0	497.31	82.49
1991	30.5	65,190.00	26.0	624.15	104.45
1992	27.1	65,190.00	.0	675.79	96.46
1993	22.5	81,510.00	25.0	784.24	103.94
1994	22.9	98,700.00	21.0	830.94	118.78
1995	20.9	118,933.50	20.5	874.86	135.95
1996	20.8	142,125.00	19.5	1,071.96	132.58
1997	18.5	172,005.00	21.0	1,082.37	158.92
1998	18.7	203,826.00	18.5	1,386.61	147.00
1999	13.4[d]	236,460.00	16.0	1,691.61	139.78
Total % increase	1,487.0	1,644.0			45.09

[a] Consumer Price Index (annual rate of inflation on consumer goods). *Source:* Banco de la República, Bogotá.

[b] Legal minimum wage decreed by the national government, in Colombian pesos. *Source:* Departamento Administrativo Nacional de Estadística, Ministerio del Trabajo y Seguridad Social, Bogotá, Colombia.

[c] Peso to U.S. dollar, average rate for June each year. *Source:* Superintendencia Bancaria, Banco de la República, Bogotá, Colombia.

[d] January to May 1999.

Representative monthly incomes from ceramics during the primary field research (1985–1990) ranged from 11,000 pesos (1985) to 40,000 pesos (1990), which consistently translated to approximately $80.00 U.S. Many La Chamba women were reluctant to reveal the prices they actually received from middlemen, and many quoted prices that were inflated, according to independent information that we had. The reluctance to discuss prices is not limited to La Chamba. In a 1994 census among craftspeople in Tolima, 54 percent refused to answer the question about their monthly income (Artesanías de Colombia 1998, 278). Although La Chamba women were hesitant to discuss their income and rarely documented it, we could record levels of monthly production and from that we could calculate approximate monthly earnings. The income figures from both agriculture and ceramics are fluctuating amounts that vary during rush and slow periods. So these figures are approximate figures that vary from family to family and from month to month during the year.

In 1985 a family's combined earnings from agriculture and ceramics could give a monthly household income of 24,890 pesos, or $176 U.S., for a relatively prosperous family in which both parents worked full-time. However, it was common for one spouse (and sometimes both) to have only partial incomes for the month. When men were without work, women increased their incomes by taking additional orders if possible. For a household of six persons, which is the average for La Chamba, this relatively high combined monthly income represented just $.98 U.S. per capita per day, barely enough to provide food for three meals. Women frequently expressed the fear that if they were to get sick and be unable to work, there would not be enough income to feed the household. When the family income declines during slack periods, members of the extended family may have to share orders for ceramics and even share food to survive. Although women complain that the income from ceramics is too low, they continue making ceramics because their income is required to meet the basic needs of the household. The market for ceramics is good and the overhead costs are low, so making ceramics is the most obvious economic decision for most women.

Sweatshop Wages for Women Potters and Their Children, 1985–1990

There are four categories of workers in the production of La Chamba ceramics: big producers, middle-sized producers, subsistence producers, and wage workers. According to Artesanías de Colombia (1998, 29), only 17 percent of the craftspeople in Tolima are big producers who sell above the minimum income level, but that figure is closer to 10 percent in La Chamba. Approximately one-third of La Chamba potters are medium-level producers whose monthly income is just under the legal minimum wage. Another one-third are subsistence-level producers whose monthly income is closer to half of the minimum wage. Finally, wage workers in ceramics, mostly burnishers, earn the least of all, but they are usually women whose husbands have higher incomes. Approximately 90 percent of La Chamba potters earn the legal minimum wage or less.

The example of Anatilde Prada de Silva illustrates the economics of ceramics making in La Chamba. Prada considers herself to be a medium-level producer, and according to our data she was in the high middle-range production bracket for local potters. The fact that she had three teen-aged children assisting her at the time of this research placed her among the more productive potters in town. Both younger and older potters, who have fewer helpers, have lower rates of production than women with several children living at home.

Analyzing the costs of a normal production cycle for tableware shows that profits depend on the unpaid labor of her children. It takes three weeks for her to make, burnish, and fire forty-four dozens of *cazuelas* at a normal rate of work. In 1985 the base wholesale price for a dozen *cazuelas* in a large order was 225 pesos, and her work for the three-week cycle could be sold for 9,900 pesos, or $70.35 U.S. After deducting the direct costs of production (slip and wood) of 1,300 pesos ($9.24 U.S.), the income for three weeks of work was 8,600 pesos ($61.11 U.S.) (see Table 11.2).

This cost structure has changed somewhat in the 1990s because the cost of wood has increased, a consequence of growing demand and a diminishing local supply. Now wood has to be trucked in from neighboring areas, adding

Table 11.2. Ceramics Labor of Anatilde Prada and Her Children

Approximate time in hours

Person	Labor	Daily	Weekly
Anatilde Prada	Make ceramics	4	20
	Burnish and other tasks[a]	4	20
Total		8	40
Aurelio	Burnish	4	20
	Assist with other tasks	—	2
Total		4	22
Martín	Burnish	4	20
Total		4	20
Maritza	Burnish	4	20
	Assist with other tasks	—	2
Total		4	22
Combined total (children)		12	64

[a] Other tasks include mining clay and firing, selling, and delivering ceramics.

to the cost of production. Increasingly people also have to buy the animal dung used in the firing of blackware, and that has also added to the rising cost of ceramics production.

The unpaid labor of children plays a crucial role in La Chamba pottery making. During a three-week work cycle, Anatilde Prada works fifteen full days (eight hours per day) on ceramics (nine days preparing, making, and selling, and six days burnishing), and her three children provide the equivalent of another twenty-four days of work (see Table 11.3). The value of the unremunerated work of her children (24 man-days by 150 pesos per day) is 3,600 pesos ($25.58 U.S.), or 42 percent of the total earnings. With the work of her children, Anatilde Prada can earn 8,600 pesos ($61.11 U.S.) for a three-week cycle of work, in contrast to the 5,000 pesos ($35.53 U.S.) per week that she would earn without it. The problem of underage children working in the crafts is not limited to La Chamba. In the nationwide census of craftspeople conducted by Artesanías de Colombia in 1994, Tolima had the second-highest number (744) of children under the age of sixteen working full-time in the crafts among all the departments of Colombia (1998, 110–11). Most of these children worked twelve months a year in the craft (ibid., 177).

This pattern of work requires a household organization in which the woman can rely on the unpaid labor of her children or other household

Table 11.3. Production Costs in Ceramic Work for a Normal Three-Week Cycle

| | | Unit value | Cost of Activity | |
| | | | --- | --- |
Input	Amount	(pesos)	Pesos	U.S. dollars[a]
Mining/preparing clay	1.5 days	300.00	450.00	$ 3.20
Making ware	6 days	300.00	1,800.00	12.79
Delivering ceramics	.5 day	300.00	150.00	1.07
Slip	5 gallons	100.00	500.00	3.55[b]
Burnishing	30 person days	150.00	4,500.00	31.98
Kiln rental	1 firing	200.00	200.00	1.42
Firing kiln	1 day	300.00	300.00	2.13
Wood	4 bundles	200.00	800.00	5.68[b]
Total			8,700.00	61.82

[a] Calculated at 140.73 pesos to $1.00 U.S.

[b] Direct costs.

members. When the 40 hours per week of the potter's work are combined with the 64 hours per week of her children, it adds up to 104 hours of work to earn 2,865.26 pesos ($20.36 U.S.), a rate of 220.40 pesos ($1.57 U.S.) per person for an eight-hour workday. Since the nationally mandated minimum daily wage at the time was 451.92 pesos ($3.21 U.S.), women and children were earning only 49 percent of the minimum wage. In communities where men make pottery, in contrast, skilled men workers can earn up to three times the minimum wage (Duncan 1998, 199). Thus, skilled men potters in Colombia can earn eight times or more the income of skilled women potters.

In a parallel case, Maria Mies (1982, 151) found that men's incomes in the Indian lacemaking industry were as much as ten times greater than women's. As in La Chamba, the low remuneration of Indian women led to their using the unpaid work of their children to increase their production, with girl children averaging ten to eleven hours of work per day (ibid., 121). Alexander Chayanov (1966, 113) explains that when rural workers need to expand their income, the only means of doing so is by increasing the number of hours worked, and this includes enlisting children and older household members to work. As Mies found in India and Chayanov predicted from his work in Russia, the women potters of La Chamba increase their production through the unpaid work of household members disguised as household collaboration.

Between 1985 and 1990 real incomes actually declined in La Chamba. Although the monthly incomes of minimum-wage agricultural workers increased from 13,557.60 pesos in 1985 to 41,025.00 pesos in 1990, the value in U.S. dollars steadily declined from $96.34 in 1985 to $82.49 in 1990. These figures are compounded by the fact that the value of the U.S. dollar also went through periods of decline on the world market during this time. The prices of ceramics during this period maintained a steady value in terms of U.S. dollars, while their value rose from 225 pesos ($1.60 U.S.) in 1985 to 800 pesos ($1.61 U.S.) in 1990. And while the monthly household income in La Chamba increased from 24,890 pesos in 1985 to 82,722 pesos in 1990, it declined in U.S. dollars from $176 to $166 during the same period.

Inflation and Price Gains in Ceramics, 1990–1999

By 1990 the Colombian national government had allowed the legal minimum wage to fall to its lowest point in dollar terms in recent history. However, the following year (1991) it decreed a 27 percent increase in relation to the dollar, beginning an effort to increase the earnings of the working class in real terms. By 1999 the minimum wage had increased, in terms of U.S. dollars, by 59 percent over 1990 rates. However, in dollar terms the increase in the price of ceramics has been even more striking. The wholesale base price for one dozen *cazuelas* increased from 800 pesos ($1.61 U.S.) in 1990 to 2,500 pesos ($2.86 U.S.) in 1995 and to 5,000 pesos ($2.99 U.S.) in 1999, or 86 percent in dollar terms. This means that in the 1990s women ceramists increased the value of their labor more rapidly than did men working in agriculture (98 percent for women in ceramics, compared to 59 percent for men in agriculture), although this faster growth must be interpreted in relation to the lower wage base for women.

However, even with the increased value of craft labor during the 1990s, earnings from crafts still lag behind the minimum wage. In the nationwide census conducted in 1994 by Artesanías de Colombia (1998, 29), 44 percent of the crafts workshops reported earning 67,000 pesos ($80.63 U.S.) or less as a monthly average. Another 21 percent reported earnings between 67,000 and 250,000 pesos, with most probably clustered near the minimum wage, which was 98,000 pesos at the time. Another 17 percent were high earners, reporting workshop earnings of 250,000 pesos or more, and 18 percent gave no information on earnings.

The attempts by the national government in the 1990s to increase the real wages of workers has had an impact on the income of people in La Chamba, and there has been a trickle-down effect for ceramics workers. However, the gender discrepancy in wages has narrowed only slightly. Women still earn considerably less than men, and the unremunerated work of children is still required for a family to provide for their food, clothing, and education.

In 1999 a family the size of Anatilde Prada de Silva's could produce 60 dozens of *cazuelas* in one month, for a total sales price of 300,000 pesos and earnings of 250,000 pesos. That equals 4,807.69 pesos per person per day of work, still well below the legal minimum wage of 7,882.00 pesos per day. These figures suggest that women and children are earning only 61 percent of the minimum wage decreed by national law. That is a significant increase over the 49 percent of the minimum wage that women and children were earning in 1985, but it is still indicates that they are severely underpaid.

By 1999 men working as day laborers in commercial agriculture could earn as much as 236,460 pesos per month during busy periods (7,882 minimum daily wage times thirty days). Colombian law requires organizations to pay full-time workers for seven days per week even though the normal work week is only five and one-half days. Similarly, the monthly salary is calculated on thirty days. Part-time workers are paid only for the days worked. When that figure is added to the 250,000 pesos that a woman with working children can earn, it gives a high-end monthly household income of 486,460 pesos ($287.57 U.S.) for 1999. The monthly household income rose from the equivalent of $176.87 U.S. in 1985 to $287.57 U.S. in 1999, an increase of 63 percent.

The 1999 income represents 2,702.56 pesos ($1.60 U.S.) per capita per day for a family of six. Between 1985 and 1999, both the minimum wage and the price of ceramics increased more rapidly than did Colombia's Consumer Price Index (CPI), which indicates there were slight gains in the economic well-being of La Chamba households. (See Table 11.4). However, relative to the larger national society, their position as the lowest-paid workers did not change, and their lifestyle remained barely above a subsistence level.

The Colombian national census indicates that 72.6 percent of the people living in rural areas and *corregimientos* (unincorporated villages) like La Chamba lived in poverty in 1985. By the 1993 census that number had declined to 62.5 percent, indicating a gain in socioeconomic levels (Departamento Administrativo Nacional de Estadística). The slight gain in income in La Chamba has been reflected in national trends, but even so two-thirds of rural residents still live in poverty.

Table 11.4. Increases in the Minimum Wage, Consumer Price Index, and Pricing for La Chamba *Cazuelas*, 1985–1999

Year	Minimum Wage[a]		C.P.I.[b]		*Cazuelas*[c]	
	Price	% increase	Index	% increase	Price	% increase
1985	13,557.60	—	50.49	—	225.00	—
1990	41,025.00	202.60	148.53	194.18	750.00	233.33
1995	118,933.50	189.90	453.26	205.16	2,500.00	233.33
1999	236,460.00	98.82	801.07	76.74	5,000.00	100.00
Total		1,644.00		1,487.00		2,122.22

[a] *Source:* Departamento Administrativo Nacional de Estadística, Bogotá.

[b] *Source:* Banco de la República, Bogotá.

[c] These are representative wholesale prices for one dozen calculated for each year.

Women Potters and Middlemen

Each woman in La Chamba is responsible for selling her own production, and the most important means of marketing is through middlemen who visit the potters' houses to place orders. June Nash (1993, 144) has pointed out that when middlemen buy directly from women, the role of the husband declines as the controller of the household income. Seventy-five percent of the La Chamba women potters reported that they sold their ceramics directly to middlemen, indicating their importance in controlling household income. Every Sunday middlemen arrive to pick up orders and place new ones, and they negotiate directly with each woman potter for the pieces to be made, the size of the order, the price, and the delivery date. They pay when the order is delivered.

During the period of this study, the prices of ceramics were normally raised each January, when the central government in Bogotá decreed the minimum wage for the new year and the new gasoline prices. Most other businesses also raised their prices at that time to offset the effect of inflation. In the 1990s additional price adjustments were sometimes made during the course of the year. There is a range of prices for commonly produced styles, such as cooking pots and tableware. Established potters and those who have access to special niche markets can claim higher prices, but most potters are limited to the going base prices offered by middlemen. The fine-ceramics potters have more latitude to negotiate prices because most of their work is single-piece production.

Since each potter specializes in making one or two forms, middlemen buy *cazuelas* from one potter, casseroles from another, fish platters from another, and so on, usually buying from the same group of potters trip after trip. In this way each middleman builds a network of contacts throughout the community and knows many different potters, and they use their networks to control the prices they pay.

The primary market for La Chamba ceramics is Bogotá, where *cazuelas* are sold in craft and tourist stores throughout the city. This market was developed in the early 1970s, when an outlet dedicated to La Chamba pottery was opened at an important downtown location in Bogotá, making it easy for both individuals and businesses to buy this distinctive ware. Today, La Chamba ceramics can be found in most of the important cities in the central part of Colombia, including Cali, Medellín, Manizales, and others. Another important market has been the eastern plains (Los Llanos) region of Colombia, an area where many agriculture workers from Tolima migrated to find work as agrarian capitalism developed there. In the Llanos they have continued buying the ceramics from La Chamba to which they are accustomed.

Economic Exploitation of Women Potters

Middlemen pick up their orders from four or five potters on any given trip, and they carry them back to Bogotá (or other cities) in flatbed trucks with wooden side boards covered by tarpaulins. Middlemen can resell their orders in Bogotá for double the cost in La Chamba, and an urban retailer may double the price again for the sale in his or her store. Depending on the structure of the middleman operation, retail prices can range from 200 to 400 percent above the prices paid to the potters.

Since middlemen take the work of several ceramists, they may earn $250–300 U.S. or more per week, while the ceramist receives only $20.00 U.S. per week. Although middlemen have the capital costs of their trucks, gasoline, and maintenance as expenses, the fact that their earnings may be fifteen times greater than those of the ceramists causes resentment in the community. Most women ceramists feel that their work is not sufficiently remunerated, especially in view of the discrepancy between their earnings and those of the middlemen.

Maria Mies (1982, 160) suggests that the combination of poverty and the social and economic marginalization of women within the capitalist system prevents them from being free-market workers, which leads to their exploitation. She calculated that the rate of exploitation of craftswomen in her research among Indian lacemakers was 300 percent, based on the sale price of the production divided by the wage earned by the women. Using Mies's calculation, the rate of exploitation of La Chamba women can also be as much as 300 percent. Mies suggests that the separation of home-based women workers from the markets leads entrepreneurs to pay them only a fraction of the market value of their production.

Anatilde Prada de Silva and other women potters expressed the feeling that they had little or no personal freedom to improve their economic status. To them the free-market system locks them into a subordinate status with low incomes. The market expansion for La Chamba since the 1960s has been based on low prices that limit potters into a cycle of poverty no matter how hard they work. Although most women protested to us about the low prices paid by the middlemen, no successful alternative has been developed. Neither Artesanías de Colombia nor the Cooperativa organized by the potters has been able to capture a significant share of the market for La Chamba pottery, and husbands who attempt to do marketing are limited to their local region by a lack of capital.

Cooperation versus Competition

Although La Chamba is a small village with a relatively homogeneous population, the women potters have not established an effective marketing organization among themselves to maintain the value of their production. As a result, potters compete with each other for the prices offered by the middlemen. Most women view pottery making as an economic activity that is supplemental to their husbands' income, so they do not define themselves as having occupations to defend. Their marginal, subsistence-level existence leads them to be conservative, and they have little willingness to risk what they do have by challenging the system. For these reasons they have not organized themselves to negotiate their prices. This absence of communal action among craftspeople is common throughout Colombia, where 82 percent do not belong to any organization that assists them in marketing or improving the technical quality of their work (Artesanías de Colombia 1998, 27).

The control middlemen exert over marketing and prices contributes to the perception of local women that they cannot change the system. The influence of middlemen is reinforced by the perceived threat of losing orders. Even though women chafe at this control, they do not see a way to challenge it. With many potters competing with each other for orders in La Chamba, they accept the low prices of the middlemen. The women do not calculate their labor, nor that of their children, as a commodity to be remunerated, but as something extra that they do in between preparing meals and caring for the family. Whatever return they receive is more than what they would receive as unpaid housewives, and thus they accept earnings that are below the legal minimum wage.

Local Stores and Markets

Forty (25 percent) of the La Chamba potters sell their work through local stores, or their husbands transport it to neighboring towns or craft fairs for sale. As in other rural communities in Latin America (Ehlers 1990, 162), La Chamba women do not travel to sell their ceramics. In addition to selling for

The Middleman

Juan Mendez is a local middleman who lives with his wife, Marcelina, on the main road entering La Chamba, near the Artesanías de Colombia complex. Marcelina is a seamstress and does not make ceramics, so they do not have a kiln. One of their married daughters makes fine ceramics, especially filters, which she fires either in the electric kilns of Artesanías de Colombia or in her aunt's kiln.

Juan was one of the first people in the community to get a motorcycle. Since he is a large man, at two meters tall and one hundred kilos, he seems to overwhelm the motorcycle. He is a Charles Bronson look-alike, and his features reflect the indigenous ancestry of this region. He has a broad smile, and his face wrinkles up around his eyes when he smiles.

His business is buying and selling small lots of La Chamba ware, sometimes even buying unfired work from widows or single women. He then fires it in a sister's kiln before the market day. He usually sells in the markets of the neighboring towns of Purificación and El Guamo. One such day he went to Purificación, leaving his house at 6:00 A.M., and once there he chose a place in the shade to lay out his ceramics. Little by little people came by asking prices and picking up pieces in order to feel their balance and weight, and some bought. By early afternoon the crowd had thinned, and he decided to pack and go home. He had only a few pieces left, and the market was essentially over.

He arrived home by four o'clock, parked the motorcycle on the front porch of the house, and unloaded the unsold pieces. He went into the house and lay down in the hammock that was stretched across the living room from wall to wall. The house is set back from the road only about two meters, so from his resting place he could watch out the door to see who walked by. As a friend or neighbor passed, he would call out to them, asking how their day had been or what they would be doing later. When he talked with us about his work, he mentioned that it was clean and that he did not have to work as hard as the field hands in commercial agriculture. He is a gregarious man, and he said that he enjoys being able to visit the markets in different towns and to interact with a wide circle of people in each one.

Photo 11.1. Carrying finished ceramics to sell. Many potters sell their production through local stores. These girls are carrying newly fired pieces to the Cooperativa de La Chamba located in the Artesanías de Colombia Center.

their wives, at any given time ten or so La Chamba men are active as local middlemen, buying from ceramists who do not have clients among the outside agents. The local men are usually not very well capitalized, so they buy small quantities. To increase their profit margin, they sometimes buy unfired greenware at a lower price from women who cannot fire their own work, then fire it and sell it. Most middlemen are male, which means that the women potters of La Chamba sell their work almost exclusively through men.

Two local craft stores are located near the Artesanías de Colombia center, on the road entering the village (see Photograph 11.1). The stores make some local sales, but they also act as intermediaries and resell ceramics outside of La Chamba. The ceramists who sell through these stores are mostly younger women who have not yet established contacts with the middlemen. Since younger women work more in fine ceramics, these stores may have these special pieces as well as the usual tableware.

The local stores accept pottery on consignment, but the young potter never knows when it will sell. In contrast, the middlemen pay in cash when they pick up orders. The potters complain about unusually long delays in

Photo 11.2. Cooperativa de La Chamba. This large showroom located at the entrance to the village permits the ceramists of La Chamba to display their work for potential buyers. Most of the ceramists in town are members of the cooperative. The wide variety of La Chamba production can be seen here.

being paid for pots that are left on consignment at the Artesanías de Colombia center and the craft stores. In an effort to bypass these problems, a cooperative, called the Cooperativa de La Chamba, was organized in 1971 to market the local production, and 240 potters joined it. Most display their work in a large, warehouse-like showroom in the Artesanías de Colombia center. (See Photograph 11.2.) However, sales are limited since few tourists come here to buy, and middlemen prefer to buy directly from the potters. The cooperative has been a passive marketing group that has not had a major impact on the market for La Chamba ceramics.

In the late 1990s buyers from Belgium, the United Kingdom, and the United States, among other countries, began to export La Chamba pottery to their countries. Today the middlemen placing orders for La Chamba ceramics frequently represent international interests, linking the potters of La Chamba even more closely to the global economy. During this international phase in the 1990s women were able to increase their prices significantly in relation to inflation, but it has not been sufficient to bring incomes up to the levels of the legal minimum wage for most.

Capitalism and Symbolic Goods

The determinants of value in a market economy are supply and demand, social status, and symbolic value. In recent decades there has been a sustained, continuing market demand for La Chamba ceramics that has been supplied by a growing number of women potters. Although the demand for their ceramics has been strong, it has not been sufficient to change the nature of La Chamba pottery as an inexpensive craft. The castelike status of potters at the bottom of the socioeconomic system means that there is little or no social value assigned to their work. The market value of symbolic goods is established not only by social status but also by the symbolic value of the commodity in addition to the cost of materials, labor, and transportation. Although the social status of potters is low, the symbolic value of their work has been strong.

Many urban consumers buy La Chamba ceramics for their value in symbolizing the local roots of Colombian culture. Although the purchase of ceramics is an economic transaction, for many urban buyers the real motive is to possess the cultural memory and heritage of a rural Colombia that seems to be in danger of disappearing. In purchasing La Chamba ceramics the customer is not only buying a pot, bowl, or jar; he or she is also acquiring an emblem of Colombian cultural identity. Since art has traditionally had value in a market economy for its symbolic value, rather than any functional value, it may be said that La Chamba ceramics is becoming more art than craft.

In Colombia there is a distinctive clientele for traditional village craft ceramics. It tends to be the new educated elite and professionals whose families have rural or small-town backgrounds. For them La Chamba ceramics represent cultural memory. Although La Chamba pottery may be used occasionally in family and holiday dinners among these urban families, its primary purpose is to represent cultural heritage. The tendency of women potters to make ceramics that are more symbolic than functional coincides with the fact that maximization of earnings is not the primary value they assign to their work.

In the terms of Pierre Bourdieu (1993, 115), village ceramics are symbolic goods of large-scale cultural production oriented toward the general public. Village ceramics communicate symbolic information about culture, ethnicity, gender, and generation within the society, and today consumers are more likely to buy La Chamba ceramics for these reasons than for their original functional purposes of cooking and storing food. In recent decades, craft has survived in many countries of the world on its symbolic value rather than its functionality.

Commerce in Cultural Memory as Art

Although traditional ceramics have become commodity goods in the markets of contemporary societies around the world, they have also come to symbolize values of social importance and cultural memory. Bernard Leach and Michael Cardew in the United Kingdom and Soetsu Yanagi and Shoji Hamada in Japan were among the first to advocate the preservation of traditional ceramics to emphasize the importance of cultural continuity with the past. They proposed that craft should retain its functional character, but it should be produced and purchased for its embodiment of cultural memory as well as its functional value. Leach and Hamada were in Colombia in the 1960s, and their emphasis on the use of traditional tableware and kitchenware for its handmade, nonindustrial quality was accepted by many potters there.

Among the Native Americans of North America, traditional arts and crafts also became commodities for the market during the twentieth century, but rather than being functional they are more symbolic of the survival and continuity of indigenous cultures. Crafts such as pottery symbolize what is traditional, and they have become a statement of pride, identity, and even defiance. María Martínez has been one of the Native American potters who most represents this ideal. Pots are made to be symbolic, political, and decorative, rather than functional, and they celebrate the cultural distinctiveness of the group that makes them. This approach to ceramics has been successful commercially for Native American potters for over a century.

In Tolima and Huila traditional village ceramics have also gained status as art in the work of people described in chapter 9, especially Eduardo Sandoval and Cecilia Vargas. Potters from other ceramics communities, such as Teodolindo Ovalle, Javier Sierra, and Reyes Suárez from Ráquira, have also gained commercial success and recognition as artistic figure makers (Duncan 1998, 91–107). Each of these potters has used traditional techniques and motifs to stimulate the cultural memory of their urban clientele. The commercial success of village ceramics in Colombia today is largely a result of its ability to communicate cultural memory.

Economics in La Chamba: Family Values over Capitalism

Although the women potters of La Chamba work within an economy of craft capitalism, they work to provide household needs, such as food, health care, education, and clothes, rather than maximizing the return on their labor. Their values are rooted in the domestic economy of the household instead of the economy of the marketplace. To the extent possible, they use capitalism to serve their family interests, rather that adjust their time and household organization to meet its demands. Although the capitalist system requires maximization of earnings, capitalization, high productivity, and full-time dedication to compete successfully with other entrepreneurs, the women potters of La Chamba cannot be successful in those terms because of the structural constraints resulting from their definition of themselves as primarily mothers and wives. Even if their incomes increased to legal minimum wage levels, they would still be paid workers at the bottom of subcontracting chains. That would not change them from being marginal workers within a market system, but their work would be more justly compensated.

The low social status of the women potters of La Chamba within Tolima and Colombian society generally has also contributed to their labor being undervalued and has led to low prices and kept them in poverty. Even though their work is beautifully designed and finished, its market value is diminished by their caste-like social position. Up to the present, the strong caste system of Tolima has maintained the status quo, keeping the La Chamba potters at the lower end of the economic ladder.

12

Women Workers

From Indigenous Craft to Mestizo Capitalism

As a part of the restructuring of the global economy, women in rural Latin America, Africa, and Asia are being actively recruited as low-wage workers through subcontracting chains that originate in the urban commercial centers. Although men in these countries are recruited as full-time industrial workers, women are especially contracted as part-time household-based workers (Harris 1990, 19). Corporations seek women laborers because they will work for lower wages, are more submissive, and will more readily accept intermittent work. The willingness of women to work under these "flexible," low-wage conditions has made them the ideal labor force in the new global industrial system (Mies 1986, 112–13). The women potters of La Chamba are such home-based workers who are contracted by middlemen to produce orders according to market demand.

Women and Global Restructuring

Global economic restructuring has shifted low-skill manufacturing work out of high-wage, developed economies into low wage countries while leaving management, finance, and research functions in the country of origin. In this process, companies have lowered their labor costs by contracting work out at less than standard wage levels, turning to workers in economically marginal areas who have few if any other alternatives for generating income. By contracting production work out to women home-based workers, companies can minimize their overhead, workers' wages, and threats of unionization (Ward 1990, 2).

Since contractors favor women over men for this low-wage work, their numbers in the labor force have increased. Although this trend may have resulted in part from women's growing interest in joining the labor market, it has also resulted from entrepreneurs actively recruiting women as low-wage labor. The feminization of the labor force was notable in the 1980s, especially in countries that had export-oriented industrialization and de-regulated labor markets (Standing 1989, 1086). As women's participation in the labor force increased in the 1980s, men's rates fell (Prugl 1996a, 46), and this decline was another factor pushing women into the labor market. When a household can no longer depend on the husband's employment or income, women turn to the informal sector, including home-based piece-work and crafts, to obtain income for their families (Tice 1995, 176).

Tracy Ehlers (1990, 19) points out that there is a long tradition in Latin America of women carrying out small-scale production and trade to help support the household, especially in weaving, basketry, and pottery. How-ever, the capitalist expansion has transformed many traditional, female-controlled, cottage-craft industries into piecework employment individually contracted to middlemen, thereby weakening and devaluing craft produc-tion in favor of commodity production. Both Ehlers (ibid., 20) and Kathleen Gladden (1993, 3) suggest that women lose power and importance in the economy when traditional cottage industries are replaced by subcontracted wage labor because they become dependent on middlemen who control the markets and the contracts. On the other hand, Helen Safa (1992, 76) sees a positive consequence of the increased economic role of women in that it gives them more status within the family and has led men to take on more house-hold tasks.

In spite of the increased role of home-based women workers, their real participation in the labor markets remains under-reported in the official statistics of many countries and international organizations (McKee 1997, 24). Shelley Feldman (1991, 66) suggests that there are at least three reasons why women's work is frequently overlooked:

1. Women's unpaid labor at home is often invisible. Since they are not regular employees, companies do not report their work, and women may also not think of themselves as "workers" (McKee 1997, 20; Weismantel 1997, 50).

2. Women's paid labor may not be considered "real" work because it is home-based and not located in an institutionalized place of employment.

3. Women may not have an occupational identity with their work; many consider it a kind of domestic task done to support the household.

The under-reporting of women's work is also affected by the perception of women primarily as "housewives," who are not considered to be in the workforce even though they perform income-generating activities. Maria Mies (198, 180) talks about "housewifization," the perception that women are dependent on the income of their husbands whether or not this is actually the case. The reality of women's work is frequently blurred by social constructs or ideologies that define what it should be. According to Mies, the concept of housewifization is economically functional in producing a low-wage, submissive labor force. If women think of themselves primarily as housewives and only incidentally as workers, they will be more willing to accept substandard wages and working conditions. In contrast, Prugl (1996b, 115–16) sees the concept of housewife as a means of political rather than economic control of women. She suggests that overlooking the importance and validity of women's work makes the degree of their exploitation less visible and allows them to be more easily manipulated. Women have been the obvious reservoir of unpaid and underpaid labor because home-based work can be adapted to the scheduling requirements of existing domestic tasks.

Capitalism and Women Workers

Capitalism has a history of underpaid labor in the form of indentured servants, slavery, child labor, and home-based women workers. Since the focus of this economic system is the accumulation of capital, underpaying workers makes it possible for the entrepreneurial class to generate larger profits, which in turn permits the accumulation of capital. The social class and educational systems are frequently structured to perpetuate this unequal relationship between managers and producers, with the former being trained in the skills of managing capital and the latter in the skills of producing goods.

Karl Marx suggested that subsistence-oriented craftspeople and peasant farmers who were in charge of their own means of production would gradually have to become small capitalists, exploiting the labor of others, or lose their means of production (McLellan 1977, 398). Indeed, the women of La Chamba have to "exploit" their own children or other family members to be able to produce a subsistence wage. The underpayment of labor that is endemic in the subcontracting system pushes mothers to use the labor of their children to survive in the money economy. Marx did not foresee the subcontracting systems that would come to characterize low-skilled, labor-

intensive production in the latter part of the twentieth century. Craft production continues intact in much of the world, but small, home-based craft
producers have been transformed from independent workers into the final
and most vulnerable link in long contracting chains that originate in remote
metropolitan centers.

As women have become the lowest-paid workers in the global free-market economy, their children have been pulled into the system as mothers'
helpers. Women and the children who work with them are the perfect labor
reserve because they can be given work irregularly on a contract-by-contract
basis. The managers and the middlemen who contract home-based women
workers through subcontracting chains are frequently "extracting surplus
value from their labor and paying less than is necessary for the worker's
subsistence" (Prugl 1996a, 43). Karin Tice (1995, 13) suggests that if we can
better understand how women become subordinated and why their work is
marginalized and undervalued in capitalistic production systems, we may be
able to prevent this transformation from happening where gender symmetry
still exists between men and women. It might even be possible to develop
strategies to correct the existing abuse of women and children as underpaid
laborers.

Women as Workers

In the small towns and villages of Latin America, women work at a number
of different levels. In research in Oaxaca, Mexico, Scott Cook (1990, 90)
described four discrete ways in which women contributed to the local
economy. The first was in being the principal decision maker in households
without a male head. The second was their work in the social reproduction
of the family, including preparing food, cleaning, caring for children, and
other household-related tasks. Third was their contribution of unpaid labor
in petty commodity production in households headed by men. The final way
was as income-producing workers, either through self-employment or as
home-based workers. The first three ways in which women contribute to the
economy are frequently not recognized as having economic value. Even their
income-producing contributions are frequently not recognized because the
work is done part-time and in the home, where it is intermingled with domestic work.

Although women make up half the workers in most human communities,
their work is often socially invisible and officially under-reported. In male-
headed households in La Chamba, men's work is viewed as the primary

income source for the household, and women's work is viewed as the surplus labor that produces a supplemental income. The interpretation of women's work as surplus is one of the justifications that induce them to accept abnormally low wages. However, in households headed by women, theirs may be the only income, and the family is reduced to poverty by the subminimal wages.

In the subcontracting system of home-based women, the greater the specialization of the contracted task, the greater is their isolation from the market, which leads to lower remuneration. Clare Wilkinson-Weber (1997, 50) studied the home-based embroidery industry in Lucknow, India, and found that the decision by a contractor whether to give a woman a subcontract for embroidery work essentially controlled her access to work. Different aspects of the work were subcontracted to various women, which assured that no single woman acquired the skill to do all of it. This meant they could not compete with the contractor, who did know the full production process. This de-skilling of craft work by breaking it down into simple, repetitive stages serves to depress wages.

Middlemen and the "Putting-Out" System

Home-based, subsistence-level craft production by women occurs in many countries today, and it is frequently based on the "putting-out" system. Here a middleman parcels out work to home-based workers, returning later to collect the finished product and pay the worker. The middleman usually relies on an established network of dependent laborers who carry all of the costs of production (Mies 1982, 34). The putting-out system is especially identified with the production of women's crafts, and it is used internationally today. It is a flexible system for the merchants who control capital because it allows them to order only what they need immediately for resale and avoid having capital tied up in inventory. But for craft producers it is an irregular and unpredictable system because their work is scheduled piecemeal.

Home-based women craft producers are the ones who have been most willing to accept the putting-out system, which frequently pays them less than established minimum wages, a reality that is masked by the fact that women are viewed as independent contractors. Women are defined as housewives doing casual craftwork in their leisure time, which legitimizes the low pay for their work (Mies 1982, 177). The practice of paying home-based women workers subminimal wages means not only that the labor of women is exploited, but also that women heads of household have difficulty earning a subsistence-level income for their families.

In Latin America the putting-out system has been used since the Spanish colonial period. In the tribute-based economy of that time, women in indigenous households produced tributary goods. Scott Cook (1990, 113) describes how the putting-out system has been used among weavers in Oaxaca, Mexico, since the colonial period, when Crown agents assigned production quotas as a form of tribute or tax. Today middlemen assign piecemeal contracts for market-oriented production. Laura Bossen (1984, 324–25) reported a similar situation among weavers in Guatemala. During the colonial period, Spanish officials distributed raw cotton to Mayan women to be spun into thread for free or for a token payment, a practice called *el repartimiento de hilazas* (distribution of the thread). Women were required to do the work as a part of their tributary obligation to the Spanish colonial state. A similar system is used today between urban merchants, who distribute the raw materials, and Mayan women artisans, who do the weaving. Since the merchants provide the raw material and contract the women's labor, the weavings belong to them, not to the weavers. The fact that women have no ownership over their finished products emphasizes their disempowerment in the putting-out system. Elisabeth Prugl (1996a, 43) documents similar putting-out arrangements for Yucatán weavers, Chiapas potters, and Ecuadorian knitters.

Government organizations have also used this system as part of economic development strategies that promote rural home-based craft production. Typically the government's craft-marketing agency places an order with the craftswoman or accepts her work on consignment, usually paying after the work is actually sold. The motivations for governmental involvement in these marketing programs range from stimulating employment, to slowing down rural-to-urban migration, to preserving crafts as national treasures (Prugl 1996a, 44). Although the agencies are established with the interests of workers in mind, they do resell the work and so are governed by market pressures. As a result, they rarely address the issues of fundamental importance to the craftspeople, which are wages and working conditions (ibid.). In La Chamba many women potters prefer to sell their work to middlemen than to Artesanías de Colombia because the middlemen pay more promptly.

Local Crafts and Global Capitalism

The potters of La Chamba are part of the global model of consumer-oriented capitalism, and they see their craft as a means of employment and income.

In the prehispanic period in the Andes, the act of making crafts was imbued with cosmological significance. However, the cultural disjunction introduced by the Spanish Conquest led to a shift in values, cosmology, and definition of crafts. This process has continued in the last century so that crafts are understood by the contemporary generation as commodities to be bought and sold in the market. Today young people think of their craft as a system of production or an occupation, and they evaluate it in terms of its potential for providing income.

Noncapitalist working relationships can coexist alongside capitalist systems of production at the village level, and both may be connected to capitalist markets (Tice 1995, 9). The noncapitalist craft relationships are characterized by the craftsperson owning the tools and raw materials of production, controlling their own labor, carrying out the full production process, and producing primarily for family or local community use. By contrast, in capitalist working relationships workers are characteristically supervised and directed by someone else, do only one specialized step in the production, do not own the tools and raw materials, and are not involved in selling the production.

In Colombian village economies, capitalist and subsistence systems of production frequently exist side by side, especially in the crafts and small-scale agriculture. This is the case in La Chamba, where women make pottery following traditional domestic craft models, but they sell it to middlemen following national and international marketing models. Stephen Gudeman (1978, 11) described this coexistence of capitalism and subsistence production in the community of Los Boquerones in Panama as follows: "Although it was generated by capitalism and proto-capitalism, the subsistence economy of Los Boquerones is not itself capitalistic. Producer, means of production and product are not separated, free labour and a labour market are not found, and surpluses are not cumulated and reinvested." The village craftsperson and the peasant farmer in Colombia frequently organize their work along subsistence lines even though the product may ultimately be sold into the larger, national market economy.

Kristin Koptiuch (1992, 153) also describes the case of traditional potters in Egypt, who continue to organize their work around household relation ships while producing for a capitalist economy. She suggests that this adaptation of the capitalist and noncapitalist systems to each other is an important mechanism for maintaining stability during the process of change. So the grafting together of the two systems is a means by which traditional household-based work can adapt itself to the demands of the international capitalist economy.

As capitalism penetrates an economy, craftspeople in local communities may adopt capitalist working relationships, or they may graft their subsistence, household-oriented working relationships onto the new system. Either way a new social order is produced. Sheldon Annis (1987, 140) describes how the adoption of capitalist working relationships by Mayan villagers led to an increased differentiation in wealth and class between households and a decline of traditional social egalitarianism and community solidarity. As the social and economic relations of the people becomes more hierarchical in capitalism, some become petty capitalists (the new wealthy ones), some remain as subsistence workers, and others fall into a kind of underclass of dispossessed workers who cannot produce a normal subsistence living (ibid., 64–65).

Since the rise of industrialism, crafts have only occasionally been able to compete as a viable economic alternative to mass production. China, India, Mexico, and the Philippines are examples of countries that have maintained a viable handicraft sector in the economy. The drawback is that these viable handicraft economies have been characterized by low wages and export-oriented production that works at the cost of keeping craftspeople poor. Crafts cannot compete with industry as a system of production, and to be economically viable they must offer something different from what industry can provide. Crafts are either important for their symbolic value (see chapter 11), or they are inexpensive goods that are of marginal economic interest to better-financed industrialists.

Craft, Caste, and Capitalism

In Colombia the separation between professional and village ceramists is a castelike separation based on differences of social status and cultural origin. The social distance between university-trained ceramists and the traditional village ceramists is apparent in their work. The former specialize in Euro-centric designs and sell their work at high prices in upscale locations, while the latter adhere to indigenous designs and sell them at low prices in stores of *artesanías*, which are identified with inexpensive crafts. In the census of craftspeople made by Artesanías de Colombia (1998, 3) in the early to mid-1990s, only 1,194 (1.9 percent) of the craftspeople in the country had university-level training, and few of those had taken courses in their craft at the university. Of the various craft media, only textile design and weaving (University of the Andes) and ceramics (National University of Colombia and University of the Andes) are taught in the major university art departments of the country. Half the artisans in the census (51 percent) had little or no formal education at all. The gulf between this majority of uneducated crafts-people, who are mostly rural and mestizo, and the 2 percent of university-educated craftspeople, who are mostly urban, is so great that it is castelike and virtually impassable.

The urban art community is Eurocentric, and it does not value local traditions. Although there is an appreciation of prehispanic and rural or village ceramics, there is a virtual taboo against the university-trained ceramists using ideas from or making reference to them in their own work. The social gap is such that indigenous esthetics are not considered an acceptable subject to treat in the "high" art of urban galleries and museums. As Dean Arnold (1985, 127) says, ceramics are a means by which ideological and social structural information is communicated within a society; and in Latin America, village ceramics communicate ruralness with its associated indigenous roots and poverty.

This is one component of a larger problem of structural racism and classism that affects the national attitude toward mestizo-indigenous communities in general. In fact, there is a structural discrimination against these communities that manifests itself in the lack of such social services as health care, roads, police protection, potable water, sanitation, electricity, and telephones. This discrimination against communities and crafts that are not European in origin is a continuation of the Conquest attitude of the inferiority of indigenous cultures. Caste in Colombia divides the Eurocentric urban artists and craftspeople from the traditional indigenous-mestizo craftspeople, forming an unbridgeable castelike separation between these groups.

Craft, Caste, and Poverty

This vertical cultural disjuncture has affected the practice of ceramics in Colombia in a number of ways. First, the poor remuneration for village crafts has led to a general problem of poverty in crafts communities. Second, village craftspeople are virtually never able to transcend class structures to become socially acceptable urban artists, although cracks in this glass ceiling have permitted a few Colombian craftspeople to achieve wide recognition in the last couple of decades, such as Cecilia Vargas in Pitalito and Eduardo Sandoval in La Chamba. Third, since village crafts are not a part of the socially acceptable world for Eurocentric classes, urban, professional artists rarely draw from the visual richness of village crafts in their own works. Fourth, village craftspeople remain isolated within small towns and villages, usually in remote rural areas. They rarely have contact with craftspeople from other regions or with the buying public. And fifth, village crafts do not have prestige as an occupation, even among craftspeople themselves. For example, in La Chamba women prefer not to work in ceramics, but if they must for economic reasons, they prefer to limit their work to the relatively clean job of burnishing, rather than the "dirty" work of making pots. However, three-quarters of La Chamba women are obligated for economic reasons to carry out the complete production process.

Clare Hendry (1992, 113) notes that every one of her informants in Atzompa, Mexico, mentioned "dirtiness" as a principal complaint about working in pottery. This deprecation of village ceramics—as dirty, lower class, or indigenous—culturally ghettoizes potters within a society and marginalizes their products within the larger national economy. Even though potters are highly productive and have low overhead, village ceramics are characterized by subsistence-level incomes. Thus, the economic logic of rural women potters is to minimize their expenditures (by avoiding capital investments in pottery production, not to mention consumer luxuries) and to increase their labor (by working as many hours as possible and enlisting the assistance of household members).

The women potters of La Chamba have little in the way of technology, capital, or social prestige to add to the value of their labor, and that is compounded by their association with low-status, indigenous-style pottery. Although they are poor and have little prestige within the economic institutions of the country, they continue the work that many accept as their destiny. Work that had a metaphysical basis in the prehispanic world has been transformed into socially stigmatized "Indian work" that consigns its producers to poverty in the Colombia of today.

La Chamba: Caste and Household Economics in a Market Economy

Given the history of social oppression in Tolima and the racially based caste system that reinforces it, the women of La Chamba have little hope for change within the existing sociopolitical system. The expansion of capitalism in the department in the last half of the twentieth century was built on the caste-based social structure. Although incomes for the rural working class have improved, the differences in wealth and income between the owners of capital and the workers have remained as great as ever.

Although the women potters of La Chamba work within a capitalist economy, their work values are more oriented to household needs than to the market. They work to provide food, health care, education, and clothes for their families, rather than to maximize the return on their labor. Their values are rooted in the domestic economy of the household instead of the economy of the marketplace. As home-based craftspeople, they work on contract in response to the demands of the market economy, and many view their substandard incomes with resentment, believing that their burden of poverty is unjustly imposed.

The demand for La Chamba ceramics has shifted from regional markets for cooking and water pots to urban markets for tableware and fine display ceramics. Although the market for La Chamba ceramics has grown in recent decades, La Chamba potters continue to be poorly paid. The exploitative prices paid to the potters and their children by merchants and middlemen threaten the future of the craft. Increasing numbers of young women are being educated, and they see migration out of La Chamba as a better choice than becoming potters, with its promise of hard work and continuing poverty. If the price gains of the early 1990s were to continue until they came more in line with national minimum-wage standards, that would be a promising sign for the future of La Chamba ceramics. If there is no room in the market economy of Colombia for the women potters of La Chamba to earn at least the legal minimum wage, one of the richest traditions of Colombian craft could be lost.

GLOSSARY OF CERAMIC TERMS

Adobe—A mixture of clay, earth, and straw that is commonly compacted into blocks and used for building walls.

Burnishing—The process of polishing and sealing the surface of a ceramics piece until it has a satin sheen.

Cazuela—A soup-sized serving bowl.

Claybody—Two or three different natural clays are mixed together to form a working clay with the characteristics needed by the potter.

Coiling—The process of building up the walls of pots with ropelike coils of clay.

Downdraft—The exhaust draft for a kiln exits into the chimney near the bottom of the kiln. The heat from the fire first rises in the kiln, but the exhaust pulls it down to exit. This guarantees a flow of fire and heat in the kiln.

Earthenware—Pottery made of low-fire clay. It is usually reddish in color.

Flashing—The changes in coloration produced by the flames from a wood fire as they lick around a pot during the firing.

Form—This refers to a particular vessel shape, such as the cooking pot or water bottle.

Greenware—A piece of ceramics that has been made and dried but not yet fired.

Leatherhard—The stage in the drying of a pot in which the clay has the consistency of firm leather.

Múcura—The prehispanic-style water bottle with long, spoutlike neck.

Oxidation—A firing environment in which the fire consumes oxygen naturally from the air.

Olla—The traditional pot used for cooking and storing of food.

Open-air firing—Pots are fired stacked on the ground, surrounded by wood, and covered by metal sheeting (formerly covered by broken potsherds).

Orton cones—Laboratory-prepared cones used by ceramists for precise measuring of temperatures.

Reduction—When combustion occurs in an environment starved of oxygen, oxygen is drawn from the ceramics being fired. Areas painted in slip can be blackened by this process.

Saggars—Ceramic pots in which smaller pieces of pottery are placed for firing.

Slip—Liquid clay of a thick, creamlike consistency.

Sprig mold—A special mold for making small, delicate pieces that are combined to make a complete piece or applied to surfaces of larger pieces.

Style—A type of ceramics defined by the use of similar designs, techniques, and forms.

Temper—Sand that is mixed into clay to give it porosity and strength.

Thermal shock—A rapid increase or decrease of temperature is characteristic of wood fires. Pots intended for cooking over wood fires must be designed to withstand the shock of these rapid fluctuations.

Tinaja—A water-storage jar.

Turning bowl—A flattened bowl or plate of 20–25 cm is set on the floor or ground, supporting and turning a new ceramics piece as it is being built up.

Wedging—Applying pressure to the clay in a repeated, systematic pattern to guarantee an even mixture and consistency and to eliminate air pockets.

BIBLIOGRAPHY

Aguado, Fray Pedro de. [1581] 1956. *Recopilación historial* (Historical compilation). Intro. Juan Friede. 4 vols. Bogotá: Empresa Nacional de Publicaciones.

Annis, Sheldon. 1987. *God and Production in a Guatemalan Town*. Austin: University of Texas Press.

Archivo General de Indias, Seville, Spain. 1584. Patronato (Patronage) 196. Sección de Mapas y Planos (Section of Maps and Plans). MP, Panama, 24. Valle del Río Magdalena (Magdalena River Valley).

Arizpe, Lourdes, ed. 1996. *The Cultural Dimensions of Global Change: An Anthropological Approach*. Paris: UNESCO.

Arnold, Dean E. 1993. *Ecology and Ceramic Production in an Andean Community*. Cambridge: Cambridge University Press.

———. 1989. "Technological Diversity and Evolutionary Viability: A Comparison of Pottery-Making Technologies in Guatemala, Peru, and Mexico." In *Ceramic Ecology, 1988: Current Research on Ceramic Materials,* ed. Charles C. Kolb, 29–59. BAR International Series 513. Oxford: B.A.R.

———. 1985. *Ceramic Theory and Cultural Process*. Cambridge: Cambridge University Press.

Artesanías de Colombia. 1998. "Censo económico nacional del sector artesanal" (National economic census of the craft sector). Santafé de Bogotá: Ministerio de Desarrollo Económico.

Avellaneda, José Ignacio. 1995. *The Conquerors of the New Kingdon of Granada*. Albuquerque: University of New Mexico Press.

Banco de la República. 1963. *Acuarelas de Mark, 1843–1856: Un testimonio pictórico de la Nueva Granada* (Watercolors of Mark, 1843–1856: A pictorial testimony of New Granada). Bogotá: Banco de la República.

Bedoya, Victor A. 1965. *Curso de prehistoria americana con relación especial a Colombia* (Treatise on the American prehistory with a special account of Colombia). Ibagué, Tolima: Imprenta Departamental.

———. 1950. *Etnología y conquista del Tolima y la hoya del Quindio: Pijaos y quimbayas* (Ethnology and conquest of Tolima and the Quindio Basin: Pijaos and Quimbayas). Ibagué: Departamento de Tolima.

Benería, Lourdes, and Martha Roldán. 1987. *The Crossroads of Class and Gender: Industrial Homework, Subcontracting, and Household Dynamics*. Chicago: University of Chicago Press.

Bergquist, Charles. 1992. "The Labor Movement (1930–1946) and the Origins of the Violence." In *Violence in Colombia: The Contemporary Crisis in Historical Perspective,* ed. Charles Bergquist, Ricardo Peñaranda, and Gonzalo Sánchez, 51–72. Wilmington, Del.: Scholarly Resources.

Bergquist, Charles, Ricardo Peñaranda, and Gonzalo Sánchez, eds. 1992. *Violence in Colombia: The Contemporary Crisis in Historical Perspective.* Wilmington, Del.: Scholarly Resources.

Bidney, David. 1967. *Theoretical Anthropology.* 2d ed. New York: Schocken Books.

Bolaños, Álvaro Félix. 1994. *Barbarie y canibalismo en la retórica colonial: Los indios pijaos de Fray Pedro Simón* (Barbarism and cannibalism in colonial rhetoric: The Pijao Indians of Fray Pedro Simón). Bogotá: CEREC.

Boris, Eileen, and Elisabeth Prugl, eds. 1996. *Homeworkers in Global Perspective: Invisible No More.* London: Routledge and Kegan Paul.

Borja, Juan de. [1608] 1922a. "Guerra con los pijaos" (War with the Pijaos). Letter to King Phillip III. Transcribed by Ernesto Restrepo Tirado. *Boletín de Historia y Antigüedades* 14 (September): 113–15.

———. [1608] 1922b. "Guerra con los Pijaos" (War with the Pijaos). Presentation of the letter to the king. Transcribed by Ernesto Restrepo Tirado. *Boletín de Historia y Antigüedades* 14 (September): 129–64.

Bossen, Laura. 1984. *The Redivision of Labor: Women and Economic Choice in Four Guatemalan Communities.* Albany: State University of New York Press.

Bourdieu, Pierre. 1993. *The Field of Cultural Production.* New York: Columbia University Press.

Bradley, Harriet. 1989. *Men's Work, Women's Work: A Sociological History of the Sexual Division of Labor in Employment.* Minneapolis: University of Minnesota Press.

Bunzel, Ruth. 1929. *The Pueblo Potter: A Study of Creative Imagination in Primitive Art.* New York: Columbia University Press.

Calderón, Camilo. 1993. "Las chivas de Pitalito" (The buses of Pitalito). In *Gran enciclopedia colombiana,* vol. 6, *Arte,* 157. Bogotá: Cordillera Editores and Círculo de Lectores.

Calderón, Pablo Mora, and Amado Guerrero Rincón, eds. 1989. *Historia y culturas populares: Los estudios regionales en Boyacá* (History and popular cultures: Regional studies in Boyacá). Tunja, Colombia: Instituto de Cultura y Bellas Artes de Boyacá.

Cardale de Schrimpff, Marianne. 1989. "La naturaleza del cambio" (The nature of change). In *Historia y culturas populares: Los estudios regionales en Boyacá* (History and popular cultures: Regional studies in Boyacá), ed. Pablo Mora Calderón and Amado Guerrero Rincón. Tunja, Colombia: Instituto de Cultura y Bellas Artes de Boyacá.

Carrillo, Charles M. 1997. *Hispanic New Mexican Pottery: Evidence of Craft Specialization 1790–1890.* Albuquerque: LPD Press.

Céspedes del Castillo, Guillermo. 1992. *América hispánica (1492–1898)* (Hispanic America (1492–1898). Barcelona: Editorial Labor.

Chaves Mendoza, Álvaro. 1985a. "Cerámica indígena" (Indigenous ceramics). In *Gotas de antaño: Introducción a la cerámica en Colombia* (Traces from yesteryear: Introduction to ceramics in Colombia), by Álvaro Chaves Mendoza,

Ronald Duncan, and Gonzalo Peláez Caldas, 60–76. Bogotá: Centro Colombo-Americano.

———. 1985b. "Cerámica popular" (Popular ceramics). In *Gotas de antaño: Introducción a la cerámica en Colombia,* by Álvaro Chaves Mendoza, Ronald Duncan, and Gonzalo Peláez Caldas, 77–94. Bogotá: Centro Colombo-Americano.

Chayanov, Alexander Vasilevich. [1925] 1966. "Peasant Farm Organization." In *A. V. Chayanov: The Theory of Peasant Economy,* ed. Daniel Thorner, Basile Kerblay, and Robert E. F. Smith, 31–277. Homewood, Ill.: Richard D. Irwin.

Collins, Jane L., and Martha Giménez, eds. 1990. *Work without Wages: Comparative Studies of Domestic Labor and Self-Employment within Capitalism.* Albany: State University of New York Press.

Colmenares, Germán. 1970. *La provincia de Tunja en el Nuevo Reino de Granada: Ensayo de historia social (1539–1800)* (The province of Tunja in the New Kingdom of Granada: Essay on social history (1539–1800). Bogotá: Departmento de Historia, Facultad de Artes y Ciencias, Universidad de los Andes.

Cook, Scott. 1990. "Female Labor, Commodity Production, and Ideology in Mexican Peasant-Artisan Households." In *Work without Wages: Comparative Studies of Domestic Labor and Self-Employment within Capitalism,* ed. Jane L. Collins and Martha Giménez, 89–115. Albany: State University of New York Press.

Cooper, Emmanuel. 1981. *A History of World Pottery.* New York: Larousse.

Cuyas, Arturo. 1962. *Spanish-English Dictionary.* 4th ed. New York: Appleton, Century, Crofts.

Deere, Carmen Diana. 1990. *Household and Class Relations: Peasants and Landlords in Northern Peru.* Berkeley: University of California Press.

Deere, Carmen Diana, and Magdalena León, eds. 1987. *Rural Women and State Policy: Feminist Perspectives on Latin American Agricultural Development.* Boulder: Westview Press.

Departamento Administrativo Nacional de Estadística (National Administrative Department for Statistics). "Censo de Población, 1985 y 1993" (Population Census, 1985 and 1993). Statistical tables supplied by Hector Mejia, coordinator, Banco de Datos, D.A.N.E., Bogotá.

Duncan, Ronald J. 1998. *The Ceramics of Ráquira, Colombia: Gender, Work, and Economic Change.* Gainesville: University Press of Florida.

Duncan, Ronald J. 1996. "De mariposas a madonas: arte y diseño prehispánico" (From Butterflies to Madonnas: Prehispanic Art and Design). In *Gran Enciclopedia Temática 5* (1996): 333–43.

———. 1993. "Arte precolombino" (Precolumbian art). In *Gran Enciclopedia Colombiana,* vol. 6, *Arte,* 15–26. Bogotá: Cordillera Editores and Círculo de Lectores.

———. 1992a. "Precolumbian Design Motifs in Inga Chumbes." *América Negra,* no. 3 (Bogotá): 133–44.

———. 1992b. "Precolumbian Art and Design in Nariño Ceramics." In *Arte de la Tierra: Nariño* (Art from the Earth: Nariño), 27–31. Bogotá: Fondo de Promoción Cultural.

———. 1989. "El arte precolombino como iconografía" (Precolumbian art as iconography). In *Arqueología: Memorias del Simposio de Arqueología y Antropología Física,* V Congreso Nacional de Antropología, ed. Santiago Mora Camargo, Felipe Cárdenas Arroyo, and Miguel Angel Roldán, 223–32. Bogotá: ICFES.

———. 1988. "Encuentro de ceramistas contemporáneos de América Latina" (Encounter of contemporary Latin American ceramists). In *Arte en Colombia* (Bogotá), no. 38 (December): 58–60.

———. 1986. "Crafts and Development in Latin America." Paper presented at the International Symposium on Handicrafts, International Development Research Centre, Singapore.

———. 1985a. "El niño rural como trabajador: Estudio de caso en La Chamba" (The rural child as worker: Case study in La Chamba). Research report for the International Development Research Centre, Ottawa, Canada.

———. 1985b. "Cuatro siglos de cerámica en Colombia" (Four centuries of ceramics in Colombia). In *Gotas de antaño: Introduccíon a la cerámica en Colombia* (Traces from yesteryear: Introduction to ceramics in Colombia). Bogotá: Centro Colombo-Americano.

———. 1985c. "Diseño y técnica en la cerámica de La Chamba" (Design and technique in La Chamba ceramics). Research report for the Program of Art, University of the Andes, Bogotá.

———. 1984. "Ceramics as Art in Colombia." *Craft International: Journal of the World Crafts Council* (New York) (July): 4.

Duncan, Ronald J., Jaime Bernal, and Ignacio Briceño. 1993. *El arte del chamanismo, la salud y la vida: Tumaco–La Tolita* (The art of shamanism, health, and life: Tumaco–La Tolita). Bogotá: Instituto Colombiano de Cultura Hispánica.

Ehlers, Tracy Bachrach. 1990. *Silent Looms: Women and Production in a Guatemalan Town.* Boulder: Westview Press.

Feldman, Shelley. 1991. "Still Invisible: Women in the Informal Sector." In *The Women and International Development Annual,* vol. 2, ed. Rita S. Gallin and Anne Ferguson. Boulder: Westview.

Foster, George. 1988. "The Validating Role of Humoral Theory in Traditional Spanish-American Therapeutics." *American Ethnologist* 15, no. 1: 120–35.

———. 1967. *Tzintzuntzán: Mexican Peasants in a Changing World.* Boston: Little, Brown and Company.

Friedemann, Nina S. de. 1995. "Anotaciones al ideario etnográfico en la obra de Fray Pedro Simón" (Notes on the ethnographic concept in the works of Fray Pedro Simón). *América Negra,* no. 9: 163–81.

———. 1993. "Arte étnico" (Ethnic art). In *Gran enciclopedia colombiana,* vol. 6, *Arte,* 145–54. Bogotá: Cordillera Editores and Círculo de Lectores.

Friedemann, Nina, Juan Friede, and Darío Fajardo. 1981. *Indigenismo y aniquilamiento de indígenas en Colombia* (Indianism and the elimination of Indians in Colombia). 2d ed. Bogotá: Ediciones CIEC.

Gallin, Rita S., and Anne Ferguson, ed. 1991. *Women and International Development Annual,* vol. 2. Boulder, Colo.: Westview.

García Canclini, Néstor. 1990. *Culturas híbridas: Estrategias para entrar y salir de la modernidad* (Hybrid cultures: Strategies for entering and leaving modernity). Mexico City: Editorial Grijalbo.

Gladden, Kathleen. 1993. "Women in the Global Economy: A Case Study of Garment Workers in Colombia." Working Paper 236. Women in International Development. Michigan State University, East Lansing.

———. 1992. "La reestructuración industrial, el subcontrato y la incorporación de la fuerza de trabajo femenina en Colombia" (Industrial restructuring, the subcontract, and the incorporation of feminine labor in Colombia). Paper presented at the Fourth Congress of Anthropology, Bogotá, Colombia.

Gómez Contreras, Emiro. 1990. "Estudio y evaluación de la artesanía cerámica en Colombia" (Study and evaluation of craft ceramics in Colombia). Bogotá: Artesanías de Colombia.

Gosselman, Carl August. [1830] 1981. *Viaje por Colombia, 1825 y 1826* (Travel through Colombia, 1825 and 1826). Bogotá: Banco de la República. (Translation of the original: "Resa i Colombia, Aren 1825 och 1826." Stockholm: Tryct hos Johan Horber.)

Gudeman, Stephen. 1998. *Economic Anthropology*. Northampton, Mass.: E. Elgar Publications.

———. 1992a. "Epilogue: Art and Material Culture." *Museum Anthropology* 16, no. 3: 58–61.

———. 1992b. "Remodeling the House of Economics: Culture and Innovation." *American Ethnologist* 19, no. 1: 141–54.

———. 1986. *Economics as Culture: Models and Metaphors of Livelihood*. London: Routledge and Kegan Paul.

———. 1978. *The Demise of a Rural Economy: From Subsistence to Capitalism in a Latin American Village*. London: Routledge and Kegan Paul.

Gudeman, Stephen, and Alberto Rivera. 1990. *Conversations in Colombia: The Domestic Economy in Life and Text*. New York: Cambridge University Press.

Gutiérrez Escudero, Antonio. 1992. "La primitiva organización indiana" (The primitive Indian organization). In *Historia de Iberoamérica*, ed. Manuel Lucena Salmoral. Madrid: Ediciones Catedra.

Haberland, Wolfgang. 1986. "Aesthetics in Native American Art." In *The Arts of the North American Indian*, ed. Edwin L. Wade, 107–31. New York: Hudson Hills Press.

Hamilton, Sarah. 1998. *The Two-Headed Household: Gender and Rural Development in the Ecuadorian Andes*. Pittsburgh: University of Pittsburgh Press.

Hanson, E. Mark. 1986. *Educational Reform and Administrative Development: The Cases of Colombia and Venezuela*. Stanford: Stanford University Press.

Harris, Betty. 1990. "Ethnicity and Gender in the Global Periphery: A Comparison of Basotho and Navajo Women." *American Indian Culture and Research Journal* 14, no. 4: 15–38.

Helms, Mary W. 1993. *Craft and the Kingly Ideal: Art, Trade, and Power*. Austin: University of Texas Press.

Henderson, James. 1985. *When Colombia Bled: A History of the Violencia in Tolima*. University, Ala.: University of Alabama Press.

Hendry, Jean Clare. 1992. *Atzompa: A Pottery-Producing Village of Southern Mexico in the Mid-1950s*. Vanderbilt University Publications in Anthropology, no. 40. Nashville: Vanderbilt University.

Hettner, Alfred. 1976. *Viajes por los Andes colombianos (1882–1884)* (Travels through the Colombian Andes, 1882–1884). Bogotá: Banco de la República.

Holloway, Ralph, Jr. 1971. "Reply." *Cultural Anthropology* 12, no. 3: 401–3.

———. 1969. "Culture: A Human Domain." *Cultural Anthropology* 10, no. 4: 395–407.

Instituto Geográfico "Agustín Codazzi." 1969. *Atlas de Colombia.* Bogotá: Litografía Arco.

Jereb, James F. 1995. *Arts and Crafts of Morocco.* London: Thames and Hudson.

Kahne, Hilda, and Janet Z. Giele, eds. 1992. *Women's Work and Women's Lives: The Continuing Struggle Worldwide.* Boulder, Colo.: Westview Press.

Kolb, Charles C., ed. 1989. *Ceramic Ecology, 1988: Current Research on Ceramic Materials.* BAR International Series 513. Oxford: B.A.R.

Koptiuch, Kristin. 1992. "Informal Sectorization of Egyptian Petty Commodity Production." In *Anthropology and the Global Factory: Studies of the New Industrialization in the Late Twentieth Century,* ed. Frances Abrahamer Rothstein and Michael L. Blim, 149–60. New York: Gergin and Garvey.

Krammer, Carol. 1997. *Pottery in Rajasthan: Ethnoarchaeology in Two Indian Cities.* Washington, D.C.: Smithsonian Institution Press.

Kruckman, Lawrence, and Michael Milligan. 1978. "La Chamba Potters." *Ceramics Monthly* 26, no. 5 (May): 55–61.

Labbé, Armand J. 1986. *Colombia before Columbus: The People, Culture, and Ceramic Art of Prehispanic Colombia.* New York: Rizzoli International.

Lackey, Louana. 1989. "Following the Book: Lessons from Piccolpasso." In *Ceramic Ecology, 1988: Current Research on Ceramic Materials,* ed. Charles C. Kolb, 117–54. BAR International Series 513. Oxford: B.A.R.

———. 1982. *The Pottery of Acatlán.* Norman: University of Oklahoma Press.

Lara Urbaneja, Carmen. 1972. "La Chamba: Análisis de una comunidad campesina en transición" (La Chamba: Analysis of a peasant community in transition). Thesis, Department of Anthropology, University of the Andes, Bogotá.

Las Casas, Bartolomé de. [1552] 1992. *A Short Account of the Destruction of the Indies,* ed. and trans. Nigel Griffin. New York: Penguin Books.

Lauer, Mirko. 1984. "La producción artesanal en América Latina" (Craft production in Latin America). Ottawa: International Development Research Centre.

Leghorn, Lisa, and Katherine Parker. 1981. *Woman's Worth: Sexual Economics and the World of Women.* London: Routledge and Kegan Paul.

LeMoyne, Augusto. 1945. *Viajes y estancias en América del Sur* (Travels and sojourns in South America). Bogotá: Biblioteca Popular de Cultura Colombiana.

León, Magdalena. 1987. "Colombian Agricultural Policies and the Debate on Policies toward Rural Women." In *Rural Women and State Policy.* ed. Carmen Diana Deere and Magdalena León, 84–104. Boulder: Westview Press.

Lister, Florence C., and Robert H. Lister. 1987. *Andalusian Ceramics in Spain and New Spain: A Cultural Register from the Third Century B.C. to 1700.* Tucson: University of Arizona Press.

Litto, Gertrude. 1976. *South American Folk Pottery.* New York: Watson-Guptill.

Llorens Artigas, Josep, and José Corredor-Matheos. 1979. *Cerámica popular española.* 3d ed. Barcelona: Editorial Blume.

Lucena Salmoral, Manuel. 1990. *América 1492: Retrato de un continente hace qui-

nientos años (America 1492: Portrait of a continent five hundred years ago). New York: Facts on File.

————, ed. 1992. *Historia de Iberoamérica* (History of Ibero-America). Madrid: Ediciones Catedra.

Mathews, Holly F. 1983. "Context Specific Variation in Humoral Classification." *American Anthropologist* 85, no. 4: 826–47.

McKee, Lauris. 1997. "Women's Work in Rural Ecuador: Multiple Resource Strategies and the Gendered Division of Labor." In *Women and Economic Change: Andean Perspectives,* ed. Ann Miles and Hans Buechler. Washington, D.C.: The American Anthropological Association, 1997.

McLellan, David, ed. 1977. *Karl Marx: Selected Writings.* Oxford: Oxford University Press.

Méndez Valencia, María Alexandra. 1993. "Las artesanías en Colombia" (Crafts in Colombia). In *Gran Enciclopedia Colombiana,* vol. 6, *Arte.* Bogotá: Cordillera Editores and Círculo de Lectores.

Mies, Maria. 1986. *Indian Women in Subsistence and Agricultural Labor.* Geneva: International Labor Office.

————. 1982. *The Lace Makers of Narsapur.* London: Zed Press.

Miles, Ann, and Hans Buechler. 1997a. "Introduction: Andean Perspectives on Women and Economic Change." In *Women and Economic Change: Andean Perspectives,* ed. Ann Miles and Hans Buechler. Washington, D.C.: The American Anthropological Association.

————, eds. 1997b. *Women and Economic Change: Andean Perspectives.* Washington, D.C.: The American Anthropological Association.

Moghadam, Valentine M. 1997. "Women, Employment, and Social Change in the Middle East and North Africa." In *Women's Work and Women's Lives: The Continuing Struggle Worldwide,* ed. Hilda Kahne and Janet Z. Giele, 87–118. Boulder, Colo.: Westview Press.

Montoya de la Cruz, Gerardo. 1990. "Comunidad artesanal de La Chamba: Aproximación a los componentes socioculturales" (Craft community of La Chamba: A consideration of its sociocultural components). Research report. Artesanías de Colombia, Bogotá.

Morland, John Kenneth. 1958. *Millways of Kent.* New Haven, Conn.: College and University Press Publishers.

Murdock, George P., and C. Provost. 1973. "Factors in the Division of Labor by Sex: A Cross-cultural Analysis." *Ethnology* 12: 203–25.

Nash, June. 1993. "Maya Household Production in the World Market: The Potters of Amatenango del Valle, Chiapas, Mexico." In *Crafts in the World Market: The Impact of Global Exchange on Middle American Artisans,* ed. June Nash, 127–53. Albany: State University of New York Press.

————. 1985. *In the Eyes of the Ancestors.* Prospect Heights, Ill.: Waveland Press.

————, ed. 1993. *Crafts in the World Market: The Impact of Global Exchange on Middle American Artisans.* Albany: State University of New York Press.

Ortega Ricaurte, Enrique, ed. 1952. *San Bonifacio de Ibagué de Valle de las Lanzas* (Saint Boniface of Ibagué of the Valley of the Lances). Bogotá: Editorial Minerva.

Perdomo Escobar, José Ignacio. 1965. "Gracia y permanencia de la cerámica en Colombia" (Grace and permanence of the ceramics of Colombia). *El Tiempo* (Bogotá), August 1: 4–5.

Pizarro, Eduardo. 1992. "Revolutionary Guerrilla Groups in Colombia." In *Violence in Colombia: The Contemporary Crisis in Historical Perspective,* ed. Charles Bergquist, Ricardo Peñaranda, and Gonzalo Sánchez, 169–93. Wilmington, Del.: Scholarly Resources.

Prugl, Elisabeth. 1996a. "Home-Based Producers in Development Discourse." In *Homeworkers in Global Perspective: Invisible No More,* ed. Elisabeth Prugl and Eileen Boris, 39–59. New York: Routledge.

———. 1996b. "Home-Based Workers: A Comparative Exploration of Mies' Theory of Housewifization." *Frontiers* 17, no. 1 (Fall): 114–36.

Psacharopoulos, George, and William Loxley. 1985. *Diversified Secondary Education and Development: Evidence from Colombia and Tanzania.* Baltimore: Johns Hopkins University Press.

Rangel de Paiva Abreu, Alice, and Bila Sorj. 1996. "'Good Housewives': Seamstresses in the Brazilian Garment Industry." In *Homeworkers in Global Perspective: Invisible No More,* ed. Elisabeth Prugl and Eileen Boris, 93–110. New York: Routledge.

Rappaport, Joanne. 1990. *The Politics of Memory: Native Historical Interpretation in the Colombian Andes.* New York: Cambridge University Press.

Rawson, Philip. 1971. *Ceramics.* London: Oxford University Press.

Reichel-Dolmatoff, Gerardo. 1988. *Orfebrería y chamanismo: Un estudio iconográfico del Museo del Oro* (Goldwork and shamanism: An iconographic study of the Museum of Gold). Medellín: Editorial Colina.

———. 1965. *Colombia.* London: Thames and Hudson.

Reichel-Dolmatoff, Gerardo, and Alicia Reichel-Dolmatoff. 1945. "Grupos sanguíneos entre los indios pijaos del Tolima" (Blood groups among the Pijao Indians of Tolima). *Revista del Instituto Etnológico Nacional* 1, no. 2 (Bogotá).

Reina, Ruben. 1963. "The Potter and the Farmer: The Fate of Two Innovators in a Maya Village." *Expedition* 5, no. 4: 18–31.

Reina, Ruben, and Robert Hill. 1978. *The Traditional Pottery of Guatemala.* Austin: University of Texas Press.

Reinhardt, Nola. 1988. *Our Daily Bread: The Peasant Question and Family Farming in the Colombian Andes.* Berkeley: University of California Press.

Rivet, Paul. 1943. "La influencia Karib en Colombia" (Carib influence in Colombia). *Revista del Instituto Etnológico Nacional* 1, no. 1 (Bogotá): 55–93.

Rojas de Perdomo, Lucía. 1985. *Manual de arqueología colombiana* (Manual of Colombian archaeology), 2d ed. Bogotá: Carlos Valencia Editores.

Rojas Escobar, Gumercindo. 1984. "Diagnóstico de las necesidades del sector artesanal La Chamba, Tolima" (Analysis of the needs of the craft sector La Chamba, Tolima). Research report. Artesanías de Colombia, Bogotá.

Rothstein, Frances Abrahamer, and Michael L. Blim, eds. 1992. *Anthropology and the Global Factory: Studies of the New Industrialization in the Late Twentieth Century.* New York: Gergin and Garvey.

Safa, Helen. 1996. "Women and Industrialization in the Caribbean: A Comparative Analysis of the Global Feminization of Labour." In *The Cultural Dimensions*

of Global Change: An Anthropological Approach, ed. Lourdes Arizpe, 135–
54. Paris: UNESCO.
————. 1992. "Development and Changing Gender Roles in Latin America and the
Caribbean." In *Women's Work and Women's Lives: The Continuing Struggle
Worldwide,* ed. Hilda Kahne and Janet Z. Giele, 69–86. Boulder, Colo.: West-
view Press.
Salvat Editores. 1988. *Historia de Colombia* (History of Colombia). Bogotá: Salvat
Editores Colombiana.
Sánchez, Gonzalo. 1992. "The Violence: An Interpretative Synthesis." In *Violence in
Colombia: The Contemporary Crisis in Historical Perspective,* ed. Charles
Bergquist, Ricardo Peñaranda, and Gonzalo Sánchez, 75–124. Wilmington,
Del.: Scholarly Resources.
Santa, Eduardo. 1988. "La guerra de los mil días" (The War of a Thousand Days). In
Historia de Colombia: La República de Colombia I, vol. 13, 1463–83. Bogotá:
Salvat Editores Colombiana.
Silverman, Helaine. 1993. "Style and State in Ancient Peru." In *Imagery and Creativ-
ity: Ethnoesthetics and Art Worlds in the Americas,* ed. Dorothea S. Whitten
and Norman E. Whitten, Jr., 129–69. Tucson: University of Arizona Press.
Simón, Fray Pedro. [1627] 1981. *Noticias historiales de las conquistas de tierra firme
en las Indias Occidentales* (Historical notes on the conquest of terra firma in
the West Indies). Vols. 1–6. Bogotá: Biblioteca Banco Popular.
Standing, Guy. 1989. "Global Feminization through Flexible Labor." *World Develop-
ment* 17, no. 7: 1077–95.
Stephen, Lynn. 1993. "Weaving in the Fast Lane: Class, Ethnicity, and Gender in
Zapotec Craft Commercialization." In *Crafts in the World Market: The Im-
pact of Global Exchange on Middle American Artisans,* ed. June Nash, 25–57.
Albany: State University of New York Press.
Stone-Miller, Rebecca. 1995. *Art of the Andes: From Chavín to Inca.* New York:
Thames and Hudson.
Thorner, Daniel, Basile Kerblay, and Robert E. F. Smith, eds. 1966. *A. V. Chayanov:
The Theory of Peasant Economy.* Homewood, Ill.: Richard D. Irwin.
Tice, Karin E. 1995. *Kuna Crafts, Gender, and the Global Economy.* Austin: University
of Texas Press.
Tovar, José Manuel. 1958. "Los Pijaos, sus ascendientes y descendientes" (The Pijaos,
their ancestors and descendants). Ph.D. diss., Pontificia Universidad Católica
Javeriana (Bogotá).
Truelove, Cynthia. 1990. "Disguised Industrial Proletarians in Rural Latin America:
Women's Informal Sector Factory Work and the Social Reproduction of Cof-
fee Farm Labor in Colombia." In *Women Workers and Global Restructuring,*
ed. Kathryn Ward, 48–63. Ithaca, N.Y.: ILR (Industrial and Labor Relations)
Press.
Urrutia, Miguel. 1985. *Winners and Losers in Colombia's Economic Growth of the
1970s.* New York: Oxford University Press.
Urrutia, Miguel, and Clara Elsa Villalba de Sandoval. 1971. *El sector artesanal en el
desarrollo colombiano* (The craft sector in the development of Colombia).
Bogotá: Centro de Investigaciones para el Desarrollo, Universidad Nacional.

Villegas, Héctor. 1986. *Testimonio histórico sobre el Tolima* (Historic testimony about Tolima). Ibagué: Editorial Atlas.

Villegas, Liliana, and Benjamin Villegas. 1992. *Artifactos: Colombian Crafts from the Andes to the Amazon.* New York: Rizzoli International.

Wade, Edwin L., ed. 1986. *The Arts of the North American Indian.* New York: Hudson Hills Press.

Ward, Kathryn. 1990. "Introduction and Overview." In *Women Workers and Global Restructuring,* ed. Kathryn Ward, 1–22. Ithaca: ILR (Industrial and Labor Relations) Press.

Weismantel, Mary J. 1997. "Time, Work-Discipline, and Beans: Indigenous Self-Determination in the Northern Andes." In *Women and Economic Change: Andean Perspectives,* ed. Ann Miles and Hans Buechler. Washington, D.C.: American Anthropological Association.

Whitten, Dorothea S., and Norman E. Whitten, Jr., eds. 1993. *Imagery and Creativity: Ethnoaesthetics and Art Worlds in the Americas.* Tucson: University of Arizona Press.

Wilkinson-Weber, Clare M. 1997. "Skill, Dependency, and Differentiation: Artisans and Agents in the Lucknow Embroidery Industry." *Ethnology* 36, no. 1 (Winter): 49–65.

Wyckoff, Lydia L. 1985. *Designs and Factions: Politics, Religion and Ceramics on the Hopi Third Mesa.* Albuquerque: University of New Mexico Press.

Zamosc, Leon. 1986. *The Agrarian Question and the Peasant Movement in Colombia: Struggles of the National Peasant Association 1967–1981.* New York: Cambridge University Press.

INDEX

African: descent, 16–17; influences, 17. *See also Mulato*

Agriculture, 54–55; family gardens, 55, 83. *See also* Capitalism; Men and work

Alvarez hacienda, 79

Arnold, Dean: burnishing, 124; ceramics and agriculture, 54; ceramics as social information, 231; hours worked, 204; pottery forms and the human body, 135; women and pottery making, 98

Art and craft: ceramics as, 167; definition of, 27–28

Artesanías de Colombia: center in La Chamba, 3, 26, 56, 218; marketing La Chamba ceramics, 89–90; national census of artisans by, 24; staff of, xvi

Asociación Nacional de Usuarios Campesinos, 47

Asociación Padres de Familia, 69

Avilés, 4; Doña Julia, 119–22, 193; Don Roberto, 120, 124, 193

Banco de la República, xvi

Barges and river commerce, 84

Belalcázar, Sebastián de, 38, 79

Borja, General Juan de, 15, 40

Bourdieu, Pierre, 150, 220

Burnishing: Anatilde Prada and children, 110–11; process of, 123–25; Don Roberto Avilés, 124; to strengthen pots, 124; by women and children, 99–100

Cabezas, Ana María: creator of fine ceramics style, 161; as an innovator, 162–63; prizes won by, 87; as a teacher, 87, 90

Calarcá, 42. *See also* Pijaos

Campesino, 21–22

Capital: cultural, 205; predatory, 205; social, 203

Capitalism: agrarian, 10, 46, 89; of crafts, 8, 10, 13, 200; expansion of, 50; family values and, 222; global, 10, 228–30; and noncapitalist working relationships, 229. *See also* Caste

Casserole. *See Cazuela, cubierta*

Caste, 21, 44; and capitalism, 230, 232; and conquest culture, 17; and rural workers, 9; system, 48, 50, 220

Cazuela, 60, 143; *cubierta*, 155; making, 109

Census, 58–59; by Artesanías de Colombia, 24; by the Ministry of Health, 59

Ceramics: as commodity goods, 221; as cultural history, 19–20, 91–93; as expression of ideology and social structure, 231

Chamba, definition of, 52, 78

Chambunos, xv, 35, 38, 65, 77

Champanes, 82, 84

Chaparral, 36, 40–42

Chapetón: area of settlement, 55, 82–83; Belalcázar attacked Pijaos at, 79; in Spanish records, 79. *See also* Magdalena River

Ronald J. Duncan is a researcher and consultant on gender, arts and crafts, *mestizaje*, and economic change in Latin America, and he has worked on projects for the International Development Research Centre of Canada, UNICEF, and the Ford Foundation, among others. He has published five books on related subjects. The most recent is *The Ceramics of Ráquira, Colombia: Gender, Work, and Economic Change* (University Press of Florida, 1998).